Love and Revolutions

Market Women and Social Change in India

Eloise Hiebert Meneses

UNIVERSITY PRESS OF AMERICA,® INC.
Lanham • Boulder • New York • Toronto • Plymouth, UK

Copyright © 2007 by
University Press of America,® Inc.
4501 Forbes Boulevard
Suite 200
Lanham, Maryland 20706
UPA Acquisitions Department (301) 459-3366

Estover Road
Plymouth PL6 7PY
United Kingdom

Library of Congress Control Number: 2007923535
ISBN-13: 978-0-7618-3667-4 (paperback : alk. paper)
ISBN-10: 0-7618-3667-5 (paperback : alk. paper)

The scripture quotations contained herein are from the *New Revised Standard Version Bible*, copyright 1989, by the Division of Christian Education of the National Council of the Churches of Christ in the U.S.A.

∞™ The paper used in this publication meets the minimum requirements of American National Standard for Information Sciences—Permanence of Paper for Printed Library Materials, ANSI Z39.48—1992 for my loved ones:

Michael, Holly, David, and Andrew

and for

Lesslie Newbigin,

who inspired this work

Contents

List of Tables and Figures

LIST OF TABLES

LIST OF FIGURES

LIST OF PHOTO CAPTIONS

Preface

This is a book that places anthropological ethnography in historical context, and that evaluates the results with a Christian moral framework. It is a "cross-over" work that integrates science with religion. The subjects of the study, who are poor, untouchable market women of India, are portrayed both in the small, detailed picture provided by ethnography and in the big, philosophical picture provided by theology. Market women can be understood to some extent in terms of the realities of their day to day experiences of life. But that understanding is incomplete unless the larger questions regarding who they are, how they are treated, and how they respond, are also addressed. Ultimately their lives and their circumstances must be understood in terms of an external evaluation. This evaluation is a moral one, whether admittedly so, or not. In this book, I admit a moral stance, the Christian one, and examine market women's lives in concentric circles of ethnography, history, and theology.

Because of the complexity of the analysis, the structure of the book needs some explanation. Roughly, the first half is ethnography, and the second half is history. At the beginning, middle, and end, are "bookend" chapters that provide the theological framework. The ethnographic chapters, 2-4, describe the lives of market women much as any work of anthropology would do. These chapters establish that market women are poor, but industrious; subject to systems of social injustice, but able to critique their circumstances; and willing to take opportunities, but generally socially conservative. The historical chapters, 6-9, trace the social movements that have affected market women's statuses as untouchables, as women, and as poor people. These chapters demonstrate that Christianity has been the primary influence in changing the circumstances of the marginalized in India. The bookend chapters, 1, 5, and 10, provide the theological argument, which is that a Christian understanding of God and of the human condition best provides for a just social and political system, one that both identifies responsibility and challenges oppression.

Acknowledgments

I have been greatly assisted in the writing of this book by others. I conducted field research in India on two occasions: one in 1983-4 funded by a Fulbright Scholarship, and one in the summer of 1995 funded by the Indo-American Fellowship program. The Institute for Social and Economic Change in Bangalore sponsored me for the first period of research, and the Department of Sociology of the University of Mysore sponsored me for the second. Eastern University, where I now work, has encouraged me to integrate my faith with my science, and gave me a sabbatical in the spring of 2000 to begin the writing.

A number of research assistants were involved in the project: R. H. Itagi, Karen Souryal, Kusuma Srinivas, Jennifer Volonnino, and Mohan Zachariah. My patient and faithful readers of the manuscript included Betsy Morgan, John Stapleford, and F. G. Bailey. Dr. Bailey has been my friend and mentor for over twenty-five years. It is not possible to express the debt of gratitude that I owe him. Despite his disagreement with me over the role of religion in society, Dr. Bailey has diligently assisted me to write this book and to think through its argument carefully. Such is to be expected of the finest of teachers.

The map of Mysore on page 29 (Figure 2.3) is reproduced with permission from the Lonely Planet guidebook South India 2 © 2001 Lonely Planet Publications. The maps on page 195 (Figure 8.2) are from India Today magazine, Dec. 15th 1997, p. 38. And the poster image of Bharatma was first put into print by the journal Manushi, vol. 76, 1993, p. 19.

Finally, I am grateful to my missionary parents, Paul and Frances Hiebert, for raising me up in the Christian faith and for giving me an interest in anthropology, and to my friends of the Ya-Ya Sisterhood, Beth Birmingham, Colleen Di Raddo, and Robin Lowery, for years of personal support. And I express here my deep love for my own family, including my husband, Michael Meneses, and my children, Holly and David Metzler, and Andrew Meneses.

Chapter One

Introduction

The assumption of this book is that the true moral law for humanity is as follows:

> You shall love the Lord your God with all your heart, and with all your soul, and with all your mind . . . [and] You shall love your neighbor as yourself. (Matthew 22:37-39)[1]

According to Jesus, our overriding, or ultimate, commitment should be to God (the first commandment), and our social commitments should be characterized by a balance between our own needs and the needs of others, (the second commandment). The balancing of these loves, like a triangle with love of God at the apex, will produce the society first envisioned by "the law and the prophets" (v. 40).

The first commandment elicits a question: who is this God? There were in Biblical times, as there are now, many gods. Jesus was drawing upon the Old Testament conceptions of Jehovah, or Yahweh, but he dedicated a good deal of his teaching to expanding and elucidating God's true nature to his disciples. He referred to God as variously as "Lord of heaven and earth" (Matt. 11:25), a King (Matt. 22:1), a vinegrower (John 15:1), and a woman searching for a coin (Luke 15:8-10) or making bread (Luke 13:20). But, his central teaching about God was that God is our "Father" (there are far too many references to list), and he warned, "call no one your father on earth, for you have one Father—the one in heaven" (Matthew 23:9).

Furthermore, Jesus identified a new kind of social order, the "Kingdom of God", characterized by a new kind of kinship, one that overrides the commitments of biological kinship that are so strong in us. This new kingdom, headed by "the Father", would be "among" and "within" its members (Luke

17:20-21),[2] and would produce an ambivalence in their relationship to "the world". It was to be "in the world", but not "of the world" (John 17; 18:36). It was to spread "to the ends of the earth" (Acts 1:8), not by the sword, as so many of the oppressed had hoped (Matt. 26:47-56), but by the simple witness of Jesus' own followers. It was to be a kingdom of love (Luke 6:27-31)[3] and of faith, i.e. trust in God's provision (Matt. 6:25-33)[4], not of material wealth (Matt. 19:23-24)[5] or worldly power (Luke 22:24-27)[6].

Both in the break with the biological principle, and in the ambivalence toward the world, Jesus freed people to become social revolutionaries in the justice tradition of the Old Testament prophets. In his inaugural sermon, he quoted Isaiah:

> The Spirit of the Lord is upon me, because he has anointed me to bring good news to the poor. He has sent me to proclaim release to the captives and recovery of sight to the blind, to let the oppressed go free, and to proclaim the year of the Lord's favor. (Luke 4:18-19, ref: Isaiah 61:1-2)

Such a revolution could not be accomplished without sacrifice of family, lineage, community, and, in general, the social life of this world. Some of his words were most disturbing on this account:

> I came to bring fire to the earth, and how I wish it were already kindled! I have a baptism with which to be baptized, and what stress I am under until it is completed! Do you think that I have come to bring peace to the earth? No, I tell you, but rather division! From now on five in one household will be divided, three against two and two against three; they will be divided: father against son and son against father, mother against daughter and daughter against mother, mother-in-law against her daughter-in-law and daughter-in-law against mother-in-law. (Luke 12:49-53)

The priority given to love of God threatens the usual social obligations. And when threatened with the loss of the benefits of these obligations, people respond with hostility, as they did eventually to Jesus himself. Still, Jesus did not shy away from this impending conflict. "Whoever comes to me and does not hate father and mother, wife and children, brothers and sisters, yes, and even life itself, cannot be my disciple", he said (Luke 14:26).[7] And elsewhere, "Who are my mother and my brothers? . . . Here are my mother and my brothers! Whoever does the will of God is my brother and sister and mother" (Mark 3:33-35).

Yet Jesus' second commandment is clear; we are to love our neighbors as ourselves. Who are these neighbors? Jesus was asked this question, and responded with the parable of the "Good Samaritan" (Luke 10:25-37). A man was traveling down a dangerous road when he was attacked and left for dead by bandits. Two priestly members of his own ethnic group passed him by, but a common man from another group, a social outcaste, bound up his wounds, took him to an inn, and paid the innkeeper to care for the beaten man. The neighbor was neither family nor ethnic mate, but pariah. Furthermore, the help was given, not received, by the outcaste, humbling the subject with both real and obligatory gratitude. It is the "other" who is our true neighbor, not just the member of our own community. And we are to love this neighbor as we would our own selves and our own people.

I would suggest, then, that Jesus viewed the strength of biological ties as potentially dangerous to his mission. Family loyalty is naturally inclined to dominate social life, and produces a kind of conservative self-defense that ranges from prejudice to ethnic cleansing. It can prevent people from taking the risks necessary to bring about structural change. Jesus saw that this natural social conservatism would inhibit the development of the revolutionary Kingdom that he had in mind; a kingdom uniting all "neighbors" through love of God, the "Father".

SOCIAL REVOLUTION

Others have felt that revolution was a necessary element in restoring morality to society, most notably, Karl Marx. Less known than his final atheism, perhaps, is the rooting of his concern for the oppressed classes in his early Judeo-Christian experience. Witness the following commentary on Jesus' words, "I am the vine, you are the branches . . ." (John 15:5) written by Marx in 1835 at the age of seventeen:

> So the union with Christ consists of the most intimate and living fellowship with him in that we have him before our eyes and in our hearts, and since we are permeated with the highest love for him we turn our heart at the same time to our brothers, whom he has bound more closely with us, for whom also he sacrificed himself. But this love for Christ is not fruitless, it fills us not only with the purest reverence and respect for him, but it also works in such a way that we keep his commandments, as we sacrifice ourselves for one another, as we are virtuous, but only virtuous through love for him." (Fulton, 1960:56)

Marx links the second commandment to the first naturally. It is out of love for Christ, the Incarnation of God, that we are to love one another. Such love for Christ produces not arrogance or intolerance, but compassion—a compassion that is free to serve others' true needs because it is not limited by the dictates of oppressive institutions.

Marx' views on the necessity of apocalyptic conflict to bring about a just social order can also be traced to the Bible (Fulton, 1960: 51). Even the abolition of private property and the family can be viewed as paralleling Jesus' description of the Kingdom.[8] Engels made the link explicitly:

The history of early Christianity has many characteristic points of contact with the present labor movement. Like the latter, Christianity was at first a movement of the oppressed; it began as a religion of the slaves and the freed, the poor and out-lawed, of the peoples defeated and crushed by the force of Rome. Both Christianity and Proletarian Socialism preached the coming deliverance from slavery and poverty." (MacIntyre, 1984:104).

In socialism as in Christianity, apocalypse would produce the liberation of those most severely affected by the oppressive structures of human kingdoms.

Perhaps the most striking parallel between the visions of Marx and Jesus is the juxtaposition of a belief in the inevitability of the coming Kingdom with a call to personal action. It is, in fact, a powerful mystery that history is gestating according to its own internal laws, and that we yet must be midwives to its birthing process. The sovereignty of God, or of history, does not produce fatalism or passivity. It produces constructive (and sometimes destructive) activity toward a partially foreseeable end (Newbigin, 1989: 101). In this and other matters, then, "Marxism shares in good measure both the content and the functions of Christianity as an interpretation of human existence, and it does so because it is the historical successor of Christianity" (MacIntyre, 1984:6).

Still, no enemy attacks more viciously than one who was formerly a friend. Marx soon rejected religion, and Christianity in particular, with all the invective that he had for the failure of ideals of justice. Under the influence of German liberal theology, and observing the capitulation of the Church to the power interests of the turbulent politico-economic times, Marx followed Feuerbach's suggestion, not just that God was dead, but that "Man" was God. Robert Tucker (1964:31) traces the line of philosophical and religious thinking that influenced so many:

"the movement of thought from Kant to Hegel revolved in a fundamental sense around the idea of man's self-realization as a godlike being or, alternatively, as God. A radical departure from Western tradition was implicit in this tendency. The centuries-old ruling conception of an unbridgeable chasm of kind between the human and the divine gave way to the conception of a surmountable difference of degree. It is hardly surprising that out of such a revolution of religion there issued, among other things, a religion of revolution."

Marx (1972a: 18) concluded, "the criticism of religion ends with the theory that man is the highest being for mankind, therefore with the categorical imperative to overthrow all conditions in which man is a degraded, enslaved, forsaken, contemptible creature."

In his concern for the fullest possible realization of the second commandment, then, Marx threw out the first. Or, more accurately, he absorbed the first commandment into the second by defining God as the alienated self of humanity. In the new utopia, the power that was to replace God was the benevolent State, a representation of the people's common interests. By reclaiming religious as well as political power over their own lives, humanity would reverse the process of alienation. "Man" would be made whole by becoming God. "The apotheosis of man" was complete (Tucker, 1964:73-4).

In Christianity, God is first and foremost other than humanity. Jesus commented, "no one knows the Father except the Son, and anyone to whom the Son chooses to reveal him" (Matt. 11:27b). What practical difference does it make whether God is "self" to us, or "other"? Both Marxism and Christianity put out a call to action in the context of an inevitable movement of history. The difference between them can be seen in the action being promoted. Jesus' call, in view of God's holy character, is to personal repentance and submission to the will of the Father.[9] God himself will champion the cause of the poor and the oppressed. The correct human action is to renounce one's own participation in evil, turn to God in complete faith, and thereby become an instrument of His loving will, rather than a hindrance to it.[10] Marx's call, given that humanity is God, is to take immediate and definite action for change. "The philosophers have only interpreted the world differently, in various ways; the point is to change it," he said (Marx, 2000: 173). The Communist Manifesto thunders:

> [We] openly declare that [our] ends can be attained only by the forcible overthrow of all existing social conditions. Let the ruling classes tremble at the Communistic revolution. The proletarians have nothing to lose but their chains. They have a world to win. (Marx, 1988: 86)

If God is self, then humanity must act on its own, forcibly if necessary, to produce justice. Patience with evil is merely delay.

In the end, Marx's rejection of the first commandment of Jesus has resulted, very ironically, in the most egregious transgressions of the second—the very one he wished to promote. The abuses of power in communist regimes are consistent with taking matters wholly into human hands. When power resides in God as other, as mystery, we are less inclined to be impatient with progress—and more hopeful of the outcome in the face of temporary resistance. Biblical depictions of God stress not only his outrage at injustice, but also his tremendous patience in waiting for repentance. A central refrain identifying Yahweh in the Bible is that he is "slow to anger and abounding in steadfast love." Hence, the first commandment, to love God, and to thereby leave matters ultimately up to him, guards against the tendency to engage in *violent* revolution in the name of the second commandment, to love our neighbors as ourselves.

ECONOMIC REVOLUTION

Since the latter half of the twentieth century, however, it has been the near elimination of the second commandment, sometimes ostensibly in the name of the first, that has produced the most bloodshed. Religious and ethnic fundamentalism has gripped the post-colonial world, as groups everywhere are defending their own people and their own gods. Hence it has become fashionable in academic circles to blame love of God for failures to love humanity.

Yet, fundamentalists everywhere see themselves as acting *in reaction* to a very great threat to morality. And there are academics who agree (Robbins, 1999). Thomas L. Friedman suggests that both communism and fundamentalism, along with other, less organized, sorts of destructive protest, are 20th century "backlashes" to the true threat to moral life, capitalism:

> . . . in the first era of globalization, when the world first experienced the creative destruction of global capitalism, the backlash eventually produced a whole new set of ideologies—communism, socialism, fascism—that promised to take the sting out of capitalism, particularly for the average working person. . . . [Now] those who can't keep up are not going to bother with an alternative ideology. Their backlash will take a different form. They will just eat the rain forest—each in their own way, without trying to explain it or justify it or wrap it in an ideological bow. (Friedman, 1999: 273)

Certainly modern capitalism eschews both commandments. Since the seventeenth century, it's proponents have announced freedom from obligation to God or to neighbor. Historically, it is true that the capitalist system was constructed with a conception of morality that included values such as honesty, frugality, industry, and even work for the glorification of God (Weber, 1976). But its strong commitment to individual liberty has done much to eliminate the benefits these values might have had to relationships.

Actually, the problem lies less in the strength of this commitment than in the peculiar conception of liberty found in the West. Here, freedom means, above all else, the right to individual choice within an established arena. Relationships, particularly in American culture, are seen to limit freedom, rather than to enable or promote it. So, freedom is the "right" to do as you wish, *despite* the needs and wishes of others. De Tocqueville identified the ethos as early as the 18th century:

> [Americans] form the habit of thinking of themselves in isolation and imagine that their whole destiny is in their hands . . . .Each man is forever thrown back on himself alone, and there is danger that he may be shut up in the solitude of his own heart. (Bellah, 1985:37)

Freedom is separation from other people, who might restrict our choices, and even from God, who might interfere with our plans.

Jesus' conception of freedom was quite different than this. At a critical moment in his career, when challenged by his followers over his identity, he declared, "If you continue in my word, you are truly my disciples; and you will know the truth, and the truth will make you free." Most of Jesus' listeners found this statement difficult to stomach. They responded, "We are descendants of Abraham and have never been slaves to anyone. What do you mean by saying 'you will be made free'?" Jesus answered, "Very truly, I tell you, everyone who commits sin is a slave to sin. The slave does not have a permanent place in the household; the son has a place there forever. So if the Son makes you free, you will be free indeed." In saying this, Jesus indicated two things: 1) that true slavery is of the heart, and to our own uncontrolled desires, and, 2) that only he, by virtue of his unique relationship to God, could offer freedom from such slavery. The incident resulted in the crowd accusing Jesus of being demon-possessed and nearly stoning him to death on the spot (John 8:31-58).

True freedom is not the right to do as we wish. It is the power to conquer our own failings, a power that *emerges* from relationships rather than being restricted by them. We need God and one another to become truly free in this sense. The capitalist model of self-interested pursuit of "tastes" (Becker, 1998) actually results in a kind of slavery. The mindless consumerism of the Western world, for instance, has not produced people who feel liberated. De Tocqueville writes:

> In America, I have seen the freest and best educated of men in circumstances the happiest to be found in the world; yet it seemed to me that a cloud habitually hung on their brow, and they seemed serious and almost sad even in their pleasures, because they never stop thinking of the good things they have not got. (Bellah, 1985:117)[11]

Single-minded focus on the satisfaction of desires leads not to freedom, but to slavery to further desiring—in fact, to slavery to self.

Ironically, capitalism bases its declaration of the "freedom" of the individual on a philosophy of natural law. Individuals are assumed to be *naturally* self-interested, prices are the result of the *law* of supply and demand, and countries that pursue their competitive advantage will *inevitably* succeed in the global market. For example, though Adam Smith (1937:144) is generally disapproving of the use of the power of monopoly over land to extract inordinate returns from tenants, he nonetheless remarks,

> "Rent, considered as the price paid for the use of land, is *naturally* the highest which the tenant can afford to pay in the actual circumstances of the land. . . .

Whatever part of the produce, or, what is the same thing, whatever part of its price, is over and above this share, [the landlord] *naturally* endeavours to reserve to himself as the rent of his land, which is evidently the highest the tenant can afford to pay in the actual circumstances of the land." [italics added]

Thus, the purported "freedom" of individuals is solely to act in accordance with a law of nature that drives them to maximize their own gain and to minimize their generosity to others. With a philosophy and resultant guiding principles such as these, it is not surprising that moral "backlashes" against capitalism have developed.

If the state became god under Marxism, then surely the market has become god under capitalism. The dictates of the market are perceived to be both inevitable and just ("efficient"). Its power is admired, even glorified. Its control over the future of humanity unquestioned. There is no real choice in the matter. The laws of the market, like the laws of nature, *must* be obeyed. But Friedman reminds us of the danger of this type of argument. He quotes the political theorist, Yaron Ezrahi, as saying:

> The most *arbitrary* powers in history always hid under the claim of some impersonal logic—God, the laws of nature, the laws of the market—and they always provoked a backlash when morally intolerable discrepancies became glaringly visible. (1999: 161-2) [italics added]

The communist and fundamentalist movements are protests, then, against the amoral character of capitalism, and against it hegemony.

The Judeo-Christian view of God is not of "some impersonal logic," but of a personal being characterized primarily by love. The Kingdom of God differs from the Kingdom of Capitalism[12] at precisely this point. A personal God requires a personal response. Response to God is the essence of response-ability. The Christian is paradoxically not enslaved by this responsibility, but freed from selfish inner demands to enter into relationships of love. In contrast, the "economic man" of capitalism is declared "free" from responsibility at the outset to pursue "natural" cravings, and chided as "irrational" if obligations to family, community, or God interfere with that pursuit. Mauss notes with irony:

> It is our western societies who have recently made man an 'economic animal'. But we are not yet all creatures of this genus. Among the masses and the elites in our society purely irrational expenditure is commonly practised. It is still characteristic of a few of the fossilized remnants of our aristocracy. *Homo oeconomicus* is not behind us, but lies ahead . . ." (1990:76)

The apotheosis of the market is yet in the making, and we are being remade in the market's image.

Does the capitalist god (the market) deliver health and happiness any better than the communist one (the state)? Capitalism's purpose is the creation of wealth. And it can hardly be disputed that the market is the most effective mechanism yet invented for the gross production of material goods. Yet, just as Marx's elevation of humanity resulted ironically in acts of violence, capitalism's elevation of material wealth has resulted ironically in poverty. The abandonment of social responsibility has produced destitution for many, many neighbors around the world. Isaiah reminds us of God's requirement:

'Is not this the kind of fasting I have chosen:
to loose the chains of injustice
and untie the cords of the yoke,
to set the oppressed free
and break every yoke?
Is it not to share your food with the hungry
and to provide the poor wanderer with shelter –
when you see the naked, to clothe them,
and not to turn away from your own flesh and blood'
(Isaiah 58:6-7)

Love of God is to be expressed as love of neighbor. The poor and oppressed must not be abandoned.

Capitalism is also a "historical successor of Christianity." Yet it too has rejected its roots, excluding religion from the public domain, and declaring all belief in God to be a private, and therefore trivial, matter (Newbigin, 1991: 13, 76ff). Weber (1976: 174) attributes this result to "the secularizing influence of wealth." He quotes John Wesley, "wherever riches have increased, the essence of religion has decreased in the same proportion" (p. 175). It appears that the ability to produce one's own wealth makes dependence on God less necessary. Thus, having declared the second commandment an illegitimate restriction on our free and natural right to selfishness, capitalism throws out the first commandment as well by declaring it irrelevant to what really counts, the pursuit of our own happiness.

MARKET WOMEN

This book's subject is the lives of "untouchable," or Dalit (the current term of respect), women who sell fruits and vegetables in marketplaces and on the sidewalks of cities in India.[13] Its argument is that these women, like all of us, would benefit from a social and economic system that adheres to Jesus' two commandments: love God, and love your neighbor as yourself. Market women are in business because they must eke out a living for themselves and their families. Despite their hard work, they remain poor and at the bottom of the market channel. Furthermore, they are stigmatized in Hindu society both as women and as untouchables. Their own adoption of conservative Hindu values completes their enslavement to systems of injustice. Yet, there have been opportunities for improvement. Over the past 150 years, due largely to Christians lobbying for change, the Government of India has enacted legislation to protect and promote Dalits, women, and other oppressed groups. Still, such opportunities have waxed and waned. In times of progressive social change, Dalits and women have been willing and able to embrace revolutionary new views of themselves. In times of retrenchment, social conservatism has been the only means of mobility. Currently, while India is opening its borders massively to the global capitalist market, it is also experiencing a backlash in the form of Hindu fundamentalism. Hence, in the main, market women are attempting to prove their value by demonstrating social conservatism, a rejection of the revolution that justice would require.

In the following chapters I will describe the character of life as market women experience it (chapters 2 and 3), place that experience in the larger context of Indian social structure (chapter 4), look to history to identify the roots of market women's circumstances as untouchables, as women, and as Hindus (chapters 6, 7, and 8), and anticipate the impact of the global economy on market women's economic circumstances (chapter 9). To this extent, the book is an anthropological ethnography. But, it is also an assessment of the human condition, which is anthropology in the theological sense. Hence, I will *evaluate* the circumstances of market women's lives, along with their own behavior, and compare to ideals of the just community that emerge out of Christian thought and values (in this chapter, and in chapters 5 and 10). Anthropologists have not hesitated to distinguish good from evil, despite their famed cultural and moral relativism. The protection of cultures and of human dignity is good. Genocide is bad. Secular anthropologists evaluate what they observe against an ethic of humanism and naturalism (Meneses, 2000). As a Christian anthropologist, I will evaluate the circumstances and events to be studied here against the two commandments of Jesus: "You shall love the Lord your God with all of your heart, and with all of your soul, and with all of your mind,...[and] You shall love your neighbor as yourself."

NOTES

1. All quotations from the Bible are from the New Revised Standard Version unless otherwise indicated.

2. "Once Jesus was asked by the Pharisees when the kingdom of God was coming, and he answered, 'The kingdom of God is not coming with things that can be observed; nor will they say, 'Look, here it is!' or 'There it is!' For, in fact, the kingdom of God is among [or within] you.'"

3. "But I say to you that listen, Love your enemies, do good to those who hate you, bless those who curse you, pray for those who abuse you. If anyone strikes you on the cheek, offer the other also; and from anyone who takes away your coat do not withhold even your shirt. Give to everyone who begs from you; and if anyone takes away your goods, do not ask for them again. Do to others as you would have them do to you."

4. "Therefore I tell you, do not worry about your life, what you will eat or what you will drink, or about your body, what you will wear. Is not life more than food and the body more than clothing? Look at the birds of the air; they neither sow nor reap nor gather into barns, and yet your heavenly Father feeds them. Are you not of more value than they? . . . indeed your heavenly Father knows that you need all these things. But strive first for the kingdom of God and his righteousness, and all these things will be given to you as well."

5. "Then Jesus said to his disciples, 'Truly I tell you, it will be hard for a rich person to enter the kingdom of heaven. Again I tell you, it is easier for a camel to go through the eye of a needle than for someone who is rich to enter the kingdom of God.'"

6. "A dispute also arose among them as to which one of them was to be regarded as the greatest. But he said to them, 'The kings of the Gentiles lord it over them; and those in authority over them are called benefactors. But not so with you; rather the greatest among you must become like the youngest, and the leader like one who serves. For who is greater, the one who is at the table or the one who serves? Is it not the one at the table? But I am among you as one who serves."

7. John Howard Yoder writes, "Modern psychologizing interpretation of Jesus has been bothered largely with whether the word *hate* here should be taken seriously or not. This is certainly to miss the point of the passage. The point is rather that in a society characterized by very stable, religiously under-girded family ties, Jesus is here calling into being a community of *voluntary* commitment, willing for the sake of its calling to take upon itself the hostility of the given society" (1994: 37).

8. According to Jesus, there will be no marriage in heaven (Matt. 22:30), nor any need to pursue wealth in the Kingdom of God (Luke 12:16-34). On the other hand, Jesus suggests that if you give up family and property in this life, you will receive "a hundred times as much" in the next (Mark 10:29).

9. Matt. 4:17; Mark 1:15.

10. See John 15:12-17.

11. St. John of the Cross (1958: 407) understood this point well: "This man, then, rejoices in all things—since his joy is dependent upon none of them—as if he had them all; and this other, through looking upon them with a particular sense of ownership, loses in a general sense all the pleasure of them all. This former man, having none of them in his heart, possesses them all, as Saint Paul says, in great freedom. This latter man, inasmuch as he has something of them through the attachment of his

will, neither has nor possesses anything; it is rather they that have possessed his heart, and he is, as it were, a sorrowing captive."

12. David Maybury-Lewis has mockingly coined this term in his film series, Millenium, episode 7, "A Poor Man Shames Us All."

13. In 1983-4, I did fieldwork in the downtown vegetable market of Mysore City, Karnataka. At that time, I was studying the market as a community and included both women and men, low caste and high, Hindu and Muslim, in my observations. But, in 1995, when I returned to do further ethnographic work, I focused my study on Hindu women, and broadened the scope to include their lives outside of the market. I did taped life histories, visited homes, and sat with them to sell. Subsequently, I delved into Indian history through library research to place what I knew in historical context.

Chapter Two

Market Life

In the small but bustling city of Mysore in south India, there are women selling vegetables on street corners and in markets. Green beans, okra, peas, potatoes, cauliflower, carrots, beets, fresh herbs, betel leaf, flowers, and especially tomatoes, are sold from baskets by women in tattered saris, sitting on the pavement. Circling around them like flies are their children, playing games, being nursed, visiting "*tayii*"[1] after school, or learning the trade. Seated next to them are their mothers, sisters, and friends, with whom they chat and exchange favors during the long day. A remarkably stable social world exists on the pavement, with an entire caste of characters, including friends and enemies, family and strangers, "good people" and "bad people," money takers and money lenders. Market women are poor, low ranking, and sometimes abused, but they are not alone. Their world is as socially rich as the whole of Indian culture is.

Looking out at the world from a spot on the sidewalk, customers necessarily get first attention. Conversations are dropped and children made to wait if a buyer is looking in one's direction. "Come here! The tomatoes are fresh. 'Ten rupees per kg." Buyers maintain a solemn face lest they appear too interested. But sellers are not fooled. A real customer has a certain gleam in the eye and will only pretend to walk away. Haggling ensues, and market women pocket their proceeds, anxiously calculating the difference between wholesale and retail prices. Customers are the lifeblood of the pavement culture, and one's financial survival depends upon negotiation skills and a steady stream of buyers.

The latter of these factors is a cause of tension among the women. One person's customer gained is another's lost! Market women have rules of territory for handling this problem and, for the most part, the rules work to keep

Figure 2.1.   Map of India

the minimal peace. But quarrels break out regularly, over customers, over loaned money, and over the ordinary irritations of working together daily for years. And, as in any close community, these quarrels are experienced as a deep hardship of life. "Good people" do not quarrel, only "bad people" do. Worse, those closest to you may pose the greatest threat. A friend in need may ask for a loan. A mother may borrow stock in short supply. A sister may ask to sit with you to sell, subdividing the customers. To refuse to help is to cut off one's own future source of badly needed emergency assistance. To help everyone is the shortcut to bankruptcy. Negotiating skills are as critical to relationships with other sellers as they are to relationships with customers, rendering market women's world a morass, as well as a mountain, of social life.

The day begins early. Mariamma[2], for instance, rises at five a.m. to take her morning bath, offers *puja*[3] to the gods on the wall, and feeds her family, before traveling by bus from her home in the government sponsored Dalit neighborhood of Gandhinagar to the regulated wholesale market downtown. There she purchases the vegetables for the day, haggling for the price and paying in cash if at all possible. Wholesalers will give credit, but they charge interest, of course, if they do. Mariamma hires a coolie to carry the vegetables the few blocks to the central retail market, the Devaraj Market, where she will wash and prepare them for sale. In the market, Mariamma "owns" a sitting spot by virtue of the fact that she has a license to sell from the city corporation, pays daily fees, and has sat at that spot for many years. She is careful to allow no new seller to sit with her for business, and her spot will be protected even in her absence by the other sellers who are also well established there.

By seven or eight in the morning, Mariamma is prepared to sell. There are two "rushes" of customers in an average day, one in the morning and one in the evening. The morning rush, at about ten a.m., brings professional vegetable buyers, such as hotel and restaurant personnel, and suburban retailers, along with ordinary household consumers. To the degree possible, Mariamma tries to create long-term relationships with these customers to insure the stability of her business. This is done by encouraging chitchat, sometimes giving the "baker's dozen", and above all else, providing fresh vegetables at market prices. The competition for customers is stiff in Mariamma's lane of the market, and she must be careful not to be too forward in calling over customers from another seller's space. Most customers walk casually down the lane asking for prices and buying in a somewhat hit-or-miss fashion. But some have known Mariamma for years and come directly to her spot. These are given the best produce and the best prices.

As the morning wears on, the rush recedes, and sellers begin to joke and quarrel with one another casually as they pass the time. Mariamma's sister, Hunumamma, sits across the lane from her. Others around are all old friends and caste-mates. Lunch is brought to her by a daughter or granddaughter in the middle of the day so that she will not have to leave her post. If she needs to use the toilet, she pays for a cup of coffee in a teashop to be allowed to go in. The market has facilities, but they are unusable. The middle of the day is hot and slow.

The evening rush, between six and eight p.m., brings a lot of husbands picking up last minute items for their households on the way home from work, along with school children and other young people looking for entertainment. The market becomes very crowded and noisy. Mariamma's prime concern is that she sell her vegetables by the end of the day. Some can be sold the next day, but she will have to hide their fading freshness and sell them to less valued customers. If there is rain, there will be fewer customers than usual. And by the third day she will lose the stock and her investment. Mari-amma is very conscious of the fact that she must make her daily and monthly loan repayments on time. If necessary, she will take out new loans to service old ones. But she hopes that that will not be necessary and that her sales will provide for her family's daily needs without putting her more deeply into debt.

At nine p.m. the city formally closes the market and all sellers are required to leave. Mariamma packs up and goes home where she prepares dinner with the help of her daughters, finishes other domestic work, and goes to bed. Her market hours are from seven a.m. to nine p.m., or fourteen hours daily, seven days per week.[4] I first met Mariamma in 1983 and sat with her for business off and on for about a year. When I returned unannounced in 1995, twelve years later, and walked into the market in the middle of the afternoon, I found her sitting in the same spot, selling just as she had been for the last thirty years.

SETTING UP BUSINESSES

There are more than 160 women among the 675 merchants doing business in the Devaraj Market.[5] Most of the men are from middle-caste Hindu or Muslim backgrounds. Their businesses are medium to large-sized shops that wholesale to retailing buyers from Mysore's hinterland. The women, on the other hand, are from low caste or Dalit background, and their businesses are small, usually conducted from sitting spots on concrete platforms or the pavement. They too sell to retailers, but more so to domestic consumers. Table 2.1 shows the predominance of low caste and Dalit affiliations of women as

Table 2.1. Proportion Of Low Vs. High Caste Traders By Sex

| Sex | Caste | | | | | | |
	Dalit	Low Castes	Middle Castes	Brahmin	Muslim	Misc.	Total
Women	86 (53.1%)	60 (37.0%)	12 (7.4%)	0 (0.0%)	1 (0.6%)	3 (1.9%)	162 (100%)
Men	24 (4.9%)	100 (20.3%)	155 (31.5%)	14 (2.8%)	192 (39.0%)	7 (1.4%)	492 (100%)

1. Low Castes include Gowda (agriculturalists), Besta (fishers), Pariwar (domestics), Kuruba (shepherds), and Nayak (laborers).
2. Middle Castes include Vokkaliga (landowners), Lingayat (landowners), Marata (traders), Shetty (traders), and Modaliyar (agriculturalists).

against the higher caste and Muslim affiliations of men. Table 2.2 shows the strong correlation between shop size, and hence wealth, and sex, men in the market being much wealthier than women.

The reasons for these differences in the status and wealth of sellers are clear. Men in the Devaraj Market come from traditional landowning or merchant castes.[6] Their communities are dominant in the city and oriented to business as a profession. Shops are passed down from father to son, or from paternal uncle to nephew, remaining within the lineage and accumulating business strength over time. For men, selling is a profession. Women, on the other hand, come to the market as refugees from other occupations that have failed to support them, such as agricultural labor, domestic help, and unskilled construction work. Their low caste status makes it possible for them to operate businesses in public, where higher caste women would be forbidden by the restrictions of purdah. And their need to feed their families gives them the reason to do it. Women too pass on their sitting spots and businesses to their daughters. But the patrilineal construction of households necessitates the division of profits, with mothers and daughters taking home money to different families. Hence, women tend not to take the long-term view of building the business. Their work is for the nuclear family; for day to day living, and for their children's futures.

Three things are immediately necessary to set up a business: a sitting spot, customers, and loans. Though they move freely throughout the market, women's selling places are segregated *de facto* into certain sections. Women are found primarily in the vegetable, betel leaf and flower sections because these are commodities easily sold by capital poor retailers. (See Figure 2.2). The lanes in these sections are constructed of concrete platforms upon which

Table 2.2.   Proportion Of Small Vs. Large Businesses By Sex

	Business Size					
Sex	Pavement Spots	Platform Spots	Small Shops	Medium Shops	Large Shops	Total
Women	42	104	15	1	0	162
	(25.9%)	(64.2%)	(9.3%)	(0.6%)	(0.0%)	(100%)
Men	14	106	316	44	12	492
	(2.8%)	(21.5%)	(64.2%)	(8.9%)	(2.4%)	(100%)

1. The market, built by the local king in the 19th century, is constructed of lanes surrounded by high walls with gates. It is a half city block wide by two city blocks long. Sidewalk spots are on the pavement in the lanes, while platform spots are on raised tables in the centers of certain lanes. All shops have concrete walls on three sides and corrugated tin roofs. Shops are of a standard size, but the business can be made larger by renting several shops in a row.
2. Daily fees are paid to the city corporation for sitting spots, while monthly rent is paid for shops. Market people view this difference as significant in indicating business size, and hence family wealth.

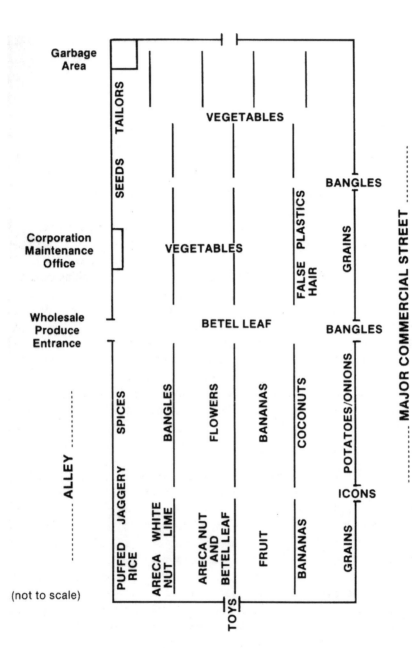

Figure 2.2.   Map Of The Devaraj Market

women sit to sell with baskets in front of them. They are tightly packed in. In the flower lane, for instance, 52 sellers sit on a platform that runs down the center of the lane about 4 feet wide and 100 feet long, yielding a spot size of two feet by four. The vegetable lanes are similarly arranged and nearly as tight. Sitting space is at a premium in the Devaraj Market.

Many women who sell vegetables in Mysore cannot gain entrance into the market at all. An estimated 30-50 of them sit to sell outside the market walls on the sidewalks of commercial streets. They are not welcome there. Periodically, constables come by to get rid of them. They duck into the market or into friendly shopkeepers' stores until the trouble has passed, and then spread out their ragged blankets and their baskets again as soon as it is safe. Elsewhere in the city, there are two other markets, in the Hindu and Muslim sections of town respectively, which are not as crowded. Women sit in these markets legally and without harassment, but the customers are fewer. And they sit on suburban sidewalks across the town if they can get the local homes and shops, and the other women selling in the area, to tolerate their presence.

Even in suburban neighborhoods, finding a sitting spot and defending it is a woman's most difficult obstacle to entering the vegetable retailing business. When Nagamma first tried to set up her flower selling business under the tree in the suburban neighborhood where she now sits, she encountered plenty of trouble. There was no one sitting on her side of the street in that block. But sellers came from as far as 2-3 blocks away to scream at her. One attacked her physically, ripping her blouse. Several of the shopkeepers were unhappy too and called the police to evict her. Nagamma went to court. Her husband had died of cancer and she had four children to support. "Since I had no other living, I got stubborn and determined to sit there to my death!" she explained to me. The court relented, and with the support of one of the shopkeepers who became her patron in exchange for sweeping work, Nagamma established herself under the tree. She has been there for over twenty years now.

But Nagamma understands the reasons for the other sellers' resistance. Girijamma, a woman who sells vegetables in the next block and who had been a good friend of Nagamma's, added flowers to her inventory in 1994. The friendship ended immediately. Nagamma was not able to prevent this encroachment any more than her own detractors had been. Nearly all the women complain that the number of vegetable retailers has grown throughout the city in recent years, with a resultant diminishment of profits for everyone.

Establishing a good location is important because it is the first element in finding customers. There is a tradeoff between choosing a central place (such as one of the markets or a major street corner) where customers are likely to come, but traders are many, and choosing a more remote place where there are less sellers, but less customers too. Given the choice, most sellers prefer

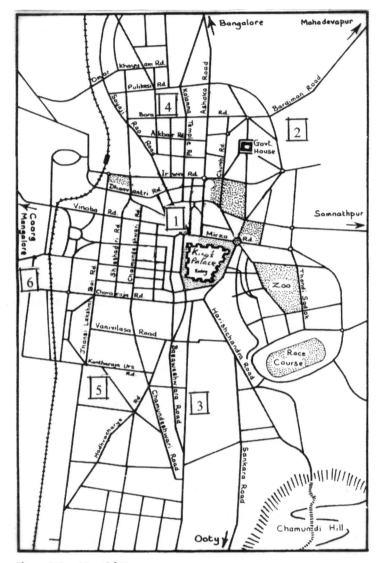

Figure 2.3. Map Of Mysore

1. Devaraj market, city center
2. Gandhinagar (Dalit neighborhood)
3. Ashokapuram (Dalit neighborhood)
4. Muslim neighborhood
5. Middle caste Hindu neighborhood
6. Suburban professional neighborhood

a central place. Despite the competition and quarrels, there are a number of benefits to be had from locating with others in the business. Price information is easier to get. Both money and stock are loaned in times of need. And, once she is accepted, a seller's spot is protected by the others from encroachment. Most importantly, customers come to central places because they prefer to purchase where the price can be bid down. A lone seller on a street corner may well be passed up by customers headed for better prices in the market. In the end, given low profit margins, the success of the business is a matter of the pure number of sales, and these are usually higher in central places.

Once a stable location has been established, a seller must develop a clientele. There are two types of customers, passersby and regulars (who visit the same seller repeatedly), and each of these may be either retailers or consumers. Opening bids will be higher for passersby and consumers, and lower for regulars and retailers, who are discounted to get or keep the business. Haggling is the norm, but is used in inverse proportion to trust levels in the relationship. The words for it, *kachu kachu madu*, and *kata pite madu*, mean "to bite or sting" and "to annoy or tease" respectively,[7] indicating both the adversarial nature of the struggle for the price and the lack of trust that necessitates it. Low trust relationships, such as those with retailing passersby are marked by a good deal of haggling, while high trust ones, such as those with regular consumers, may eliminate it completely.

Haggling begins with the seller calling out an initial bid to potential buyers. Buyers who are interested approach the seller and observe the produce, often asking skeptical questions about its freshness. Sellers make lavish claims for the vegetables, sometimes by snapping them in half, and may begin slowly dropping their price if they feel that the buyer is genuinely interested. Buyers, who lack market price information, resist counter bidding as long as possible, but will finally be forced to do so by the seller in order to secure a commitment. To the last, the buyer's strongest bid is to walk away, and sellers are sensitive to face and body movements that might indicate this is about to happen. If signs are positive, the seller may begin packing the produce in advance of an actual agreement in order to complete the transaction.

Despite the natural antagonism of the haggle, market women speak of the necessity for "love and affection" in relationships with customers. From their end, the women express this "affection" by offering small gifts: an extra measure of vegetables, a cut on the price, or even a cup of tea and a conversation about family. Kalamma explains:

> [Customers] come to us if we call them . . . We ask them with love about the welfare of their wife and children, [or] whether they have finished lunch, breakfast, or coffee. For ladies, we ask about the welfare of their husbands and children, about the educational level of their children, about the behavior of their

children, about the marriage of their children, etc. Then they reply to our questions happily—that the daughter is not engaged because a suitable boy has not been found yet, [or that] a suitable girl had not been found yet, or rituals have not been conducted yet. They will say with a deep sigh that God has to see to those things. They talk to us with love . . . We have to speak with respect to those who come to us. Then they will be happy.

Thus, in gifts of conversation as well as of material goods, market women are setting up relationships of trust with potential clients.

But, things do not always go so well. Sellers sometimes tire of have to constantly appease customers. Cheluvamma says:

> If we quarrel, they will scold us. Old ladies [i.e. sellers] usually quarrel. They have been doing business for a hundred years. They have earned a lot. If the customers do not take the produce at the asking rate, the old ladies scold them. If they [i.e. the customers] are good natured people they won't say anything, treating [the seller] like a mother. But, if the customers are not good people, they will also quarrel . . . Then we have to interfere and apologize [for the seller] to the customers.

Buyers expect lowered prices from regular sellers. Sellers expect, in return for their gift of price reduction, the counter-gift of the customer's faithfulness. A client is expected to come only to his or her matron for all needs related to the commodity. The matron must supply these needs, if necessary by borrowing stock from another seller, at market price or lower. Nothing breaks off incipient reciprocity as quickly as passing spoiled vegetables or charging an artificially high price, on the seller's part, or purchasing elsewhere, on the buyer's part.

Still, if all goes well, a relationship of real duration, sometimes for as many as 20-30 years, combining social and economic mutual gain, will be established. In such cases, it is not unusual for a market woman to ask for and receive loans from her client, and to expect significant gifts at critical times in the life cycle such as marriages, illnesses, or deaths. Luxmamma has been sponsored for many years by a Brahmin woman who lives in an apartment above the spot where she sits, and Kalamma has been sponsored by the wife of the shopkeeper who has permitted her to sit in front of his store. Clients such as these are characterized as "good people" by the pavement subculture because they make businesses viable for the long run, thereby "feeding" poor people.

Loans are *the* central preoccupation for market women. Almost none of the 23 women that I interviewed in 1995 was functioning without them. Indebtedness ranged from Rs. (rupees) 2,000 to Rs. 25,000, with most women juggling several loans at once to accumulate the needed capital. To put this amount in perspective, the average take-home profit for a day of work is about Rs. 25-30, so most women owe between six months and two years of work to the moneylenders. Interest rates are well established. A twenty-four hour loan incurs one rupee in interest per ten rupees in principle (3,650% per annum), but women avoid these. A 100 day loan is the most common type, and incurs Rs. 200 in interest on Rs. 800 in principle (91% per annum). Bank loans are available for lower rates of interest, but they require the sponsorship of a government employee—a nearly impossible requirement for low caste women to fulfill. Some women have joined mutual savings associations that will loan for little or no interest to those who pay into the fund in monthly installments. But, in addition to the fact that the money must be contributed up front, the rigidity of these associations makes them less attractive than moneylenders, who may be counted upon to be flexible in times of financial loss.

Loan repayments are made on daily, weekly, and monthly schedules. No financial matter concerns the women more than the repaying of loans. If they fail to do so, punishments range from quarrels to beatings to refused future loans. It is the last of these possibilities that women most fear. They simply cannot operate their businesses without cash for stock and credit for times of loss. When I asked about lifetime goals, several of them responded that their keenest desire was to pay off all of their loans. "I want to die with a good name and no loans!," said Hanumamma. Responding to a question about reincarnation, Nagamma remarked, "If I am in debt [when I die], I want to return, even if as a worm. I have to clear my loans by doing business. If I die inbetween [i.e. with loans outstanding], what can be done? My children are not in a position to clear that loan."

The loaning business is more than a little lucrative for the moneylenders, as can be seen not only by the interest rates (given very low rates of default),[8] but by the wide variety of types of people willing to offer loans. In the beginning, I was at a loss to identify who these lenders were. Eventually, I discovered that nearly anyone and everyone with spare cash might be making loans to vendors. Shopkeepers, landlords, Brahmin wives, customers, and fellow sellers were all potential moneylenders. Moneylending was anybody's game, and well worth the investment. Yet, for all this, capital was scarce in the market, and market women were constantly on the lookout for who might supply them with much needed cash.

Moneylenders are not seen by market women as "sharks." For sellers, the fear is not of high rates of interest, but of the inability to get enough capital. "Good people" give loans out of compassion, even at high rates of interest. "Bad people" do not "help" at all. Furthermore, the nature of the relationship between moneylender and seller is complex. Though they make every effort to pay on time, most women are late on some occasion or another due to business losses. When that happens, sellers can ask for and receive extra time without further interest. The personal nature of the relationship makes this possible. Sellers ask for clemency, and moneylenders give it. With some exaggeration, Nagamma says:

> They don't say anything if we take extra time to repay the amount. If we say that there has been no business, they don't complain. I have not paid [on my loans] for one and a half months. But there has been no comment from them. They just ask us to give back the amount [eventually].

Still, if the delay is for too long, moneylenders will begin to pressure for repayment. They may come to the market and harass the sellers verbally. Sellers plead for pity, and when that doesn't work, may scream at and even physically attack lenders to impress upon them the reality of their inability to repay. In the end, either the lender backs off and gives more time, or the seller takes out new loans to pay off old ones. Default is very, very rare. Moneylenders are exploitative without a doubt. But market women are convinced of their need for them, are able to negotiate effectively with them, and hence, have remarkably few complaints about them.

LONG-TERM SUCCESS

Beyond the immediate requirements of a sitting spot, customers, and loans, other factors, such as tacit business skills, support from family and friends, and even luck, ensure long-term success in business. Most women have had little or no education. There were 162 women in the Devaraj Market when I did a census in 1983-4. Of these, 137 (84.6%) had had no education whatsoever. A further 21 (13%) had had no more than a few years of schooling, so over 97% of the women had not gone beyond the elementary level. This is in spite of the Government of India's long history of encouraging education for women and Dalits. Poverty had made it impossible for market women to take advantage of government sponsored schooling, and had necessitated their beginning to work at a very early age, learning how to buy, sell, and manage money by doing it along side their mothers.

Since this latter "education" is informal, market women do not view it with much regard. Yet, from an outsider's perspective, these women are anything but unskilled! They handle complex relationships with customers, moneylenders and colleagues. They manage the finances of the business, including loans taken and credit given, without written accounts. They calculate daily gains and losses, estimating the prices that they can or cannot afford to give. And they haggle effectively, using skills such as tact, knowing when to hold fast and when to let go of a bid, and even strategic outbursts of anger, to achieve their objectives. Such tacitly learned skills are important to doing well in business.

Family and friends provide support both in the establishment of sitting spots and in covering times of financial exigency. To locate centrally, a new seller must have a network connection to the more established sellers in the area. Usually the connection is kin-based. But friendships also provide the ties that allow entrance to particular locations. In the case of the betel leaf sellers who sit on the central steps of the Devaraj Market, a single woman controls who will and will not sit there for business. In 1982, a merchant received permission from the city corporation to build a kiosk and open a mid-sized business where the betel leaf sellers sit. He began construction. Three times, the betel leaf women came in the middle of the night and deconstructed (literally) the day's work on his shop. In the end, despite the city's support, he gave up and went elsewhere. The pavement community sometimes wins out against local powers by persistence born of desperation and by the strength of the network.

When loan payments must be made, when produce has been lost to poor weather or lack of customers, when personal or family crises require cash payments, and when stock is needed during times of short supply, reciprocity prevails between women related to one another through blood or long association. So, neighboring sellers on the sidewalks and in the market are paradoxically both competition and support. And, it is important to be a "good" person to others in time of need, thereby insuring help for one's self in the future.

When asked, market women themselves identify luck, i.e. circumstances outside of their own control, as being the most significant factor in both short-term and long-term successes or failures of businesses. Kalamma, who is in the betel leaf business, said:

> One day we have a good business of 50,000 leaves and [another] we sell 20,000 leaves. At times it is even difficult to sell 1,000 leaves. . . . Business is difficult. One day we get Rs. 10 as profit and sometimes we even lose Rs. 1000 [because] there is no business. The people who do the areca nut business are our regular customers. If they do not come to buy, then the whole day we won't have business. In marriage seasons we have good business. One to two thousand leaves will be sold. Otherwise, they take 10 leaves . . . during auspicious occasions, marriages, or religious festivals. We can keep leaves for three or four days. But they will be spoiled in a week. They will rot.

A multitude of factors combine, in daily, seasonal, and even longer-term cycles, to bring greater or lesser profits. Sellers try to anticipate these when they can. Calendars are kept of Hindu and Muslim festivals by those whose products are needed. Marriage season is anticipated in like fashion. Production and sales of one product has a secondary effect on others: promoting them, as when areca nut sellers buy betel leaves to make pan for marriage season, or crushing them, as when artificial flowers replace real ones. And, the weather impacts sales for everyone in the produce business. Daily, skies are watched anxiously, lest heat wilt the vegetables, or too much rain keep customers away. So, many things are out of sellers' control, and in the hands of God.

I asked market women whether they thought God helped them in their business practice. The answers ranged tremendously. Some responded affirmatively, making comments such as, "God gives us whatever we ask of him. He helps in times of difficulty," and "How can we live without God? We are here [only] by God's help!" Others were more ambivalent, remarking, "Sometimes we prosper and sometimes we lose. I believe in God. He helps us sometimes and yet sometimes he will not!" And still others were cynical, saying, "He hasn't helped me. We have to earn our own bread. God has not helped me. We have to work hard for a living," and "Would I be living like this if God helped?" None of the women suggested that God deliberately desired their poverty or their failure, nor did any question his existence. But some expressed concern, even complaints, over his seeming neglect of them. Varunamma summed it up, "One can't know how God helps [because] we can't see God. If we have good business, we say that God has helped in the business. If we fail in business we say God has not helped."

Still, most women prayed daily for their own and their family's sustenance. Some even went on pilgrimages to entreat specific gods for help. Hanumamma had a success story:

> Yes, . . . we are helped by Tirupati Venkataramana Swami. We used to live in acute poverty. So my father went to Tirupati and prayed to the god [in the temple there] for good things to happen. Our financial problems were solved to some extent. If there is no food today, by tomorrow we can get some by worshipping God. If the children have problems, then they will be solved. When there is a lack of food, we can at least get porridge. These are the benefits we get by worshipping that god.

In business, as in life, eliciting divine intervention is at least worth a try.

HOUSEHOLD FINANCES

Once a business is set up and thriving, the yield is in money taken home each day for basic needs. Market women live on a shoestring, carefully calculating each expense. Their needs are for food, clothing, housing, utilities and, for the long-term, dowries. Of these, they must put food first, with basic nutritional needs accounting for an estimated 60-80% of their monthly income. Women say they need Rs. 10—25 per person per day for food.[9] With children and other family members to feed, total family food needs are at Rs. 20-50 per day, or "Rs. 60-70 when relatives visit!" Poor families in India have a diet consisting largely of boiled grains with occasional vegetables and other condiments. Meat (which is permissible for the low castes) and fruit are usually beyond their financial reach. So is rice, which was selling for Rs. 11-12/kg in 1995, as against the cheaper grains such as finger millet, which was selling for Rs. 5-6/kg. It is not uncommon for people to indicate their level of wealth or poverty by describing what they eat. One middle class merchant complained to me of his expenses due to the fact that, being rich, his family "has to eat all of these things!" Many poor women indicated their poverty by the fact that they eat only porridge. Even the morning greeting indicates the centrality of food, *"Uuta aitaa?,"* "Have you eaten yet?" The proper response is to reassure the greeter, *"Aitu!,"* "I've eaten," lest the other feel obligated to feed you. People everywhere link food to social status and to reciprocal obligations. But poverty brings a certain power to the symbolism that is lacking for those who are not as aware of their own need to eat.

Payments for shelter and utilities vary significantly depending on the home. Poorer women live in homes containing one or two rooms with no electricity or running water. They get water from neighborhood taps and sometimes borrow others' toilet and bath facilities. For rentals, their monthly payments range between Rs. 50 and Rs. 100, with an advance deposit of Rs. 500-1000. Women who are better off live in homes with three or more rooms, including a kitchen, bathroom, and storage, and have utilities. Their utilities cost them Rs. 30-50 per month, and their rent ranges between Rs. 300 and Rs. 500 or more, with an advance deposit of Rs. 2-3,000. A few women have managed to purchase or build homes. Others have aspirations of owning their own homes, but little real hope of achieving the goal. Most are simply too strapped financially to consider the matter. Minimally, then, Rs. 100-200 per month is needed to cover housing.

The long-term financial goal toward which women work the hardest, though, is not purchased housing, but dowries for daughters. In the urban Dalit community, the standard rate for a dowry is Rs. 20,000. Most mothers are carefully pinching pennies in order to accumulate the needed money. In addition, they take out loans at the time of the marriage, and pay these off later. The social implications of this practice will be considered in the next chapter, but here I only note the pure size of the amount needed, relative to income, and the hardship that women are willing to endure in order to accumulate it. Even at Rs. 10 saved per day, an amount most women can only achieve with difficulty, it takes 5½ years to accumulate one dowry. Multiple daughters mean multiple dowries. Chennamma, who had not received a dowry herself at all, managed to marry her daughter with one. "I gave Rs. 20,000 for my daughter's marriage by begging from rich people. Since her marriage we have found it difficult to eat!" Puttabasamma's situation is similar. Referring initially to her own marriage, she says:

> There was no dowry at that time. Forty-five years ago, there was no dowry. But now, I had to give Rs. 1,000 for a watch [for the groom] and Rs. 6,000 dowry for my daughter's marriage. I have taken Rs. 20,000 as a loan [for all wedding-related expenses] and am paying interest on it. We are suffering a lot now. My daughter would have to stay home if we didn't give a dowry. There is no life for girls without dowries. That is why we have taken a Rs. 20,000 loan and are paying interest on it.

After business loans, dowries are the chief financial concern that women have for the long-term.

There are a few miscellaneous expenses. Business costs, beyond the purchase of stock, are relatively minor. Rs. 1 is paid to the daily collector in the Devaraj Market, but nothing is paid for sidewalk spots elsewhere in the city. The bus to get to the market costs Rs. 1-2, though with heavy baskets of vegetables, women sometimes pay the Rs. 5-10 for a motorized rickshaw. Baskets for holding the vegetables are cheap and there are few other necessary supplies. In terms of domestic needs, clothing can be requested as gifts from known "rich people," and the same clothes are worn for years, sometimes decades. Children's school costs are covered by the Government's sponsorship of Dalit education. Religious expenses can be adjusted according to the ability to pay. A few rupees will cover the incense and flowers for worship of gods whose posters are on household walls, while pilgrimages can be engaged for Rs. 50—500, depending on how far away the temple is.

Money is not kept in banks. Given the less than respectful way that a ragged, untouchable women is usually treated in a bank, most women simply do not think of a bank as being accessible. Small amounts of money are kept at home under the bed or hidden in bags around the house. Larger amounts are converted into gold jewelry and worn, in time-honored Indian fashion, in ears and noses, or around the neck. These can be cashed in in times of critical need. And finally, loans to others can also be a means of accumulating a savings for the future. Money lent out will come back with interest.

Table 2.3 posits a hypothetical household budget based on the financial information given above.

Of course, most often a market woman's income of Rs. 30-50/day, or Rs. 900-1500/month, is not the only income for the household. Employed hus-

Table 2.3. **Reconstructed Monthly Household Budget For An Urban Dalit Family Of Four**

1. Food	Rs. 1,800	(81%)
2. Housing	Rs. 150	(7%)
3. Utilities	Rs. 30	(1%)
4. Dowry savings	Rs. 100*	(5%)
5. Misc. Business	Rs. 80	(4%)
6. Misc. Domestic	Rs. 50	(2%)
Total:	Rs. 2,210	(100%)

* This figure is highly variable, with some families probably saving more, and others not at all.

bands and grown children may contribute as well. But where these are lacking, circumstances for women and small children can be desperate.

To illustrate the range in financial circumstances, I will compare two women's situations: Kalamma, who is relatively well off, and Jayamma, who is poorer. Kalamma sells betel leaf in the Devaraj Market together with her elderly mother who sits beside her. She entered the market at age seven with the help of her brother, who wholesales betel leaf to the entire market, and her aunt, who taught her the work. Due to her brother's support and her own industry, Kalamma has built a relatively large and stable retail betel leaf business. She buys the leaves for Rs. 800/10,000 and sells them for Rs. 900, a 12.5% profit. Daily sales are highly variable, depending upon the weather and the season. But, Kalamma is able to keep up with her domestic expenses, which include Rs. 1500/month for food, Rs. 500/month for the rent of her two room house in a Dalit neighborhood, and Rs. 50/month for electricity. In addition, she is sending her two daughters to school, and is saving for their dowries with great energy by making small loans to neighbors against the marriage dates. She also supports her own younger siblings and their families, and sponsors other poorer people by giving them food and small loans.

Jayamma sells flower garlands in the smaller Vanivilas Market of the Hindu section of town. At twenty years old, she is about half Kalamma's age and has a baby to support. Jayamma was raised literally in the market by her grandparents who both did business there till they died when she was ten years old. Since then she has made and sold garlands by day, and slept under the crumbling market walls by night. She works together with an aunt who has a home and lets her visit once in a while. Flower garlands are sold by the *maru*, a measurement of outstretched hands. They sell for Rs. 5-6/*maru*, yielding a profit of about one rupee per sale. Jayamma's aunt buys the flowers in the Devaraj Market and brings them to Jayamma for weaving. Jayamma has a loan of Rs. 1,000, and is expected to pay Rs. 10 on it daily. But, her income ranges from Rs. 25-30/day and she needs Rs. 20 for food, so she gives the remainder to the money lender and pleads for clemency when it is not enough. Some days she loses in business and cannot pay at all. So, Jayamma accepts the charity of patrons who give her a bit of extra money or a used sari out of pity for her or her baby. Monthly, Jayamma's income is approximately Rs. 800 and her expenses for food and loans are Rs. 900. She makes up this difference by accepting gifts, but she has no home and is considering giving up her baby to an orphanage.

Neither Kalamma nor Jayamma have responsible husbands. But both have depended heavily upon family connections. Kalamma's brother is her sponsor. Jayamma's grandparents were hers until they died. She views that event as having been pivotal. "I have suffered a lot since childhood doing business . . . I lived happily in my childhood days. My grandmother passed away ten years ago. We were all fed by my grandmother." Kin connections are vital to financial success, both in terms of startup and the ability to weather periodic losses. Recognizing the importance of these, Jayamma comments, "I want to be reborn the daughter of a rich couple . . . [In this life] I just want to build a house of my own and continue the business. But I cannot get money. Nobody will step forward to help . . ." True poverty, then, is not only of money, but also of kin. In the next chapter, I will describe the nature of market women's family lives.

NOTES

1. "Mother"

2. Throughout this work, I have used pseudonyms for the women's names to protect their identities.

3. "Worship." This is done by offering incense, flowers, vermilion, rice, and, if financially possible, a coconut, to a picture of a deity on the wall. A bell is rung, an oil lamp is lit and circled clockwise in front of the deity, and prayers are said, asking the god for a blessing.

4. One woman, when asked whether she takes any days off from work during the week, replied sardonically, "No, ours is not a government job."

5. These numbers and the following ones, including those in tables, are based on a census of the market that I took in 1983-4. I interviewed 654 merchants. Another 21 merchants declined to be interviewed.

6. Sellers do not typically come from Brahmin background. The few Brahmins that I did encounter either tried to hide their caste background or denied hotly that caste was relevant any longer in India.

7. See Meneses (1987:236). The dictionary definitions are from Bucher (1983). For descriptions of the haggle, see Cassady (1974) and Alexander (1987).

8. International aid agencies have identified the low rates of default on loans by poor women worldwide. As a result, many have established banks modeled after the Grameen Bank in Bangladesh to provide low interest loans for economic development. See Yunas (2001).

9. All expenses in this section on finances are 1995 rates. At the time, U.S. $1.00 = Rs. 32.

Chapter Three

Family and Social Mobility

When they go home at night, market women enter another world. They walk or take the bus from the market to lower class neighborhoods such as Gandhinagar or Ashokapuram where others are also returning from work. Such neighborhoods are constructed of lanes lined with whitewashed, government-sponsored, two-room, row houses. Some homes have plumbing, but most do not, so people meet at the central tap for water and conversation, much as villagers do at the well. After dusk, the lanes begin to fill with chatting neighbors, running school children, chickens and dogs. Roaring sounds of the surrounding traffic and of the many birds settling in trees for the night overlay conversations. The spicy aroma of the evening meal cooking over a cow dung fire or kerosene stove fills the air, mingling with dust, exhaust, and other city smells.

As the evening progresses and darkness settles in, things quiet down, and everyone drifts into homes for dinner at 9 p.m. and bed at 10. Now is the time for family and hearth. But families everywhere are a mixed blessing: "When they're good, they're very, very good, and when they're bad, they're awful!"[1] Hence, the peacefulness of the night is broken by the sounds of quarrels heard through thin plastered walls. Husbands are sometimes faithless, extended family is often critical, and children constantly require attention. At night, in the place of the daytime's financial challenges, women have relational ones.

REMEMBERING CHILDHOOD

Most market women have grown up in neighborhoods in Mysore. In the survey of the market that I did in 1983, 145 (89.5%) listed Mysore as their home, while only 14 (8.6%) mentioned surrounding villages, and 3 (1.9%), other states. Yet, even those well established in town have links to home villages of parents and grandparents. Husbands' family villages are important too. "[I am from] Mysore," Nagamma says, "But I am married to Mandhya." Visits are made to villages, money is sent back and forth, and further marriages are arranged.[2]

For Dalits, the contrast in the socio-economic circumstances of cities as against villages is sharp. In villages, Dalits make a living primarily from agricultural manual labor. Many parents of market women, female and male, worked full-time in the fields of landowners. In addition, they tended their own gardens to meet subsistence needs. Only a very few owned land. In cities, Dalits do various kinds of unskilled work that are typically better paid and less demanding than agricultural labor. Parents of market women from Mysore worked as coolies, as domestic help, and, of course, in marketing. The attraction of working in city markets can be seen in the following shifts: from back-breaking work in fields to the physically less strenuous work of selling; from the power and influence of landlords to the independence of owning one's own business; from strong caste and gender restrictions to the relative freedom of the public arena; and from heavy-handed immutable communities to the potential, at least, for upward mobility. All of this is not to say that there are no losses. Shivamma describes the combination of risk and opportunity that city life represents:

> It is very difficult to live in villages, but in cities, somehow or other, we can earn a living. We can earn as maids. We can also sell flowers. [But] nobody will step out to help in times of emergency. In villages, we can get a mouthful of food at least once from others. But in cities, everything depends on money. Since I have a job, I am staying here. I like city life. There are limits[3] in villages, but not in cities. That's why I like to stay here.

The ties that bind in the village also provide in times of need. But, given the stigma and limits that such ties impose, most Dalits see the city as a way forward, for themselves and for their children.

As they remember their childhoods, market women identify two interlinked factors making times "happy" or "sad": 1) the relative wealth or poverty of the natal family, and 2) the age of death of siblings and parents. Dalit families of market women's parents' generation typically produced 4-10 children, but lost many to diseases and malnutrition. Most market women had lost at least one or two siblings in childhood. Mariamma's mother lost 10 of her 12 children. Parents themselves sometimes died young, leaving the family desperate for its subsistence. Nagamma lost her mother when she was just six years old. Her father remarried, but subsequently died himself, along with three of her siblings. As a result, Nagamma raised the surviving siblings, including providing for them financially. So, deaths, especially of parents, brought poverty and sent children to work early. In "happy" families, parents were alive, subsistence was adequate, and children did not have to work. In "sad" ones, productive members of the family died, the family experienced real lack, and children had to take up adult responsibilities.

For girls, marriages were arranged very early. Most of the women I interviewed were garlanded (i.e. engaged) by age 7-9, and married by age 12-18. Of fourteen women for whom I have the information, two were married at 7 years old, six at 10-13 years old, five at 14-17 years old, and only one at 20 years old. Nagamma was married at 13 and had four children by the time she was 18. Kalamma was garlanded at age 7, and had to stand on a chair to receive the flowers. She was married at 12. Chelluvamma remembers:

> My mother arranged [my marriage] when I was seven years old . . . I started my periods after six years of marriage. I wore a skirt because I did not know how to wear a sari. At the wedding, somebody held me up to receive the *tali* [wedding pendant].

Chelluvamma's mother gave her no advice about married life "because I was too small to understand." And a number of other women reported that they did not remember any of the arrangements for their marriages because of their young ages.

To the degree possible, Dalit communities imitate higher caste communities in carrying out the rites of passage. Normally, the process of arranging a daughter's marriage begins with the public announcement of a girl's readiness by the celebration of maturation rites. The girl spends 16 days seated on a wooden platform in the household sitting room, under a pandal constructed for the occasion, and in front of the family god. The leaves of various trees, especially the coconut tree, are hung above her, yielding the ceremony's name, *soppuhakkoudu*, or "putting on the leaves." Married women assist her during this time by doing *puja*, or worship, to her and to the god.[4] Her maternal uncle, as male representative of the mother's lineage, must come, either bringing gifts to take her himself as a bride, or releasing her to marry another. Her family gives her clothing and sweets. On the 16th day, she is decorated elaborately and photographed for the making of marriage arrangements.

Such is the ideal for low caste women as for high. But in the lower castes, poverty affects the degree to which these ideals can be realized. Most Dalit women have only 1-3 day *soppuhakkoudu* ceremonies, or sometimes none at all. Dire poverty may delay the ceremonies for a biological reason, namely the late onset of menarche due to poor nutrition. Kalamma remarks:

Usually [girls mature] at the age of 12. My daughter matured at the age of 14. Girls who have happy lives usually mature earlier than poor girls, who mature at 14 or 15 years old.

So, physical deprivation can be the reason for failure to live up to ritual expectations.

In the interim between maturation and marriage, Hindu women are instructed directly by their mothers, and indirectly by society at large, in the ideals of womanhood, which are: 1) being married, 2) becoming the mother of sons, and 3) having a 'good temperament,' especially expressed as not causing quarrels in the patrilineal family. Shivamma's mother told her, "Don't quarrel, you have to lead a good life." Varunamma's mother told her not to get into bad company, to do anything mischievous, or to quarrel with others. Kalamma was told "You should understand your husband's feelings. You should worship him like God." And Jayaluxmi's mother told her to "develop good relationships with everyone." There was some evidence of mothers' ambivalence over the difficult role their daughters were about to take up. Mariamma's mother, when confronted with her daughter's desire to marry a lover, supported her rejection of conventional arrangements, and told her to "marry him if you wish." But most mothers were conservative in their advice, impressing upon their daughters the importance of conformity.

In upper caste Hindu communities, marriage arrangements are initiated and conducted by the brides' families and dowries are paid. Upper caste women are commonly placed in *purdah* for the protection of their own purity and their men's honor. As they are restricted to the home, they cannot be expected to bring in an income. Dowry, it is said, provides for their future upkeep. The wedding itself is an enormous expense. It consists of three days of ceremonies. A pandal is erected outside the bride's family's house for the rites. The bride is decorated as richly as her family is able to do, with new saris, jewelry (including ear, nose, and finger rings, ankle and wrist bracelets, and a silver or gold waistband), jasmine flowers in her hair, and henna markings on her face, hands and feet. In addition to cash payments of dowry, expensive gifts are given to the groom and his family. Brahmin priests are invited to conduct the marriage, and are given gifts of rice, coconuts, and money. Musicians are hired. And as many as several hundred guests are housed and fed for the three day period. All in all, weddings are the most conspicuous display of wealth in Hindu society, and can establish the bride's family's prestige in their local community, or destroy it, sometimes for generations.

None of the market women I interviewed had had a marriage like this. In fact, in the past, the Dalit community did not follow this set of customs at all. Marriage arrangements were initiated by grooms' families, and bridewealth, not dowry, was paid. Dalit women's status as 'untouchables' precluded any pretensions to purity. And, in any case, Dalit wives could not have afforded financially to remain secluded in homes. Bridewealth, then, compensated their natal families for the loss of their services. Even wedding expenses were covered by grooms' families, though these were relatively brief and unceremonial affairs. So, market women were married as children, with simple ceremonies, and sent straight to work.

MARRIED LIFE

In higher caste families, a newly married daughter-in-law is placed under the authority of her mother-in-law. The young wife is expected to be subservient to the whole of the patrilineal joint family throughout the years in which she raises her own children. But joint families are the luxury and the bane of the well-to-do. Landholdings or business assets provide the income to support everyone and are the inheritance which unites them. In poorer families there are few, if any, such assets, and people separate easily because of quarrels or to look for work. So, while they were generally married into joint families as young girls, most market women moved out with their husbands early and managed nuclear families until the time of their own children's marriages. In nuclear families, it is husbands, rather than mothers-in-law, who have the most influence over women's lives. Chennamma says, "The husband is the most important thing. He is like God."

Few of market women's husbands are much like God, though. Of 22 women, only 6 (less than 1/3) had husbands present in the home at all when I interviewed them. Eight were widows, but a further eight had been abandoned. In homes with a husband present, reports of quarrels, of other women, of drunkenness, and of refusal to give financial support abounded. Shivamma tells her story:

> My husband 'married' another woman within the first month of my marriage. Afterwards, I had two children [by him] and she also had two. But he has left me and is staying with her . . . My second husband is my brother-in-law. My [first] husband was a drunkard, a vagabond, wicked. He lost all our property. He got my signature and took Rs. 50,000 by threatening me with a knife and with leaving me for another woman . . . I have been with my second husband for seven years. Now he has left with all my gold ornaments, saying that he has no children by me. Where can I go, being a woman? I cannot earn money elsewhere [than the market] by myself.

Kalamma's husband was a drunkard and beat her regularly. Twice she had to recover her children from having been sold for money for liquor. Kalamma left this husband, and took another. But, she says:

He doesn't do anything. He drinks. I need a husband just to protect me from others. There are vagabonds in the market who are always harassing women. Sometimes I have even thought of committing suicide. But we should not do that. God will not excuse us for that. We have to go [i.e. die] whenever we are called by God. We have to tolerate whatever difficulties we have.

Papanni was being beaten by her husband. She describes the final quarrel that led to their separation:

I asked him why he was not feeding our three children? "How can I earn [enough] money?," I said. And I told him not to drink. So he beat me. Daily we need Rs. 30 for the children. Just for lunch, we need Rs. 30-50. So I asked him, "How can I earn the money?" He beat me very much and told me not to ask such questions again. Since that day he hasn't shown his face [at our house].

Market women cannot depend, financially or otherwise, on husbands for support. Frequently they end up in sub-nuclear families for which they are themselves the only means of subsistence.

The reasons for men's failure to support their families in Dalit communities are the same as those found in poor communities around the world. Men are not able to get enough work to provide for their families' subsistence needs. Furthermore, the poorly paid and transient work that they are able to find is usually of very low prestige. Daily they suffer the abuses of higher caste or higher class men, an experience which encourages them to find relief in alcohol and in one another's company. Their frustration is expressed as neglect and abuse of their families. Still, despite the pressures, some men in the Dalit community had been successful as husbands and fathers. Chennamma, who elevated her husband to the status of a god, has had a good marriage. Rangamma, Hanumamma and Jayalaxmi say that they were "very happy" in their marriages. And Mariamma has had a husband who worked hard, assisting her to build a home and to send all five of their daughters to school.

Significantly, three of these five happily married women are widows now, and the other two have husbands who are physically incapacitated and completely dependent upon them. Perhaps no single factor sends a woman to work in the market more definitively than the lack of steady financial support from a husband. And those women who are able to find such support either cut down their business hours or eliminate them altogether in order to take care of their children. A steady husband provides a woman with a life that is less bound by financial concerns, hard work, and exploitation.

The death of a husband brings social and religious, as well as economic and personal losses. In Hindu society, widows are held responsible for their husbands' deaths. The loss is considered so great that only the sins of a previous

life can explain a widow's misfortune. In the past, women of higher castes
who wished to redeem themselves, especially queens, would commit *sati*, or
suicide by being tied on to their husbands' funeral pyres. Such women were
worshipped, both before and after their deaths, as goddesses. *Sati* is now out-
lawed, but the stigma of widowhood remains in full force. A woman must
shave her head, don a white sari, and wear no "feminine articles," such as
make-up, flowers in the hair, or jewelry. She must not attend any social functions, especially not weddings, because of the bad luck her presence incurs.
Most importantly, she must not remarry. Her celibacy is held up as a symbol
of purity and rank for the whole caste.

When asked, market women nearly uniformly report that "In our caste
women do not remarry." To their minds, the question is a matter of caste propriety, and they respond by reciting the high caste norm. But actually, many
market women are remarried, sometimes after divorce and sometimes after
widowhood (at least 6 of 22).[5] Second marriages are called *kudawali*, or "stay-
ing together," and are generally not celebrated.[6] They are recognized as matters of convenience for the partners involved, rather than as arrangements between families and lineages. So, while some market women who are widows
wear the traditional white sari that declares their celibacy, many continue to
wear colorful saris and jewelry, announcing their availability for another
match. Javaramma explains that as her husband did not support her adequately,
she does not feel that she need take on the status of widow on his account:

> My husband had left me . . . He failed in his responsibilities. Afterwards I had a
> baby girl by my maternal uncle. Then [my husband] died. I did not perform any
> rituals for him. That is why I am wearing vermilion powder and bangles. In our
> caste, one should not wear anything [ornamental] after the death of a husband.
> My husband had six children from his second wife. He was working for the rail-
> ways and [yet] did not give me any money. I looked after my child with great
> difficulty. Somebody helped me to do business in the market.

This is not to say that the ideal of paying for the sin of "killing" one's husband through austerities is not present and significant in low caste women's
lives. Puttabasamma's ambivalence is strong:

> There is no second marriage for women. But men have married for the second
> time. But a woman who has been married once is not fit for a second marriage.
> Women can have 'love marriages' the second time around. But no one does any
> rituals for a second marriage. That is difficult for women. There is no second
> marriage. Marriage is only once in their lifetime.

And Mariamma is proud of the fact that she has kept her young daughter a
proper widow. "My daughter lost a 28 year-old husband. My daughter is

beautiful. Still we have not arranged a second marriage for her . . . People don't arrange marriages for their children for the second or third time." Despite the difficulty imposed on women widowed early, Dalits emulate the higher caste practice of confining widows when possible.

RAISING CHILDREN

If widowhood is the primary shame of an Indian woman's life, the birth of a child is her primary honor. Contrary to the West, where children are sometimes received with ambivalence, the birth of a child is nearly always a happy event in India. For women, it legitimizes their status within family and community. A barren woman is no woman at all, and may be divorced freely. A woman with children has made a contribution to the patrilineage, especially if the children are sons. So, with their own worth almost entirely in their status as mothers, most women view their children as their most valuable social asset.

In poor families, children are an economic asset as well as a social one. Children who are not sent to school, can be sent out to work early, commonly bringing in more wealth than they consume by age six. Those children who are educated are expected to care for parents in old age. Thus, having children makes good financial sense in circumstances of poverty, so long as parents can expect to receive reciprocal aid. Caldwell (1982:145) notes, "High fertility remains rational in nonagricultural urban conditions as long as the flow of wealth is predominantly from the younger to the older generation." Market women expect their children to carry on their businesses or to take up relatively well-paying jobs after being educated. Hence, despite the difficulties associated with childrearing, poor women want children. Of 22 women whose life histories I collected, nearly half (10 women) had four or more.

Still, with access to government sponsored family planning, market women do make choices about how many children to have. Five women of 22 had only 1 child, and a further 6 had only 2 or 3 children, with no correlation to the age of the mother. Two women spoke freely of choosing to stop having children by getting an "operation." Infant mortality rates are low due to the healthcare provided for Dalits in cities, and market women are increasingly expecting to educate the children they have. Both of these factors incline toward having fewer children. Yet, the benefit of having children is not lost. Children who are better off can better care for parents. Mariamma says of her children:

> I want them to get educated and to stand on their own feet. Then, I hope that they
> will keep me happily with them. We have taken care of our children. I expect

nothing but a morsel of food from them when I am old. With great difficulty, I have looked after my children, without a single beating or scolding, and with good clothing, satisfying all their wants - everything they asked for. Now, out of compassion, they have to provide a morsel of food for their mother. That is what I want.

With unstable or absent husbands, women have children to establish life-long relationships of mutual support.

The birth of a baby is accompanied by celebratory rituals. Some time after the seventh month of pregnancy, priests are consulted to determine an auspicious time to send the mother-to-be home to her natal family. When members of her family come to collect her, the woman is presented with a special meal and a sari by her mother-in-law. At home, she is given ceremonial "worship" and pampered with her favorite foods. She marks her happiness by wearing multi-colored bangles. For city women, the birth takes place either at home with a midwife or in the government hospital. Eleven days after the birth, the naming ceremony is held for the baby. A cradle is richly decorated, neighbors are invited who bring gifts, music blares over a constructed loudspeaker to the community, and a lavish meal is served to the guests. The baby is placed in the cradle for the first time by five married women, and a name is chosen, usually from the names of family gods. After a few months, the new mother is sent back to her husband's home, again with gifts: a new sari for herself, and clothing, jewelry and the cradle for the baby.[7]

But children are valued differently depending upon their sex. In the upper castes, sons, who bring in a dowry, stay with their families after marriage, and provide for parents in old age, are more valued than daughters. This does not mean that daughters are not loved. Sandra Murray (1984) and Lynn Bennett (1983) have both described the affection given to daughters in childhood, the sorrow with which they are sent off to husbands' families at marriage, and the ritual honor given to sisters returning to natal homes. Yet, the economic burden of having daughters under the dowry system is real and produces significant distortions in the larger society. India's female to male ratio is 0.93, one of the lowest in the world. Most disturbingly, that ratio has *fallen* dramatically in the last century, from .97 in 1901 to .93 in 1991, producing a "particularly serious" problem of "missing women" (Dreze and Sen 1995: 140). Surprisingly, the decline is most evident not in the upper castes, but in the lower and untouchable ones, a fact that Dreze and Sen attribute to lower caste emulation of upper caste practices, such as "female infanticide, child marriage, seclusion, dowry, *sati*, *johar*,[8] levirate, polygamy, and related patriarchal practices" (p. 157). These days, the abortion of female fetuses is so prevalent that ultrasounds have been declared illegal where not medically necessary. The imbalance is worst where upward mobility is occurring, leading Dreze and Sen to remark, "economic growth and poverty reduction may, in some respects at least, be a source of intensified female disadvantage" (p. 158).[9]

When questioned on the matter, market women uniformly report that they have "no joy" in birthing a daughter as compared to birthing a son. Nagamma is unequivocal:

> There is more happiness when a male child is born. 'A lot of affection for the male child. The birth of a female child makes everyone unhappy. No one likes a female child. All are happy when the first child is male. When a female child is born, people say things like "There is no use for this child. Throw it away."

Yet, it is clear from my own observations that, contrary to what happens in higher caste families, lower caste mothers' relationships with growing and grown daughters are much closer than their relationships with sons.[10] Daughters commonly follow their mothers into market work, becoming stable income producers. Even if in school, daughters care for younger children and cook meals for the family in the evenings. Sons, on the other hand, get involved in gambling, drinking, and other vices that anesthetize men's painful circumstances at the bottom of society. They cannot be fully trusted to support their mothers, now or in the future, any more than husbands can. Shivamma says of her own son, "I want him to lead a good life and to look after his parents, but what he has in mind, that I don't know."

As a result of the fact that they can trust daughters more than sons, market women invest heavily in their daughters' futures. Two investments are made: education and dowry. Market women educate their daughters if anything more readily than their sons. Mariamma has five daughters and is educating them all. One daughter has a B. A. degree, one a P. U. C. (Pre-University Course), two have finished high school, and the youngest is yet in school.[11] Puttabasamma has sent her son to work doing plastering and is paying Rs. 50 per month to a tutor to help her daughter finish her P. U. C.. Four other children, three of them daughters, are still in school. Referring to herself, her husband, and her son, she comments, "Three people are working hard for the education of the others." One of Javaramma's sons is unhappy with her because she has removed him from school and has sent him to work to finance the education of her other two children, one of them a daughter.

Market women's sacrifice of time and money to educate their daughters does make financial sense. Caldwell comments,

> Poor people have limited investment opportunities in such societies and economic and political caprice can upset what appears to exist, so educational investment in children is thought to be the best investment . . . (1982:146)[12]

But the education of daughters is not merely for economic purpose. In Hindu
society, educated daughters can be placed in better families at marriage. So,
education becomes a kind of dowry savings, one that will assist the entire
family's social mobility.

DOWRIES AND MOVING UP

Market women save more energetically for *varadakshina*, or dowry, than for
any other long-term expense. This is in marked contrast to their own parents,
who expected bridewealth at the time of their marriages. Jayaluxmi says simply, "There were no grand scale marriages 45 years ago . . ." Many women
reported to me that, "There was no dowry at that time." Varunamma notes the
shift in practice:

> [Formerly] we did not search for the groom. In our caste they had to come and
> ask for the marriage. The grooms were coming when a girl passed nine years
> old. This was the case at that time. Now the situation is totally changed and
> everything works with dowry. At that time, they [i.e. the grooms' families] were
> giving everything and marrying the girls. Now the girls must give everything in
> marriage.

Table 3.1 compares market women and their daughters with respect to dowry.
    The size of a dowry given in the Dalit community depends on two factors:
1) the relative wealth of the bride's family, and correspondingly the amount
they are able to offer, and 2) the relative prestige of the groom's family, along
with the type of work he is expected to do. A coolie will not be given a dowry
at all, but an educated man with a government job will certainly demand it.
In 1995, the 'market rate' for a Dalit dowry was uniformly reported to be Rs.
20,000. With market women earning *annual* incomes in the neighborhood of
Rs. 10,000 – Rs. 18,000, a single dowry, never mind more than one if there
are several daughters, is a major investment. Furthermore, some of the costs

Table 3.1.   Dowry Given for Daughters vs. Mothers

	No Dowry or Bridewealth	Dowry Given or Planned	Unknown or Irrelevant (no daughters)	Total
Mothers' Marriages	16	0	6	22
Daughters' Marriages	1	9	12	22

Note: The count for daughters' marriages is not by the number of daughters *per se*, but by the number of
    families anticipating the giving of dowries.

of the wedding are above and beyond the dowry itself. A list of expenses for the bride's family might include the following:

Table 3.2. Potential Marriage Expenses Born by a Dalit Bride's Family

Dowry in cash	Rs. 5,000
To the bridegroom:	
Watch and ring	Rs. 2,000
Suits	Rs. 2,000
To the bride:	
Jewelry	Rs. 5,000
Saris	Rs. 8,000
Cooking utensils	Rs. 4,000
Procession and band	Rs. 3,000
Rented hall and priest	Rs. 2,000*
Miscellaneous (eg: food)	Rs. 5,000
Total:	Rs. 36,000

*This charge is low compared to what it would be for wealthier families because poorer families share the expense by joining 'group marriages' that may include as many as twenty or more couples at once.

On an income of Rs. 30-50 per day, most of which goes to immediate consumption, this is an astronomical figure.

There are some expenses on the groom's side as well. For instance, the groom's family is expected to provide the wedding pendant and toe rings that are the symbols of a married woman for the bride (about Rs. 3,000 – 5,000). And, some grooms' families will contribute further to the cost of the wedding as needed. Most will not, however, and brides' families without wealth have a harder time finding a groom and must conduct less elaborate marriages. Kalamma says,

> For my daughter's marriage, I told them that I couldn't give anything because we are living in acute poverty. So, I gave a suit, a watch, and Rs. 1000 at the time of her marriage. Four years ago, I conducted the marriage of my [other] daughter, giving a watch, a suit, and Rs. 2000 to her.

Despite their poverty, market women have fully adopted the expectation that they will finance their daughters' marriages just as higher caste families do.

Mindful of the strain of saving for dowries (or paying on dowry loans), and of the concern for family honor and for a daughter's future happiness, Nagamma complains about the burden of raising daughters:

> [Interviewer] How do you feel when a daughter grows up?
> [Nagamma] Worries. More money has to be earned for the marriage. There will be more expenditures. Worries start over the demands that the boy will make.

Our worry is that we have to work hard. I have conducted my daughter's marriage, so the worries have stopped. But now something has to be purchased for the grandchild. I need at least Rs. 5000 for her.

It is the marriage of daughters, more so than the marriage of sons, that establishes and maintains family reputation (Mandelbaum, 1972:108). Hence, given the expense, the emulation of the higher caste practice of dowry by lower caste and untouchable families is a clear sign that the urban Dalit community is attempting to improve its standing in Hindu society.

NOTES

1. The psychologist Mary Stewart Van Leeuwen applies this rhyme to family life as a warning against undo veneration of the family as an institution.

2. South Indian society does not have the rule of village exogamy that North Indian society has. Furthermore, marriage to maternal kin is valued, with some women, including two whom I interviewed, being married to mothers' brothers.

3. The word Shivamma uses here is *maryade*, which Bucher (1983) translates as "1. a limit, border. 2. the bounds of morality, moral law; rule of decency; propriety of conduct; reverential demeanor, respect, civility." My research assistant translated the word as "caste discrimination." So, Shivamma combined, in good Hindu fashion, caste hierarchy with moral order and social decency, which produce, for her, "limits."

4. In Hinduism, nearly everyone is worshipped in the context of one ritual or another. Even inanimate objects (the tools of one's trade) are worshipped on *Ayyudha-puja*, the annual festival celebrating work. Such 'worship' does not indicate more than a kind of appreciation for the status the person occupies for the moment.

5. I strongly suspect that more women in the sample were remarried. As it was a sensitive subject, I did not press the matter much in interviews, and only discovered one woman's remarriage accidentally by visiting her home.

6. Chennama reported, though, that there can be a small ceremony, in which the *tali*, or wedding pendant, is tied on the bride under a tree.

7. This description is from market women themselves. Kalamma reports that an insect is buried in front of the house at the baby's naming ceremony. She knows of no other reason for this than that it is "for the welfare of the child."

8. *Johar* refers to the mass immolation of women to avoid capture by an invading army. Both *johar* and *sati* were practiced especially in medieval North India.

9. Dreze and Sen go on to say that this negative effect of economic development can be mitigated by encouraging "women's agency" through education, independent income, and property rights (p. 159-60).

10. Mothers and sons are particularly close in higher caste families. For a psychoanalytical analysis of this feature of Hindu society, see Carstairs (1975).

11. In the Indian educational system, 10 years earns a high school degree, a further 2 years earns a P. U. C. (Pre-University Course), and yet another 3 years earns a B. A. or B. Sc. degree.

12. Elsewhere, Caldwell establishes that mass education is a primary factor in reducing fertility rates as parents invest in their children's futures and consequently lose tangible benefits to themselves, at least temporarily (1982:310).

13. A caste's ability to obtain the services of Brahmins is a litmus test of its place in the Hindu social hierarchy. Now, with more than 50 years of anti-caste rhetoric and legislation in India, most castes can find a liberal Brahmin priest who will conduct their marriages. Still, the lowest groups cannot get a Brahmin to serve at their funerals because those rites are considered highly polluting.

Chapter Four

Caste and Religion

Market women do not live in isolated communities. Both of their worlds, the market and the Dalit neighborhood, are highly constructed by larger systems and processes. The market is a node in local, regional, national, and international systems of exchange that will be investigated in chapter nine. The neighborhood is a concrete instance of the Hindu caste system that will be investigated here.

Few complex social structures have been as heavily studied by anthropologists as the caste system. Early interest centered on the functions of the various castes and on the organic economic and social whole that castes together create at the village level (Dubois, 1999; Basham, 1959; Mandelbaum, 1972). Castes are occupational groups with membership inherited by birthright alone, and marriage outside prohibited. So, individual castes, known as *jatis* (Beteille, 1996), are stable, but not self-sufficient. They owe their existence to the exchange of goods and services traditionally prescribed to take place between them. In villages across India, families of landowning *jatis* enter into patron-client arrangements with families of artisan and service *jatis*, exchanging shares of the harvest for blacksmithing, barbering, pottering, weaving, carpentry, laundering, and agricultural labor. Such relationships extend through generations and are regulated with the help of the village council. The result is a stable village structure that has endured for literally thousands of years.

Jatis are arranged in a hierarchy that is legitimized by prevailing Hindu beliefs about purity and pollution. Ancient texts, the *Vedas,* identify four caste categories, or *varnas* (literally "colors"): Brahmins (priests), Kshatriyas (warriors and kings), Vaishyas (merchants), and Shudras (farm laborers).[1] Brahmins, at the top, are born pure and are to engage in sacred work.

They are forbidden to do certain types of profane work, such as commerce or manual labor, lest they pollute themselves through contact with the material world. Brahmins, then, are the epitome of the system, the image of purity it presents to the rest. The other *varnas* are arranged in descending levels from Brahmins. Kshatriyas are powerful as kings, but are metaphysically polluted, and therefore spiritually denigrated, by their engagement in this-worldly concerns, such as administration and warfare. Vaishyas are even lower, due to their polluting contact with money. And Shudras are still lower yet for their engagement in manual labor. The Vedas only indicate four *varnas,* but later texts refer to the emergence of a fifth (*panchama*), the pariahs or untouchables, so named for the degrading work they do in carrying away refuse, nightsoil, and the dead. These are the very most polluted of all, born hopelessly defiled, and even defiling others by association.

The *varna* system functions to organize *jatis* hierarchically and to arrange the ritual relations between them according to the nature of the work exchanged. Work itself is pure or polluting, depending upon its degree of involvement with polluting things. The purer castes must have the services of impure castes to carry away their refuse, wash their cloths, shave them, and do their manual labor. If they do these things for themselves they will become polluted. Impure castes are 'naturally' polluted by birth, and can redeem themselves in part by serving those above. In return for their services they receive their sustenance, along with the blessings of purer people, blessings they could not possibly give to themselves. So, in this manner, the economic structure of village life is given strong religious sanction.

The ideology of the caste system is more overt, and more manifestly religious, than the legitimizing ideologies of most other complex social structures. Religious objectives trump social, economic, and even political ones. And religious hierarchy is openly valued. Dumont (1970: 20) defends this viewpoint out of Hinduism:

> To adopt a value is to introduce hierarchy, and a certain consensus of values, a certain hierarchy of ideas, things, and people, is indispensable to social life. This is quite independent of natural inequalities or the distribution of power. No doubt, in the majority of cases, hierarchy will be identified in some way with power, but there is no necessity for this, as the case of India will show. Moreover it is understandable and natural that hierarchy should encompass social agents and social categories. In relation to these more or less necessary requirements of social life, the ideal of equality, even if it is thought superior, is artificial.

According to Dumont, caste, as an honest expression of hierarchy, reflects "a fundamental social principle" of life (p. 2), and, in fact, "should be seen as less 'exploitative' than democratic society. If modern man does not see it this way, it is because he no longer conceives justice other than as equality" (p. 105). A hierarchical system is the natural result of a community with values, and provides justly for all of the parts by incorporating them into the whole.

While Dumont's work is widely acknowledged, many theorists have critiqued it as being unduly absorbed with cultural ideals as against observed realities, and overly influenced by the Brahmin, or top-down, view. In his effort to portray sympathetically the beauty and logic of the system, Dumont too easily glosses its injustices. In fact, villages are commonly hotbeds of caste-based disputes, and the treatment of Dalits has ranged from abuse at best to outright slavery at worst.

Significantly, some of the less idealized portrayals of the caste system come from sociologists who are themselves Indian. Ghurye (1993) introduces conflict and historical context to the model in his analysis of the 19th and 20th centuries' "nonBrahman" protest movements in the south. There, castes have been amalgamated into political associations under the democracy. Yet even he views conflict and change as contemporary deviations from an earlier period in which the caste system was a stable, functional, and harmonious, if hierarchical, form of organization. Srinivas goes further by suggesting that the middle castes have always vied for position by manipulating symbols of purity. "It is clear that vagueness or doubt regarding mutual position is not accidental or unimportant, but is an essential feature of caste as an ongoing system" (1969: 4). The jostling for rank that occurs between the middle castes (*jatis*) is not a weakness of the system, he suggests, but a mechanism for making necessary adjustments to changing economic circumstances. Yet even Srinivas is reluctant to critique the effects of the system as a whole on those at the bottom.

The theorists most critical of injustice in the caste system have been, not surprisingly, the Marxists. Joan Mencher has suggested that "caste has functioned (and continues to function) as a very effective system of economic exploitation . . ." She bases her argument on field research with Dalits, offering a bottom-up view of the system, and suggesting that much of what has passed for social science theory in the study of caste has merely been the uncritical adoption of high caste rationalizations:

> The notions of *dharma* and *karma* (or duty and fate) are more useful as rationalizations of the system from the viewpoint of high-caste people . . . Untouchables may accept these notions to some extent, but it is important to distinguish between the overt acceptance of such values and the holding of other values usually unexpressed to outsiders. (1974: 476)

According to Mencher, Dalits are skeptical of the received explanations out of Hinduism for their degraded status, and, when others are not around, express that skepticism freely.

Mencher's point has not gone uncontested. Moffatt, a student of Dumont's, has also done research with Dalits. He offers two types of evidence to demonstrate the existence of a Dalit "consensus" on caste ideology: 1) the complementary roles that Dalits are willing to play with respect to higher castes, indicating their inclusion in the system, and 2) the Dalit "replication" of Hindu institutions in their own communities, including the arrangement of their own subcastes into purity and pollution-based hierarchies, and the worship of Hindu gods:

> In their definition of their own identity and its lowness in *toRil* (caste duty) and myth, then, the Harijans [Dalits] of Endavur are in fundamental consensus with the higher castes. They define themselves as low for the same reasons as the higher castes do, and they agree with the evaluation that persons with their characteristics should be low. [1979: 129]

According to Moffit, who is entirely sympathetic to their circumstances, Dalits believe that they are in fact degraded, both by birth and by occupation, and therefore are complicitous with the system.

Lacking in either approach to Dalit representations of themselves is any concept of agency. If Mencher views Dalits as helpless victims of political and economic oppression, Moffatt completes their victimization by suggesting that they subscribe uncritically to the system that so abuses them. Bailey, whose work stresses agency, suggests that Dalits and other low caste people oscillate between acceptance of their social lot, and defiance of it, depending upon circumstances (1957; 1960:151ff and 191). Where opportunity exists to benefit from protest, Dalits may attempt a challenge. But where benefits can be gotten from a feigned acceptance of the status quo, they will comply.

My experience is that Dalits will, in fact, take advantage of some opportunities. But, their concern with their standing in Hindu society, and especially their attempt to escape its stigmatization, may cause them to sacrifice other opportunities. Being poor, Dalits must strategize about their own survival and do what is necessary to ensure it. And, they make skeptical remarks about Hinduism and its justifications for their circumstances. Yet, the Dalits I know typically *believe* the foundational assumptions of the religion in which they have been reared, and try to make the best of their lives within the constraints they have been given. When new opportunities come along, Dalits are not completely unwilling to give them a chance. But, the risks involved in taking those opportunities are often underestimated by outsiders. So, on the whole, Dalits, like the rest of us, have a tendency to choose the socially conservative path for as long as they can bear it, and only resist or protest when that path offers them absolutely no hope.

MARKET WOMEN AND CASTE

In the census I took in 1983, women in the Devaraj Market reported membership in the following castes (*jatis*) in approximate descending order of rank:[2] Lingayat, Shetty, Vokkaliga, Modaliyar, Gowda, Kuruba, Rajpariwar, Besta, and Adi Karnataka (including Holeya, Madiga, and others). There were no Brahmins, and only one Muslim woman.[3]

The first four of these castes are middle-ranked, and there are a few women from each of them minding family shops in the market that are generally managed by men. Members of middle-ranked castes are landowners, merchants, or urban professionals. Three women reported they are Lingayats, a highly respected religious community, second only to Brahmins in Karnataka.[4] Five women are Shettys, a high trading caste originally from the neighboring state of Andhra Pradesh. Despite its "foreign" origin, marked by continued use of the Telugu language at home, the Shetty community in Mysore is large and powerful. Three women are Vokkaligas, a dominant landowning caste of Karnataka, and a further three are Modaliyars, a powerful landowning caste of Tamil Nadu, the state to the south. Most women of castes such as these can afford to be at home full time. So, in the Devaraj Market, such women constitute only 14 of the 654 merchants (about 2%).

Table 4.1.   Castes Represented among Market Women

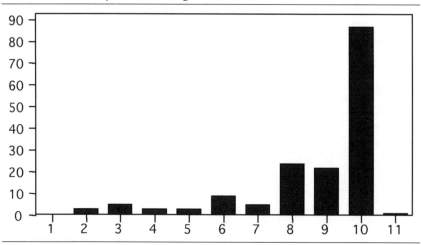

Key: 1 = Brahmin (0)   6 = Gowda (9)
       2 = Lingayat (3)   7 = Kuruba (5)
       3 = Shetty (5)   8 = Rajpariwar (24)
       4 = Vokkaliga (3)   9 = Besta (22)
       5 = Modaliyar (3)   10 = Adi Karnataka (87)
                               11 = Muslim (1)

The next four castes in Table 4.1 are low-ranked and have significantly more women represented. Members of low-ranked castes are fishers, shepherds, domestic workers, agricultural laborers, and tribals. All are classed as Shudras in the *varna* system. They perform at least mildly polluting services, and are presumed to eat meat and drink liquor (signs of their degraded position). Nine women are Gowdas, a relatively superior low caste involved in agriculture and business in and around Mysore. Gowdas are said to have originally been Tulu speakers from southern Karnataka, an area of impenetrable forested mountains. Five women are Kurubas, who, as per their name, are traditionally shepherds, and are local to Karnataka. Some Kurubas were originally of tribal background. Currently many are subsistence agriculturalists in villages (Parvathamma, 1971: 53). Twenty-four women are Rajpariwars (also called Nayaks[5]), a low caste of laborers from Rajasthan and Haryana to the north. Twenty-two women are Bestas who are, again as per their name, traditionally fishers from the Mysore area. As fishing is polluting work, many members of the caste have attempted to move into wage labor and business.

The Shudras are all low and polluted, but none are classified as untouchable because they are members of the *varna* system, albeit at the lowest rank. True untouchables are *avarna*, strictly speaking "without *varna.*" They are below the ranking system altogether. In Karnataka, there are a sizable number of untouchable *jatis*, having occupations such as construction worker, agricultural laborer, sweeper, leather worker, etc. Some groups have migrated from other parts of India. But most are indigenous, such as the Holeyas. *Hole* means "pollution, defilement, impurity, and meanness" (Bucher, 1983:68). The separate street on which Holeyas must live in towns and villages is called a *holegeeri,* or "Holeya place." Both terms have strong stigma attached. Hence, most Dalits of Karnataka prefer to be called AKs, Adi Karnatakas, or "first" Karnadigas, in the same manner in which indigenous people around the world prefer to be called "natives". Eighty-seven women in the market are AKs, 13% of the total number of merchants, and 54% of the women represented. Including both low and untouchable ranks, over 90% of women in the market are of low prestige backgrounds and are considered to be highly polluted.

CASTE SYSTEM LEGITIMACY

Market women display a variety of views, from liberal to conservative, on the legitimacy of the caste system. None of them question the legitimacy of having caste *per se*. That is, none suggest that *jati* affiliations should be eliminated entirely. Nor do any dispute the notions of purity and pollution. In general, market women accept higher caste moral and aesthetic values. Yet many of them do say that, "There should be no caste *discrimination,*" by which they mean exclusion from various social and political arenas. And nearly all of them try to present their castes as equal to higher ones by virtue of conformity to Hindu values. Where they disagree with one another, it is usually a matter of the degree to which the woman is identifying with conservative high caste values as against liberal government policies.

Conservative views of caste tend to be expressed in cultural terms, that is, by appropriating Hindu values, such as caste endogamy, the ban on the remarriage of widows, and the observance of strict commensality rules.[6] Nagamma (who is Gowda) bemoans the fact that she has had to marry her daughter down:

> My daughter is married into a different caste, so she is not allowed to be in our caste [anymore]. They have to live separately. No one is teasing [me] that she married a boy of different caste, [but] I cried with my relatives because I still have the responsibility for two more daughters. So they are helping me to find suitable grooms for my daughters. I wanted to conduct the marriage to my caste people.

Mariamma (AK) stresses her orthodoxy in not remarrying her widowed daughter, and attributes this orthodoxy to the superior performance of the lower castes in cities: "In villages, even for widows with two children they do *kudavali* [living together]. But we do not conduct marriages even for widows without children." Chennamma (AK) affirms caste commensality rules: "We do not take food from Madigas [leather workers].[7] Acharyas [crafts producers] are superior to us . . . We take food from the rest of the castes. We even take food from the Agasa [washers] group." And Cheluvamma (Besta) emphasizes, "Some people marry into other castes. We won't talk to those people. We do not even take water from them. They are excluded from the caste . . . we do not take food from other castes."

Liberal views of caste tend to be expressed in political terms. Some market women have clearly adopted the rhetoric of the stated anti-caste position of the government. "Now there is no discrimination with regard to caste," says Puttabasamma (AK), and she refuses to admit any knowledge of her caste's origins. Women with this perspective often mix their progressive views with a tired belligerence toward the whole matter. Mariamma (AK) says, "Ours is a superior caste," and Luxmamma (AK) says, "Our caste was started by super-human beings." Both women identify themselves not as Holeya, nor even as AK, but as "Harijan," the name given to Dalits by Gandhi as the "children of God." Siddamma (AK) tries to return the usual high caste accusations of impurity when asked whether her own low caste remarries widows: "No," she says, "but widow remarriage is practiced by Brahmins, Lingayats, and Gowdas . . . it is not allowed in our caste."

When questioned about this clearly inaccurate statement, she washes her hands of the whole matter, saying simply, "Our problems will all be solved when we die."

This contrast between culturally conservative views and politically liberal ones is evidenced most clearly in market women's responses to my question about caste origins.

Varunamma (Besta) gives a traditional explanation:

Interviewer: How did your caste originate?

Varunamma: I don't know in detail. Gangadevi [the river goddess] rose up here. We are her children. She is the mother of our caste. We are all born to her, and Lord Ishwara [Shiva] saved all . . . In the past, Ganga came and talked to her children.[8]

Javaramma (AK) gives a political explanation:

Interviewer: How did your caste originate?

Javaramma: Those who stick together have a good life, and they want to put down poor people. This is what is happening in my caste. The caste hierarchy in Karnataka is not good . . . Those who are poor like us do not have anything. We have to do manual labor for food. If we ask for loans, we are beaten by them. Even after being paid back, they say that we have not cleared the loan.

And, Sannamma (AK) expresses her disgust with the whole matter:

Interviewer: How did your caste originate?

Sannamma: Who knows.

Neither education, nor age, nor relative caste rank, nor rural vs. urban origins, nor any other regular feature that I can identify distinguishes market women as regards their opinion of caste. Presumably for individual reasons (agency), some women prefer to identify more with traditional high caste values on purity and orthodoxy, and some more with contemporary political values on democracy, citizenship, and human rights.

Still, market women agree on one thing. They are adamant that they share a common humanity with higher caste people. This is no small matter. Brahmanic ideology legitimizes rank by positing such essential differences between the *varnas* that the model approaches one of speciation. Against such a view, the recognition of a common humanity does much to threaten caste hierarchy. Kalamma takes up the challenge by responding to a question about higher caste treatment of lower caste people saying, "We are also human beings with blood and flesh." And Nagamma does the same when she describes the complexity of her own relations to the higher caste families whose homes she cleans:

> We are well looked after by some Brahmins. Daily, I come at five in the morn-
> ing to wash vessels and sprinkle water in front of the house and drink coffee if
> it is given. . . . Sometimes they are willing to give something for breakfast,
> thinking that *'They are also human beings.'* Not all Brahmins are alike. They
> have different temperaments. . . . [In one house] the daughter-in-law, in the ab-
> sence of the mother-in-law, takes and arranges the vessels in the kitchen even if
> they were cleaned by me. But, the mother-in-law, before taking the vessels,
> sprinkles water [to ritually purify them]. She asks me to empty the stored water
> if I touch it. After that she once again sprinkles water on [the container] and col-
> lects [fresh] water. [Emphasis added.]

Nagamma recognizes variations in the attitudes of upper caste people, along with changes that are occurring due to urbanization. On the whole, she is philosophical about the discrimination she receives. But, she insists that higher and lower castes are of one humanity and that discrimination is illegitimate. "We are also upper caste people," she says, "We also take purifying baths daily. But still they won't allow us in."

DEVOTION TO HINDUISM

Hinduism is the larger framework that ultimately legitimizes the caste system. It posits a hierarchy of being in which the human social hierarchy is only a segment. Below humans are animals, plants, and the material world. Above them are spirits and demons, gods, and ultimately, the cosmic force. In such a chain of being, caste hierarchy makes sense. Divisions among people are necessary to fill the various requirements of an orderly socio-economic system, and ranking is simply an acknowledgement of varying inborn abilities that fit the people to the duty. A Vedic origin myth describes the sacrifice of the primeval man that produced the *varna* system.

> When they divided the Man, into how many parts did they apportion him? What
> do they call his mouth, his two arms and thighs and feet? His mouth became the
> Brahman; his arms were made into the Warrior ["rajanya"], his thighs the Peo-
> ple ["vaishya"]; and from his feet the Servants ["shudra"] were born. (*Rg Veda*
> 10.90, O'Flaherty, 1981:31)

As the head is considered pure and the feet polluted in Indian culture, the myth legitimizes a theory of innate differences by identifying castes with relatively pure or polluted body parts. Furthermore, it implies that such differences are valuable in the constitution of society as a corporal whole. The Hindu concept of *dharma*, variously translated as "righteousness," "duty," and "cosmic order," provides the mandate to remain in rank. In the Kannada dictionary, the Sanskrit-derived word is glossed as,

> 1. Ordinance, law; duty; right, justice; charity; liberality; a pious act. 2. usage, custom. 3. virtue, merit, good works; religion, piety. 4. almsgiving; alms; gift. 5. harmlessness. 6. sacrifice. 7. nature. 8. the god of justice. (Bucher, 1983)

Law, religion, and nature are equated, legitimizing the high value on custom. Virtue lies in doing one's duty with generosity and sacrifice. Failure to follow custom is, by implication, harmful to others. Ultimately, the performance of *varna*-specific duty is what maintains cosmic order. And *dharma* limits justice to a kind of conservative piety.

While market women do not read at all, much less read the Vedas which traditionally have been forbidden to untouchables and to women, they are certainly familiar with the concept of *dharma*.[9] The word is a common one in the language, and folk stories, proverbs, and songs extol the value of doing the duty of one's station. In every village and town across the country, annual productions of *The Mahabharata*, and *The Ramayana*, epic dramas from India's medieval history, reinforce the centrality of the concept. *The Bhagavad Gita*, the central song of *The Mahabharata,* admonishes the hearer at length to perform *dharma* faithfully no matter the consequences. It declares, "One's own *dharma*, imperfect though it may be, is better than the *dharma* of another, however well discharged. It is better to die engaged in one's own *dharma*, for it is risky to follow the *dharma* of another" (Nabar, 1997:18).

In villages, contemporary *varna dharma* mandates the following roles for Dalits with respect to higher castes: doing manual labor, removing night soil, disposing of the dead, and performing as musicians in funerals. But in cities, Dalit roles are necessarily less closely associated with particular duties. The market and the government structure working relationships along different lines, and *dharma* is left to be expressed as piety in the form of religious devotion to gods. Market women pursue this devotion with great vigor. They worship posters of gods at home daily, visit temples weekly, celebrate Hindu festivals with their families annually, and go on religious pilgrimages when finances allow.

Even the poorest woman keeps posters of gods on a wall at home and offers daily *puja*, or worship, to them. *Puja* consists of decorating the icon with flowers and a vermilion forehead dot, offering it rice and a coconut if possible, burning incense and an oil lamp, and saying prayers.[10] The picture itself is a print, manufactured from an artist's rendition, and sold in the market for 2-3 rupees. There are a wide variety of such renditions, but all are well within a genre of painting: displaying the god with many arms and face forward, eyes to the viewer; using bold colors; identifying the god with characteristic symbols (the conch shell for Vishnu, the trident for Shiva, etc.); indicating its mood by conventional arrangements of hands and legs (palm up for peace and blessing; bent leg forward for battle, etc.); and surrounding it by other images and symbols with specific meanings (the swastika for Aryan heritage; the "om" symbol for Hinduism, etc.). Below is a poster of Laxmi, the goddess of wealth, commonly worshipped by both women and men in the market:

Figure 4.1.   Laxmi, the Goddess of Wealth.[11]

Some of the gods that market women worship are family deities. These are important because they mark patrilineal lines and link family to place. As the gods are associated with specific temples, annual visits must be made during festival times, reuniting the family for social as well as religious purposes. By stories and names, local deities are identified with the cosmic pantheon. Nanjundeshwara is the form of Shiva resident in the city of Nanjangud, for instance, and Biligiri Rangaswami is the form of Vishnu who sits on the Biligiri mountain.[12] Puttamma describes how the Goddess (Parvati, wife of Shiva) came to reside in her village:

> Malageshwari is the name of the Goddess residing in a village . . . Originally Malageshwari was at Kanyakumari [the cape] in Tamil Nadu. According to the legend, she moved away from there. After touring the country, [she and her brother] came and settled in my native place, Nagarley . . . The so-called superhumans came to ruin Malageshwari. Then both Eerananna [her brother] and Malageshwari sank in the river, in order to hide from them. Their clothes were taken away. Afterwards, she came through an underground tunnel and appeared in a forest. Since the Goddess came through a *malige* [underground tunnel], she was named Malageshwari [the Goddess of the cave] and both of them were installed.

The local goddess, named for a tunnel, *malige*, becomes the cosmic Goddess, *-eshwari* (i.e. the wife of *eshwa*, or Shiva) and is said to have taken up local residence. In Mysore, the Goddess is Chamundi (known elsewhere as Durga), who, in terrible form, saves the world by slaying the buffalo demon. She sits in her temple on Chamundi hill, receiving tourists from all parts of the country, and overlooking the city named for the demon she slew, Maheshasura. Buses leave every ten minutes taking worshippers up the hill to the temple where they can look out over the town with the Goddess' conquering perspective. In like fashion, each and every locality is rendered sacred by stories, temples, and depictions of the gods. And the worship of these gods links families corporately to their places of origin.

Some of the gods market women worship are personal favorites. Varunamma's favorite god is Shiva "because he has given everything; he is the head of the universe." Hanumamma says, "I trust Chamundeshwari. There are various gods and goddesses in different villages. But I trust in the god of Nanjangud and the goddess of Chamundi Hill." A few market women hold exclusive loyalty to one god or another, but most are thoroughly polytheistic, proclaiming as Mariamma does, that "We believe in all gods. We bow respectfully to all the gods that are found in the world."

Faithful polytheism requires participation in all the festivals of the Hindu ritual calendar. So, despite the expense, market women celebrate: *Ugadi,* the new year, *Divali*, the festival of lights, *Shivaratri*, in honor of Shiva, *Dasara*, for the Goddess as Durga the world-saver, *Gowri-Habba*, for the Goddess as Parvati the dutiful wife, *Dhanurmasa*, the ninth solar month, and many, many others. "We cannot celebrate to the level of rich people," says Kalamma, "but we celebrate beyond our capacity." Celebrating involves the preparation of special foods that are offered to the god in question and then consumed. In addition, there are festival specific duties. During *Shivaratri*, daily ablutions are let go in favor of morning prayer for eleven days; during *Gombehabba*, dolls are dressed, displayed, and worshiped; during *Ayudhapuja*, flowers and brightly colored vermillion are used to decorate everything from craft instruments to buses; and during *Dhanurmasa*, fasting is observed. Kalamma (who is AK) describes her daily routine during this last festival time:

> [I drink] only milk. We should not eat anything till evening. We have to get up early in the morning, at 5 am, and we should not see others. After bathing, we put on clean clothes, worship an ant hill, and make three rounds of a pipal tree.[13] This ritual is done for 48 days, and we get some peace of mind [from it]. Though we do not have any wealth, we get some satisfaction from worshipping God.

Urban life facilitates the participation of untouchables in Hindu festivals. And so, urban Dalits, though segregated into their own neighborhoods, emulate middle and upper caste popular Hindu practices in the streets and in their own homes.

Pilgrimages, to temples near and far, are a form of religious entertainment in Hinduism, and market women engage in them whenever finances will allow. Siddamma says:

> We go to see that god [Mahadeshwara] when we have money. We cannot go when there is no money. It is a long journey, and we have to go by bus. Mahadeshwara is in Nanjangud, and the Mahadeshwara hills are very far off.

Money must be spent on travel, food, and the gift to the priest. More significantly, income must be foregone due to lost work time. But family and friends, including children, go along on these ventures, and the trips are much anticipated as opportunities for a break from the humdrum of ordinary life. The monotony of work, market and domestic, is left behind. Special snacks are purchased and eaten along the way. The scenery is new and interesting. There is plenty of time for gossip on the bus. Sleep is out in the open. And entering the temple, the highlight of the trip, is the occasion of seeing a god!

For Dalits, visiting temples is also a matter of upward mobility. Prior to Gandhi's campaign in their favor, untouchables were forbidden to enter most Hindu temples and could not receive the services of priests. Even now, there are many village temples from which Dalits are barred, despite the law that they be allowed. To walk in with other Hindus, then, to the inner sanctum where the god is seen,[14] and where the priest serves by receiving offerings and bestowing a blessing, is to shed pariah status and become a full member of Hindu society. Market women are aware of the fact that they are being permitted something denied in the past, and take full advantage of this opportunity when they can.

Yet, religion is never merely a social instrument; it has personal significance. The Kannada word commonly used to indicate devotion to a god is *nambike*, glossed as "confidence, trust, fidelity, faith, belief; faithfulness" (Bucher, 1983). Trusting in God is the essence of devotion, and devotion is the essence of religion. Kalamma describes the moment of peace she gets from daily worship:

> I sit there [in the temple] for ten minutes. It may be the Raghavendraswami temple, or a mosque, or a church. I will go wherever I wish, whenever I wish to go . . . I will sit there to get some peace of mind. Afterwards I will go back home.

In moments such as these, women receive nothing more nor less than personal religious benefit.

Still, there is a tremendous variance in the degree to which market women are willing to place their trust in God.[15] I asked them whether God had given them any help. Of 20 respondents, 11 described how God had blessed them, 7 expressed doubt as to whether God was really helping, and 1 remarked that we cannot know whether God helps or not. The common understanding is that devotion persuades God to bestow good luck upon the devotee. But there is no correlation between the relative wealth or poverty of the woman and her credulity or cynicism in the matter. Women of faith perceive God's hand in sustaining them, regardless of their poverty. Shivamma, who lost her mother at age six, was left by her husband with four children, and has had to struggle to feed herself and her family, says:

> I worship God. How can we live without God? There is no life without God. We live by believing God, that he will definitely give us whatever we ask. We cannot do anything without God.

Women of doubt question God's willingness to help them, regardless of their better circumstances. Nagamma, who has earned enough money to marry all of her daughters and build a new home for herself, says:

> He has not done anything. We gain something if we work hard. My complaint is "Why has God made me to suffer like this when I believe in him?" I cry daily, trying to feed my children.

But, qualifiers are added in both directions. Women of faith express fatalism. "He gives whatever we ask him; He helps us in times of difficulty," says Girijamma, and then adds, "Whatever is stored in destiny will happen." And women of doubt express trust. "God has not helped us; We are not living as well as others," says Laxmi, but then remarks, "I trust [God] hoping that he may help me some day or another." In the end, appealing to God is always worth a try. "I light one incense stick in front of the god," says Siddamma, "and pray for food, clothing, and shelter."

UNTOUCHABILITY AND REBIRTH

The promise given to the lower castes is that by following their *dharma* they will be reborn into a higher station. The law of *karma* legitimizes people's circumstances in two ways: on the one hand, the conditions of one's current life are explained and justified in terms of meritorious or reprehensible acts committed in past lives, and on the other hand, rewards and punishments for acts committed in this life are projected into future ones as promises and warnings. The ancient Laws of Manu state, "One duty the Lord assigned to a Cudra [Shudra]—service to those before mentioned classes, without grudging" (I.91).[16] The text describes in great detail the rebirths that result from one's willing service, or lack thereof (XII:16-69). The one who "practices in the main what is right," receives "happiness in heaven (XII: 20)," but the one who "cultivates in the main what is not right," (XII:21) is first tortured in hell by Yama, the god of death, and then "enter(s) upon base transmigrations" (XII:52). The slayer of a Brahmin, for instance, "enters the womb of dogs, boars, asses, camels, cows, goats, sheep, forest animals, birds, Candalas and Pukkacas[17]" (XII:55). The one who violates caste restrictions is reborn a ghostly servant of enemies (XII:70-2). Manu warns against any effort to determine the moral good apart from Brahmins: "If fools, whose nature is darkness, declare any rule of right when they know nothing about it, the sin resulting therefrom, becoming an hundredfold greater, enters into them who declared it" (XII:115). So, "let that which well-instructed Brahmans may declare be regarded as an undoubted rule of right" (XII:108).

Once again, market women are aware of the concepts of *dharma*, *karma*, and *samsara* (rebirth). Girijamma (who is AK) is able to explain the entire philosophy:

> We have not seen rebirth. [But,] something that is good will happen to us in this life if we have done something good in our previous life. God will send us through another person to this earth. Or we are thrown out if we have not behaved properly . . . So we should always walk on a right path.

And Hanumamma says simply, "We have to eat in our next life the fruits of what we have done in this life." Furthermore, some women make positive anticipatory statements about rebirth. Papanni reports, "Yes, I believe in rebirth. I pray to God . . . not to give [me] troubles in my next birth. I wish to live happily at least in my next birth." Puttamma says, "I want to live peacefully at least in my next birth." And Luxmi, who had no parents growing up, says, "I want to be born a daughter of a rich couple."

Still, many market women are deeply ambivalent about the doctrine of rebirth. While all affirm the Hindu pantheon both in belief and in ritual practice, accept the concept of *dharma* as a generalized call to living a righteous life, and make efforts to emulate the purity laws of middle and upper caste Hindus, there are many who question or outright deny the existence of the afterlife. "I don't believe in such things," says Kalamma when asked about rebirth. "I don't know," says Puttabasamma, and Mariamma responds with "No, I don't believe." Even those with a belief in rebirth deny the absolute law of causation implied in the doctrine of *karma*. They do this by adding an element of the accidental to their explanations and a hope that God will forgive their mistakes (a thoroughly unHindu idea). "We are suffering now because of the mistakes we made in the last life. [But,] we are praying to God for good in the next life," says Jayaluxmi. Of 18 women interviewed in 1995, 8 gave credence to the concepts of *karma* and *samsara*, while 10, more than half, either declared they did not believe or disclaimed any knowledge of the matter.

Further rejection of the doctrine of rebirth as justification for low rank can be seen in Dalit origin myths. Every *jati* in the caste system has an explanation for its existence in the form of a story. Dalit stories frequently posit a time in the mythical past when the group was of higher rank. The central part of the story tells of a mistake made by a caste-mate. But commonly the mistake is of a minor nature, far exceeded by its punishment, and often committed by accident of a well-intentioned person (Kolenda, 1964: 75). It is all "a terrible misunderstanding" (Moffatt 1979: 122). In the end, it is actually sad fate that is to blame for the caste's current degraded position (Moffatt 1979: 122; see also Deliege, 1993; Gough, 1973).

At least some of the stories told in Karnataka fit the usual Dalit pattern. According to one myth, Holeyas once had the privilege of riding elephants, a kingly mode of transport, but were accidentally deposed (both literally and figuratively) by the very height of their animals:

> The Holeya chief, Honnayya, was riding on an elephant in a procession to a temple, one day. When the procession went through the temple gates, Holeya found that the portal was too low for him and his elephant to pass through. While the others went in, Honnayya and his followers were forced to remain outside, thereby losing forever the privilege of temple entry.

In another myth, Rajpariwars had once been assigned the high prestige job of
holding the umbrella for the king, an account that is supported by their name,
"king's family." Since then, say caste members, they have simply fallen on
hard times. And, the following explains why Holeyas eat meat:

> Shiva and Parvati employed a servant, Holeya, to tend their cow. The servant
> tasted some of the cow's churned butter and greedily tried to obtain more by
> killing the cow. Shiva punished the servant by requiring him to eat the cow.
> When the servant complained that he could not do it alone, Shiva relented and
> allowed two others to help him, Madiga and Bedar. Bedar left the meat and ac-
> companied Shiva into a temple. But Holeya and Madiga preferred to stay out-
> side eating carrion, and were therefore condemned to be outcastes, becoming
> "right-handed" and "left-handed" respectively according to the position they
> had taken in relation to the temple door.[18]

Greed resulted in sin (the killing of a cow), which was punished with a mandated degraded activity (eating beef), and consequent outcasting.

So, at best, origin myths reflect the ambivalence Dalits feel for high caste
explanations of their defiled condition. In the absence of ideological alterna-
tives, oppressed groups can only hope to gain by contending that they are
conforming to accepted values more than is believed by others. Most Dalits
lack the grounds upon which to contest, at the deepest level, the basis for their
own oppression.

NOTES

1. These colors, white, red, brown, and black, respectively, are said to refer to skin
colors. Lighter skin indicates more purity and Aryan blood, while darker skin indicates more pollution and Dravidian blood (see chapter six).

2. It can be notoriously difficult to determine the "real" rank order, as informants
do not always agree, and as castes bear different names and have subdivisions. I am
especially grateful to Kusuma Srinivas, Karen Souryal and R.H. Itagi for assisting me
to research the castes that I describe here.

3. Muslim women are not prevented from taking up market work, but are restricted
from leaving their neighborhood freely. Hence the market in the Muslim section of
town has many Muslim women, but the downtown market has only one.

4. Lingayats are members of the Virasaiva sect founded by Basava in the 12th century and characterized by exclusive worship of Shiva (Sastri, 1994: 435; Parvathamma, 1971: 84-116). They are identified by the wearing of the Shivilingum,
Shiva's phallic symbol, and the worship of Nandi the bull, Shiva's vehicle in mythology. Theoretically, they have an anti-caste ethic and contest Brahmin superiority by
using their own priests. In fact, however, they have reconstituted "an entire comple-

ment" (Kolenda, 1978:22) of caste specialists within the community, including their own untouchables.

5. This group was very difficult for me to identify. Some informants equated Rajpariwar with Nayaks of the north, and some with Bestas of Karnataka. Not a few said "they are all the same," lumping all low castes together.

6. Higher caste people may not eat with lower caste people without polluting themselves. Hence, the willingness to eat together, especially in formal situations, is a sign of relatively equal rank in the system.

7. Chennamma is perpetuating the centuries old tussle for rank between the Holeyas (her own caste) and the Madigas (the one directly beneath hers). In describing this competition, the Census Report of 1891 remarks, "the caste inequalities even amongst the lowest levels are infinite and there is no depth among them below which there is not a lower."

8. The full name for the Bestas is Gangematha-Bestaru, hence the reference to the river, Ganga (Ganges), and to fishing.

9. Fuller describes the relationship between sacred texts and popular religion: "Popular Hinduism can be distinguished from 'textual Hinduism,' the 'philosophical' religion set out and elaborated in the sacred texts that are the principal subject matter for Indologists, Sanskritists, historians of religion, and other textual scholars. The sacred texts of Hinduism—and the concepts, ideas, and speculations contained in them—are often vitally important to popular religion, and the latter cannot be studied successfully unless textual scholarship is taken into account . . . Nevertheless, themes central in the scriptures are not always central in ordinary people's beliefs and practices, and textual scholars' conclusions do not necessarily provide good guides to the workings of popular religion. For the anthropologist of popular Hinduism, ethnography - not scripture - is both the major source of evidence and the touchstone of interpretation" (1992:6).

10. Whether in home or in temple, *puja* involves care for a god similar to that given to humans: waking, bathing, eating, entertaining, and bidding farewell. Fuller comments, "*Puja,* at its heart, is the worshipers' reception and entertainment of a distinguished and adored guest."

11. A triad of god-families predominate in popular Hinduism. Brahma is the creator god, and together with his consort, Saraswati, the goddess of learning, is worshipped almost exclusively by Brahmins. Vishnu is the sustainer, and he has Laxmi, the goddess of wealth, as his consort. Vishnu incarnates himself periodically, usually as an animal, but also as Rama and as Krishna. Shiva, whose consort is Parvati (to be described in chapter seven), is the destroyer. But he is also the primal procreator, and hence is worshipped in the form of the phallus, or *lingum.* Shiva is the god most widely worshipped in south India. A rich mythology accompanies them all.

12. Bhairava, Mahadeshwara, and Parameshwara refer to Shiva, with "eshwa" being the identifying component of the name. Venkataramanaswami, Narayanaswami, and Narasimhaswami refer to Vishnu, with "rama" or "narayan" as identifying componants. And Chamundeshwari refers to the Goddess Parvati, also known as Devi, Durga, Kali, or Shakti, who is the prime activating force in the pantheon. All of these names were given to me as examples of family deities by market women.

13. The worship of anthills, monkeys, snakes, *tulsi* plants (basil) and pipal trees is common in popular Hinduism, and circumambulation of everything from trees, to gods, to temples, to funeral pyres, is central to the ritual.

14. The sight of the god produces a blessing known as *darshana*. This blessing is the primary purpose of the visit.

15. Market women hold the monist belief developed by Hindu philosophers that a single god-force is behind the various gods and goddesses of the pantheon. The Kannada word for God, *Devaru*, is plural, but is used with the singular pronoun when referring to God generically.

16. All quotes are from Hopkins (1995), with translator's parentheses removed for easier reading.

17. Candalas and Pukkacas are of mixed-caste birth, "the basest of men" (X:12, 18). The term Candala is one of the earliest references to untouchables in the Hindu literature.

18. The reference to "right-handed" and "left-handed" indicates the higher rank of Holeyas as against Madigas. This distinction is found in other castes as well in south Indian society (see Beck: 1970).

Chapter Five

Love and the Other

The Kingdom of God, as announced by Jesus, establishes a triad of relationships between God, the self, and the other. The second commandment of Jesus suggests that love of self, or of one's own people, must not supersede love of others. Hence, the Christian conception of the Kingdom is potentially disruptive of all other 'kingdoms,' or systems of ultimate loyalty, such as family, lineage, caste, ethnic group, and nation—i.e. of all "principalities and powers" of this world.[1] These structures demand a loyalty to one's own at the expense of others. And, they rely upon a social construction of the other as enemy to enhance internal solidarity. The problem comes when heightened fears result in conflict between groups who have defined one another as enemies. Without a commitment to love the other, peace can be maintained only locally, and that by being sacrificed at the extra-local level.

LOVE OR FEAR?

Elizabeth Colson, responding to the Hobbsian theory of the social contract, has identified the role of fear in the establishment of progressively higher levels of socio-political order:

> Fear, to most of us, seems a poor basis on which to found a society or develop a system of law. But we are unrealistic if we ignore the fear and concentrate solely on the advantages people see in their associations. A dynamic picture must include them both. (1974: 45)

According to Colson, it is fear that motivates people to form the reciprocal ties that ultimately create political institutions. To illustrate her point, Colson tells of a Tonga woman who gave generously of her precious supply of grain to a visitor who was a virtual stranger, someone she was unlikely to encounter again. Initially, Colson took the gift of grain to be a simple expression of generosity. But she later discovered that the woman was afraid of becoming a victim of sorcery. The Tonga woman explained, "It is not safe to deny them. You saw me give grain to that woman who came the other day. How could I refuse when she asked me for grain? Perhaps she would do nothing, but I could not tell. The only thing to do is give" (p. 49). An act of generosity was found to be rooted in fear. Such behavior derives from a pessimistic view of humanity. Most foraging and tribal societies expect the worst from people. The human heart is believed to be naturally self-centered and prone to passions that result in violence.[2] Colson remarks:

> Like the Tonga, the Chimbu, the Abelam, the Australians, the Pomo, the Makah, and the Iroquois, the Eskimo believe that conflicts are likely to arise from jealousy, envy, and resentments over insults. . . . [Anthropologists] find scanty ethnographic evidence for actual feuding in societies said to rely upon self-help, but good evidence for a pervasive fear of feud. (1974: 41-2)

Hence, fear of retaliation preempts conflict, or works toward its resolution. And personal restraint is emphasized to avoid the "violence that brings more violence" (p. 40).

Yet such restraint is both exhausting and expensive—exhausting because of the need always to evaluate the other's emotional state and contain one's own, and expensive because of the need to keep up the reciprocal exchanges that cement relationships (as in the above case of giving grain to avoid a sorcerer's attack.)[3] The establishment of socio-political institutions, from family to state, while limiting people's freedom to act in ways defined as illegitimate or criminal, provides a freedom from fear of reprisals that allows people to behave more overtly and directly in their own interests. Hence, argues Colson, *there is in most people a kind of social conservatism that prefers even an oppressive order to no order at all.* On the whole, people are willing to trade freedom for safety, and as a result, they have constructed increasingly larger socio-political units, with increasingly stronger internal structures of authority, over the course of human history.[4]

There are two costs involved in this process, one that Colson recognizes in her analysis and one that she misses. The first is that the safety from one's neighbor bought with socio-political order must be paid for by enduring that order's infringement upon one's ability to do as one wishes.[5] Once an authority has been put into place, people find that,

> It is no longer enough to restrain themselves to avoid embroilment with neighbors. They have now both to avoid behavior that will embroil them with au-

thority and to find ways to escape the demands that reforming or encroaching officials make upon them. (1974: 6)

The price to be paid is that of the demands of the authority itself. Yet, says Colson, even under colonialism, people have been willing to pay this price for the peace that it buys. "Whatever their quarrels with government, they want good government rather than less government" (p. 8).

The second cost, the one Colson misses, is that, quite in line with the foraging and tribal view of human nature, the purely political solution to the problem of fear creates a safe place for selfishness. While institutions are functioning well to prevent the conflict that would destroy the social order, individuals and groups can fight, and fight hard, for their own interests. Such aggressive pursuance of interests is legitimate so long as it is carried out within the established rules of the order. So, for instance, the political framework supporting the market economy permits a very blatant and unapologetic defense (and offense!) for business. The only requirement is to act within the law. Political regulation of interests substitutes for the moral injunction to *care*.

To be sure, in foraging and tribal societies, moral injunctions are very time and energy consuming. It can be a relief to let go of social obligations in favor of a simple and direct statement of one's own needs. But without the injunction to care, political machinery can sacrifice a designated segment in the interest of the smooth running of the whole. It is not that institutions merely need a bit of help from morality. To avoid sacrificing people, good will toward others or love, rather than fear, must be the driving force in the creation of these institutions, as well as in the structural changes that are necessary along the way.

Love is a matter of the heart. The apostle Paul defines it as follows:

Love is patient; love is kind; love is not envious or boastful or arrogant or rude. It does not insist on its own way; it is not irritable or resentful; it does not rejoice in wrong-doing, but rejoices in the truth. It bears all things, believes all things, hopes all things, endures all things. Love never ends. (1 Cor. 13:4-8a)

Love, then, is a set of responses rooted in a disposition of concern for the welfare of the other. Christians have always understood that such love can only be the result of a transformation of the heart, which is indeed naturally inclined to selfishness.[6] Efforts to keep the peace in foraging and tribal societies also call for transformation of the heart. Colson (1974: 92) remarks:

. . . in examining the ethnographic data on reform movements among Americans [sic] Indians and in Central Africa, I have been struck by the extent to which they stress the need for individual reform and purification. . . . In more egalitarian systems, the reform of *all* is demanded, since the burden of order is assumed to rest with all. The individual is made to conform to the ideal standard of the good person.

So, if the problem is evil in the heart, the solution is the conversion that makes love possible, and thereby prevents the war of all against all.

Colson sees such thinking as detrimental to the construction of benevolent political orders. She cites African witch finding movements, which scapegoat anti-social individuals, suggesting that the emphasis on individual reform inhibits the creation of "a new formal order, which will make it impossible for the Old Adam to reemerge" (p. 96). But, I would argue, new formal orders are constructed by the same old people. There is no reason to suspect that human beings will be more generous and enlightened in the planning and building of socio-political systems than at any other time. Indeed, there is good reason to think they will be less so, given the significant interests that are at stake.

Loving orders can only be constructed by loving people, and loving people are the result of a process of inner transformation — one that produces a different kind of freedom, the inner freedom from fear.[7] Of course, it is not that there is no love in the "Old Adam." People everywhere love their families, their social and ethnic groups, and their nations. But this is merely the love of self extended. Love of the *other* is what Jesus commanded. Such love comes exclusively from God and is truly revolutionary in the sense that it turns people around from distrust to trust, from fear to willingness to give.

The willingness to relinquish the protection of self (or, more accurately, to leave that protection to God) has, in fact, been a source of power for social movements in history. Martin Luther King Jr. led such a movement born in the churches of the American south despite the segregation that was, and is, deeply illegitimate to the very concept of the Church. He was able to do this because he melded love to the political question:

> One of the great problems of history is that the concepts of love and power have usually been contrasted as opposites, so that love is identified with a resignation of power, and power with a denial of love. It was this misinterpretation that caused the philosopher Nietzsche, who was a philosopher of the will to power, to reject the Christian concept of love. It was this same misinterpretation which induced Christian theologians to reject Nietzsche's philosophy of the will to power in the name of the Christian idea of love.
>
> Now we've got to get this thing right! What is needed is a realization that power without love is reckless and abusive, and that love without power is sentimental and anemic. Power at its best is love implementing the demands of justice, and justice at its best is love correcting everything that stands against love. (King, 2001a)

Christian love is not "sentimental and anemic." It is an inner power "implementing the demands of justice." It transforms the inner lives of individuals, who then challenge those human institutions that misrepresent God's rule on earth.

Furthermore, Christian love aims not only at inner personal transformation, and not only at the transformation of oppressive structures, but ultimately at altering the course of human history. More than one scholar has identified the Judeo-Christian religious tradition as having given birth to the very notion of history, based as it is on an irreversible linear, rather than a nature-based cyclical, or oscillating, sense of time (Eliade, 1991; Newbigin, 1989; Leach, 1961). According to Eliade (1991: 104), the concept of history is a result of the Hebrew prophets' interpretation of Israel's experiences with other nations. The prophets interpreted these experiences as God's intervention, both blessing and punishment, for their salvation. This caused the Israelites to:

> place a value on history . . . transcending the traditional vision of the cycle (the conception that ensures all things will be repeated forever), and [discovering] a one-way time . . . It may, then, be said with truth that the Hebrews were the first to discover the meaning of history as the epiphany of God, and this conception, as we should expect, was taken up and amplified by Christianity.

In the Christian era, anticipation of God's salvific epiphanies, first as the Messiah, then as the Second Coming of Christ, has produced a worldview in which events are perceived to be part of an unfolding story (Newbigin, 1996: 32ff). Martin Luther King understood his own movement to have historical significance within that broader story. In his last speech (King, 2001b), given hours before his assassination, King depicted himself being asked by God to choose a century for his own birth. Mindful of the liberating hand of God in producing nationalist freedom movements around the world, he chose the 20th century for the key role he might himself play in influencing the course of the development of God's Kingdom.

For Christians, then, history is the story of the growth of God's redemptive Kingdom. As Jesus indicated in his metaphor of the mustard seed (Mark 4:30-32), the Kingdom of God is growing into a mighty tree in which "the birds in the air make nests in its branches," i.e. in which the powerless find protection. Christianity has produced movement after movement down through the centuries for the marginalized, due in part to its ongoing discomfort with human political authority, and in part to its strong teleology (Troeltsch, 1992).[8] At their best, these movements have been the result of the inner transformation of individuals from fear and selfishness to love of God and love of others.

To summarize, then, if the transforming power of love of God and neighbor has not been encouraged or realized, institutions will be built primarily upon a concern for safety and a "refusal of history" (Eliade, 1991:117). That is, natural social conservatism will cause people to invest in the creation and maintenance of orders that are based on an ideal of structural and temporal stasis. These orders will function to keep the peace and provide for needs, but not without the moral expenses of permitted selfishness and sacrificed others. When stasis is the answer to fear, love cannot reach across the social and political boundaries. Such is the conservatism, in my view, of the concept of *varna dharma* (caste duty) that undergirds and legitimizes the caste system.

CASTE OR CHURCH?

Dumont to the contrary, *dharma* makes morality serve the cause of order rather than justice. For maximum stability, the Hindu worldview declares that all things in the cosmos, including society, are static. Time is circular and change an illusion. The Gita, the most beloved and popularly read of Hindu scriptures, says, "That which does not exist [*asat*] can have no becoming, while that which exists [*sat*] can never cease to be" (Nabar and Tumkur, 1997, 2:16). Timelessness is the philosophical foundation that legitimizes *varna*.

Varna is the institutional means of relating non-kin to one another in Hindu society. The principles of hierarchy and exchange of services inherent in the concept function together to establish the rules of interaction between *jatis*.[9] Out of this interaction emerges an order which has survived centuries, if not millennia, of invasions by various central Asian groups, with accompanying culture clashes. Certainly there is conflict within the order. Minor incidents of inter-caste violence are common. But this is violence that serves to maintain the system, even as it adjusts the system to changing political and demographic circumstances. So, the virtue of the caste system is surely in the stability it provides for village India. It has both kept the peace and provided for social and economic needs. It has, in fact, maintained a viable order.

Yet, within that order, selfishness is permitted and designated people are sacrificed. The rules of caste are legitimized by a belief in natural differences, including differences in moral capability. According to the Gita, "The order of the four *varna*s was created by [God] in accordance with the differences in their qualities and actions" (4:13). Brahmins are naturally sober and virtuous, while Shudras are lazy and inclined to vice. Therefore, privilege is accorded by virtue of birth to some, while inferiority is accorded to others. *Varna dharma*, the carrying out of the duties of one's caste, is in accordance with one's own essential nature and reflects one's place within the whole unchanging order. In the next chapter, I will document the effects of this cosmology on Dalit people's lives. Here, my point is simply that the ideology of the system completely supports differential treatment, and that it does so in order to provide security by positing stasis.

Stasis requires that everyone engage in the perfect performance of duty. But how is one to handle the desires or passions that must be frustrated because they would hinder that performance? Worse yet, what if the dictates of one's *dharma* necessitate the performance of some sinful act, such as killing in the case of a warrior? It was to answer this existential question that the Gita was written. The solution is to choose duty over desire, action over consequences, that is, to do what one must do dispassionately:

> You have a right to the performance of action alone, its fruits are never within your control. Do not perform action with an eye to its fruits, nor let there be in you any attachment to the non-performance of action. . . . Therefore, always perform what you have to do without attachment, for the man who performs action without attachment attains the highest state. (2:47 & 3:19)

These are the words of the god Krishna to the hero Arjuna who is on the eve of a battle against his own paternal kin for the throne of a kingdom. Arjuna has objected that he cannot possibly carry out his duty to fight because he will have to kill his own "brothers." This surely is against all morality. He protests, "My mind is confused about my duty . . . I shall not fight" (2:7-9). Yet, for the rest of the text, Krishna encourages Arjuna to proceed in the interest of *dharma:*

> Any action prescribed by one's *dharma* should not be renounced. Abandoning it because of ignorance is described as *tamasa* [darkness, gloom, sin] . . . When a prescribed action is performed as a duty, O Arjuna, having given up attachment as well as the fruit, such abandonment is held to be a *sattvika* [truthful] one. (18:7-9)

The performance of duty, done dispassionately and without concern for consequences, is morality. Hence, the subjugation of morality (justice) to the social order is complete.

It must be said, that if the Gita sacrifices the lives of others, it sacrifices the interests of the self just as easily. Detachment ultimately destroys all meaningful connection to life.

> Indifference to the objects of the senses, negation of the self, awareness of birth, death, old age, ill-health and pain as evils, non-attachment, not holding on to one's son, wife, household and such things, a constant equanimity amid all desired and undesired occurrences . . . all this is said to be knowledge, all else is ignorance (13:8-11).

The self-abnegation seems extreme. Yet, the individual is promised both self-realization and salvation through identification of the soul with God:

> He whose soul is not attached to external contacts finds that bliss which is in the Self. Such a man, disciplined in yoga through his union with Brahman [God], enjoys unending bliss . . . He who has thus found happiness within himself, who has also found his peace and light within, such a yogin has become godlike and attained the release that comes of being one with Brahman. (6:21-24)

In contrast to Jesus' injunction to balance the love of self and others, the Gita exhorts people to eliminate all such loves, to engage in thoroughly disinterested action, and thereby to receive the bliss of self-obliteration in the Godhead that comes from having served the order completely.

In the end, Krishna makes it clear to Arjuna that he really has no choice. He is, in fact, a puppet to his destiny, which is unchanging and unchangeable:

> If, resorting to self-conceit, you maintain 'I will not fight', your conviction regarding this is baseless: nature will compel you to do it. Being bound by the action arising out of your nature, O Son of Kunti, you will have to do that which, contrary to your nature and through delusion you do not wish to do. The Lord dwells in the hearts of all beings, Arjuna, and by His divine illusion makes all creatures whirl as if placed in a machine. Go unto Him for shelter with all your heart, O Bharata [Arjuna]. By His grace you shall attain supreme peace and an everlasting home. (18:59-62)

The perfect performance of duty is thus revealed to be not only natural, but utterly inevitable, since God "by His divine illusion makes all creatures whirl as if placed in a machine." Internal peace is the reward for the sacrifices involved in living out one's fate. But it is fate that rules circumstances in the end, and conformity is the only real option.[10]

To sum up then, the virtues of the caste system have included social stability, effective economic exchange, and political order—all the benefits of stasis. But its vices have included the exclusion, subjugation, and stigmatization of those at the bottom. Furthermore, philosophically it accomplishes its goal of legitimizing order by sacrificing all human passions, including love—the very love that might mitigate the ill effects of its hierarchical cosmology. This is surely the social conservatism born of fear that Colson identifies. And, in the end, that conservatism produces an order that consistently sacrifices the other to the self.

In concrete terms, where the Hindu ethic of *varna dharma* produces *jati* as a social unit, the Christian ethic of love produces the local church. Churches invite new members and encourage personal, social, and even political growth. They are composed of "patient revolutionaries" (Newbigin, 1989:

209)[11] intent upon changing both people and the institutions that they have built through history. This change is oriented to a future in which the Kingdom of God, already present in hidden form, will be fully "revealed" (I John 3:2). The hope implied therein permits people to let go of their self-protecting social conservatism in favor of liberating concern for others.

For Dalits and women in India, the choice is just this: whether to join the church or remain in the *jati*? *Jatis* provide their members with work, marriage partners, neighborhoods, social support, and legal defense, not to mention a fundamental identity. Churches, especially in India, attempt to provide many of these same things, but are inclusive rather than exclusive, and refuse the stigmatization of caste and pollution. This is not always perfectly so. The church in India has struggled to remain free of caste, just as the church in America has struggled to remain free of racism. Still, despite failures, the Christian Church is, in fact, an institution founded on a paradigm of love-based change rather than fear-based order.

The apostle John links together the two commandments of Jesus thus:

There is no fear in love, but perfect love casts out fear . . . We love because he first loved us. Those who say, "I love God," and hate their brothers or sisters, are liars; for those who do not love a brother or sister whom they have seen, cannot love God whom they have not seen. The commandment we have from him is this: those who love God must love their brothers and sisters also. (I John 4:18-21)

One cannot claim to love God without a demonstrated love of others. Obedience to the second commandment of Jesus is to be taken as evidence of obedience to the first. In the next chapters, I will demonstrate that historically it has been a Christian conception of love for, not detachment from, others that has improved the circumstances of Dalits and women in India. This has not happened without conservative reaction from the defenders of the caste- and gender-based order. But real progress has been made for the marginalized in Hindu society due to the influence of the Church.

NOTES

1. The term belongs to the Apostle Paul, and is rendered "rulers and authorities" in the New Revised Standard Version of the Bible. Paul's point is that the social and political structures of this world are given only temporary authority over us and will themselves be judged in the end of time. In Ephesians 3:8-10, Paul identifies the Church as the conscience of the social order: "I should preach . . . that now the manifold wisdom of God might be made known by the church to the principalities and

powers . . ." And in Colossians 2:13-15, he reminds the new Church that earthly institutions will finally be dethroned: "And you . . . He has made alive together with
Him. . . . Having disarmed principalities and powers, He made a public spectacle of
them, triumphing over them in it." (Both quotes are from the New King James Version.)

2. See, for instance, Lee's (1969) story of the attempt to control a hunter's dangerous, even homicidal, pride through group joking and scorn.

3. The prestige economies of Melanesia are a case in point. In these economies,
people "overproduce" yams and pigs in order to fund the elaborate exchange system
from which political leaders emerge. As much labor may go into the production of
food crops for exchange as for consumption. So, in the absence of authority structures, maintaining the peace becomes literally expensive.

4. I am writing these words within a week of the Sept. 11, 2001 terrorist attacks
on the World Trade Center in New York City. Fear is pervasive, and politicians are
scrambling to reestablish systems that will restore a sense of security. The construction of a world order with centralized power has never seemed so likely!

5. Colson is referring to government, but says at the outset that her model is based
on the study of central African clan systems (p. 25). I will be applying this analysis to
the study of the caste structure.

6. I am thinking here not only of contemporary Protestant pietism and its stress
on immediate conversion, but also of centuries of Catholic work on "divinization,"
which is a longer process of conversion from selfishness to God-centeredness and
love.

7. See F.G. Bailey's (2001b: 102-113) analysis of the various philosophical
stances possible with regard to morality and institutions. I take the third stance, the
one of Mahatma Gandhi, who "did assume that human nature is not rock-like, not a
given, but is a *potentiality*, something unformed that can be shaped in such a way that
we will all be able to get along" (p. 106).

8. I would cite here, not only modern movements such as the anti-slavery and
civil rights movements, but pre-modern ones such as those spawned by the monastics,
non-western ones such as the T'ai-p'ing Rebellion of China (Van Leeuwen, 1964:
369-72), and women's movements all over the world.

9. *Jatis*, of course, contain non-kin. But they would not exist at all were it not for
the *varna* system which provides them with internal solidarity by way of opposition
to other *jatis*. Without *varna*, lineages (*gotras*) would be the highest level of social organization.

10. The Gita also contains a strong theme of worship, or love of God, as a means
of attaining the detachment necessary in the performance of earthly duties. I am not
insensible to the parallels here between Christianity and Hinduism (in fact, among all
the world religions) as regards the priority given to love of God. It is the link between
loving God and loving neighbor that I am investigating, and on this score, Hinduism
regards loving others as a *hindrance* to loving God, while Christianity regards loving
others as *evidence* of loving God.

11. Newbigin's full comment is deeply relevant to my argument here, and runs as
follows: "We [Christians] are not conservatives who regard the structures as part of

the unalterable order of creation . . . and who therefore suppose that the gospel is only relevant to the issues of personal and private life. Nor are we anarchists who seek to destroy the structures. We are rather patient revolutionaries who know that the whole of creation, with all its given structures, is groaning in the travail of a new birth, and that we share this groaning and travail, this struggling and wrestling, but do so in hope because we have already received, in the Spirit, the first fruit of the new world (Rom. 8: 19-25)."

Devaraj Market Gates

Lanes Inside the Market

Sellers Outside the Market

Sellers Inside the Market

Tomato Seller

Flower Sellers

Seller with Established Space

Seller Subletting Space

Market Transaction

Kalamma at Work

Mariamma at Work

Mariamma at Home

Chapter Six

History of Untouchability

Market women are working hard to promote their own and their children's welfares by adopting Hindu symbols of high rank. They are, in fact, members of whole communities of urban Dalits that are beginning to be upwardly mobile, that is, to "sanskritise" (Srinivas, 1966).

Sanskritisation does not refer to economic mobility, though a gain in wealth commonly precedes and makes possible the social move. It refers rather to the emulation of high caste ritual practices in the hopes of gaining prestige for the whole group. So, sanskritising castes commonly forbid the consumption of meat and alcohol, restrict the remarriage of widows, refuse food from lower castes, gain the services of Brahmin priests, wear the sacred thread of "twice-born" castes, and avoid being polluted by untouchables. In addition, since movement is supposed to be impossible, they reinvent their origin myth. Caste leadership suggests they have found new evidence revealing a noble past that was forgotten due to hard times. Now, they say, the time has come to "reclaim" their original status. So, the practice of purity laws and the newly refurbished origin myth legitimize a claim to higher rank.

There is no implied criticism of the caste system in the sanskritising process. In fact, caste values are actually reinforced by their adoption in the attempt to move up. And, the necessity of constructing a new origin myth demonstrates that the notion of change has been rejected in favor of a cosmology of stasis. Hence, as Srinivas points out, such movement produces "positional change" without producing any "structural change" (1966: 7).

In the past, this form of mobility was found only among the middle castes. It simply was not possible for those below the especially rigid line of untouchability to move up. But now, changed political circumstances have permitted untouchables to challenge their traditionally debased position. India is a democracy with a constitution that specifically outlaws caste discrimination. Furthermore, the government provides a wide variety of benefits intended to promote Dalit advancement. Given the strength of the caste system, it is not surprising that real progress, in terms of health, wealth, and education, has been slow, and that improvement in social standing has been even slower. But change has occurred. Dalits across the country are recognizing that this is a time of unprecedented opportunity to improve their circumstances.

Dalit sanskritisation necessarily involves some new features. These include the adoption of higher caste clothing and ritual practices that have been expressly forbidden to untouchables in the past, the refusal to do traditional polluting work, the demand to be given access to public places including Hindu temples, and the exchange of the practice of bride wealth for dowry payments (which I will interpret more fully in the next chapter). On the one hand, Dalits are using the apparatus of the democracy to obtain resources, representation, and ordinary good treatment. "We are human too." Yet, on the other hand, most are *not* challenging the fundamental Hindu values or cosmology that support the caste system any more than have the middle castes. They are merely attempting to better their lot, using, in fact, the very symbols that previously degraded them. Deliege remarks, "Their resentment is not directed against the system as such, but rather against their own position within it. They therefore do not try so much to eliminate the system as to improve their place within it" (1999: 63).

THE ORIGINS OF CASTE

Contemporary popular mythology has it that the caste system is a product of the intermarriage of the invading, pastoral Aryans with the indigenous, civilized "Dravidians"[1] 3,500 years ago. The higher one is in the caste hierarchy, the more Aryan, the lower, the more Dravidian. One might think that the original inhabitants, who had built cities, formed centralized government, and developed refined arts, would have had higher prestige than the invading tribals in the resulting synthesized culture. But the honors always go to the conquerors rather than the conquered. Hence Aryan pride is millennia old in India, symbolized by the swastika, by relatively light skin, and by the popular twin epic military poems, the Ramayana and the Mahabharata.[2]

The degree to which these historical circumstances are in fact responsible for the origins of the caste system has been debated. Currently, one school of thought is suggesting that "orientalist" colonial scholars, whose written works were used by the British government for administrative purposes, are responsible for imaging caste in overly rigid terms and for projecting it backward into history (Bayly, 1999: 21-23; Dirks, 2001; Raheja, 1999). Furthermore, it is said, the British directly influenced the nature of caste over the more than two centuries of their presence in India. The census, taken every ten years, required all Indians to identify themselves by *jati*, sometimes with benefits in the off-ing. And the policy of encouraging Brahmins in administration increased their real power over other castes. Current conceptions of caste in academia, then, are said to be tainted by the colonial construction of caste.

In truth, there is a difficulty with writing an accurate history of caste, due to the lack of pre-colonial historical documents. India boasts some of the oldest writing in the world, but little of it is historical in nature before modern times. Religious poetry and myth predominate. Of these works, the oldest are the Vedas, orally transmitted works that were written down in the 9th century B.C. The Vedas are ritual texts which make only indirect reference to daily life. The philosophical Upanishads of the 7th – 5th centuries B.C. fail like-wise to describe the social system in which they are set. It is not until the laws of Manu, written in the 1st – 5th century A.D., that caste regulations are sig-nificantly outlined (Hopkins, 1995: xix ff). Hence, accurate knowledge of the origins of the system, as against contemporary popular mythology on the point, is difficult to come by, and probably will remain so.

Still, it is clear that caste is not an invention of the British, nor are purity and pollution laws the product of modern times. Feudal India was built upon values of hierarchy and exchange. Agriculture was the economic base, and the local village the primary social arena. Pauline Kolenda notes,

> The caste system is related to a different economic and political context – a stag-nant paleotechnic agrarian economy supporting some craftsmen, priests and re-ligious mendicants, a monarch, his bureaucracy, and an army in a chronically unstable political condition. (1985:4)

Under feudalism, the caste structure provided the division of labor needed for agriculture, as well as the chain of command needed for moral order and po-litical defense. This is not to say that the system was entirely static. It would not have survived the centuries if it had been. At least three kinds of change occurred: 1) expansion of the system, 2) oscillations caused by structural ten-sions and 3) adjustment to the social and natural environments.

First, as caste spread from the north to the south of the subcontinent, it in-corporated aboriginal peoples by a complex process of inclusion usually, but not always, at the bottom of the ladder as untouchables. One of the likely re-sults of this expansion was the *varna-jati* distinction, as the pure numbers of castes grew, along with the need to classify them. The other result, of course, was simply the fact that by the time of their arrival in the 16th century, Euro-peans found caste-like structures from Kashmir to Tamil Nadu, and from Rajisthan to Bengal, an area of almost three million square kilometers. Caste and its accompaniments of hierarchy, Hinduism, and the agricultural village, replaced tribal order and its accompaniments of egalitarianism, animism, and horticulture or foraging (Bailey, 1971).[3]

Secondly, the uneasy balance of power between the Kshatriyas (warriors), who had political control, and the Brahmins (priests), who had religious control, tilted back and forth, depending largely on the piety of the particular king. Technically, the Brahmin at court served the king as an advisor of ritually superior standing. But Brahmin control was never so complete as to prevent kings from using religion to sacralize their own purposes, or even to eliminate kings' participation in nonBrahmin religious cults (Bayly, 1999:76-79). Hence, Brahmin and King were engaged in a perpetual swing of the pendulum between religious and political values and control.

Finally, the system would not have survived if it had not been able to adjust to the vicissitudes of economic life such as changes in technology, new natural or social environmental circumstances, and demographic shifts. Hence *jatis* were formed, split apart, or died out, depending on the viability of the occupations they monopolized. Still, in the main, the structure was relatively stable through the feudal period and functional for settled, agricultural life. It was, says Beteille, "a more or less complete system . . . both meaningful and morally binding" (2000: 160).

That stability was purchased, however, at the expense of those at the bottom of the order. The place of untouchables was oppressive in the extreme. Taken collectively from various parts of India, the following practices marked untouchability in the pre-British past:[4]

1. The necessity of taking a ritual bath if touched by an untouchable.
2. The requirement that untouchables ring bells as they walk to warn others of their approach.
3. The requirement that untouchables wear spittoons to avoid polluting the ground.
4. The requirement that untouchables operate at night to avoid being seen.
5. The forbidding of untouchable men or women to wear shirts or shoes.
6. The forbidding of untouchable women to wear jewelry or face powder.

---

7. The segregation of untouchables into separate hamlets.
8. The forbidding of untouchables to walk through the caste village.
9. The forbidding of untouchables to use major roads or wells.
10. The refusal to seat or to serve untouchables in tea shops and restaurants.

---

11. The forbidding of untouchables to read the Vedas (or learn to read at all).
12. The refusal of priests and artisan castes to serve untouchables.
13. The forbidding of untouchables to enter Hindu temples.

———

14. The requirement that untouchables remove the village people's night soil.
15. The requirement that untouchables remove carcasses and corpses.
16. The forbidding of untouchables to own land.
17. The slavery of untouchables to land owners for agricultural labor.

Such practices reflected a number of intertwined themes: a) symbolic stigmatization (#'s 1-6 above), b) social exclusion (#'s 7-10), c) religious restriction (#'s 11-13), and d) degraded economic status and tasks (#'s 14-17). Like the strands of a rope, these themes were wound together to produce a very strong means of controlling untouchables for caste purposes.

THE CHRISTIAN CRITIQUE OF CASTE

There is evidence that untouchables protested their circumstances on occasion in medieval India. But, in the main, it took outsiders, arriving in the 17th and 18th centuries to bring real change. The French Catholic missionary, Abbe Dubois (1792-1823), encountering caste in the early 19th century, was horrified by the harshness of the treatment of untouchables:

> . . . their masters may beat them at pleasure; the poor wretches having no right
> either to complain or to obtain redress for that or any other ill-treatment their
> masters may impose on them. In fact, these Pariahs are the born slaves of India;
> and had I to choose between the two sad fates of being a slave in one of our
> colonies or a Pariah here, I should unhesitatingly prefer the former. (1999: 51)

European Christians had certainly not failed to engage in their own forms of exploitation and oppression. Nonetheless, it was Christian critique that piqued the conscience of high caste Hindus and subsequently spawned the movement against untouchability.

The first Europeans to arrive in India were traders, but the first to critique caste practices were the missionaries who followed. Missionary objections to caste emerged out of their own conceptions of the moral community. Forrester comments,

> . . . it was the insurmountable barrier to ordinary acts of humanity between those
> of different caste which aroused the deepest sense of moral outrage . . . The mis-
> sionaries may have been quite incapable of appreciating the emotional and ma-

terial support which a *jati* provided for its members in their horror at the moral effects of this kind of social organization, but their attitude was based not on simple individualism but on a notion of a caring community in which the individual had a considerable degree of liberty to follow the dictates of his conscience and develop his talents to the full in the service of his fellows. (1980: 26)

The Christian ideal for community was characterized not by an abstract, universal set of rights of the individual, but by a love of each for all, producing a freedom within service for every member. The barrier to "ordinary acts of humanity," along with the regular practice of ordinary acts of inhumanity, such as those marking untouchability, denied not only the intrinsic value of the person, but the full value of that person to others in society. The commandment to love one's neighbor was at stake. And missionaries took such social evils as untouchability to be clear evidence of the need in India for the Gospel (i.e. "good news") of Jesus Christ.

Missionaries of the time did not see themselves as cultural imperialists, nor even as colleagues of their compatriots in colonial government. The earliest Protestant missionaries to India included William Carey, who arrived under heavy restrictions in 1793, hid in Calcutta to avoid East India Company police due to a ban on proselytizing, and had to retreat to Serampore in order to be able to preach unobstructed. In fact, as it developed from a trading company to a mercantile government, the East India Company not only restricted missionary activity, but actively supported Hindu temples by giving them sizable monetary contributions (Harper, 2000: 101). The specter of missionary activity resulting in conversions that would threaten local unrest was feared to be bad for business. At the outset, then, missionaries and company officials were at odds with one another.

The company soon discovered the value of missionaries' linguistic abilities, however, and, yielding to pressure from London, gave permission for them to enter India with a license in 1813. Further, it removed the requirement for licenses in 1833. But the tensions continued. Missionaries were not only preaching for conversion, they were encouraging a wide variety of socio-cultural reforms, such the elimination of infanticide, child marriage, slavery, child labor, *sati*, and untouchability. Though the government did respond slowly with reform legislation, its first priority was always the maintenance of civil order for purposes of trade. An Anglican missionary, Rev. George Mattan, commented in 1851:

... stray fears exist among all classes of people, that the enlightenment of slaves will be followed by their liberation, and the consequent ruin of the interests of agriculture. We are therefore being regarded as *enemies* to the best interests of the country. (Forrester, 1980: 107) [emphasis added]

William Wilberforce protested that, despite its faults, missions to India had in
fact been "an Angel of Mercy" in the context of "godless colonization"
(O'Connor, 2001:76). To the colonial government, missionaries were an an-
noyance at best, dangerous at worst.

The matter came to a head with the revolt of 1857 which galvanized the administration into firmly choosing political control over social and religious
change. In a clear policy move, Queen Victoria crowned herself "Empress of
India," and declared that it was,

> . . . our royal will and pleasure that none be in anywise favoured, none molested
> or disquieted, by reason of their religious faith or observances, but that all shall
> alike enjoy the equal and impartial protection of the law; and we do strictly
> charge and enjoin all those who may be in authority under us that they abstain
> from all interference with the religious belief or worship of any of our subjects
> on pain of our highest displeasure. (Wolpert, 2004: 238)

Wolpert remarks of this proclamation that it was "couched in high-sounding
phrases that made this policy of indifference to the plight of women, untouchables, and exploited children sound as noble as Victoria" (ibid).

The primary missionary purpose was a simple one: to convey the news, to
those who had not yet heard it, that God is in the process of redeeming the
world, and that this redemption is made possible by the life, death, and res-
urrection of Jesus Christ. Actually, this news had reached India as early as the
first century A.D. with the arrival of the Apostle Thomas whom the present
day Syrian churches of Kerala count as their founder. But, over the centuries,
the Syrian church had fallen into a syncretistic adaptation to caste. Syrian
Christians were engaging in some of the most egregious untouchability practices, including forbidding entry to their sanctuaries. Undoubtedly, the adaptation to caste was in part responsible for the Syrian church's survival in
Hindu society for over 17 centuries:

> The Syrian Christians, like the Jews of Cochin and the Bene Israel of Bombay,
> survived and indeed flourished because they accepted the social system within
> which they found themselves, and observed its norms. The life of the church, the
> Syriac liturgy in its fullness, and a rounded theology in the Eastern tradition were
> all maintained, and tolerated by society at large, because no incompatibility was
> discerned between the gospel and a social order based on notions of hereditary
> pollution and purity. There was, as far as can be discovered, no attempt to pro-
> duce a distinctively Christian legitimization of the caste system; but neither was
> there any attack on it based on Christian grounds. (Forrester, 1980: 100)

From a contemporary missions point of view, the failure to challenge caste
and the tolerance of Hindu social conservatism had produced a "domesti-

cated" gospel (Newbigin, 1989: 142ff). That is, social acceptance had been purchased at the price of God's justice and consequently of the growth of the Church. And, the moral community of the Church had been compromised, with detrimental effects upon both oppressors and oppressed.[5]

The Roman Catholic church, following the initial Portuguese traders to India, and encountering the Syrians in the 17th century, took exception to Syrian liturgical practice and attempted to coerce acknowledgment of the Roman pope. It did little, however, to challenge caste. With centuries of missions behind it, the Catholic Church was very aware of the matter of cross-cultural sensitivities. As early as 1659, Pope Gregory the XV instructed his missionaries with the following propaganda:

> Do not regard it as your task, and do not bring any pressure to bear on the peoples, to change their manners, customs, and uses, unless they are evidently contrary to religion and sound morals. What could be more absurd than to transport France, Spain, Italy, or some other European country to China? Do not introduce all that to them, but only the faith, which does not despise or destroy the manners and customs of any people, always supposing that they are not evil, but rather wishes to see them preserved unharmed.
>
> It is the nature of people to love and treasure above everything else their own country and that which belongs to it; in consequence there is no stronger cause for alienation and hate than an attack on local customs, especially when these go back to a venerable antiquity. This is more especially the case, when an attempt is made to introduce the customs of another people in the place of those which have been abolished. Do not draw invidious contrasts between the customs of the peoples and those of Europe; do your utmost to adapt yourself to them. (Neill, 1971: 179)

The Pope's concern was certainly a valid one! Respect for culture is far from being an unchristian idea. Even the Apostle Paul had said "I have become all things to all people, that I might by all means save some" (I. Cor. 9:22). And, with this philosophy in mind, Roberto de Nobili, the Jesuit missionary to Madurai (in south India), had donned an ochre robe, taken up the study of Sanskrit, and entered Brahmin society as much as possible as a Brahmin man to convey the news of Jesus in culturally appropriate terms.

But, adapting to local sensibilities meant, in the Indian case, accommodating high caste prejudices. De Nobili, with papal permission, began his missionary work by cutting off all contact with other Christians in the area (who were largely of low caste origin) in order to avoid offending Brahmin converts. Later, in churches under his oversight, he allowed caste segregation to the point of constructing walls down the middle of sanctuaries to separate high caste members from low. In a 1599 decree, the pope permitted Christians across India "to refrain from touching persons of inferior caste, when in the company of heathen of superior caste . . ." (Hardgrave, 1969: 91). For the Catholic Church, then, adaptation to "manners, customs, and uses" in India included accommodation to caste.

It was Protestant missionaries of the 18th and 19th centuries, then, who most profoundly challenged caste. Protestantism was not in its origins a mission-minded movement. It had had as its first agenda the internal reform of the Church. But with the advent of German pietism in the 17th century and the Great Awakenings of America and England in the 18th century, a plethora of missionary societies were founded, many of them interdenominational due to the lack of interest among denominational leaders. These para-church mission agencies collected funds, printed literature, and sent out as missionaries single men, couples, and later, many single women who had been excluded from leadership positions in the churches at home.[6] Women's associations of local churches in the United States and England funded much of this work, catapulting the 19th century into a major Protestant missionary movement.

Pietistic and evangelical missionaries stressed the power of personal transformation through "new birth," citing Jesus' words to Nicodemus, "Verily, verily, I say unto thee, except a man be born again [or, 'born anew,' or 'born from above,' in various English translations], he cannot see the Kingdom of God" (John 3:3, King James Version). This emphasis on religious experience produced a number of results. The first was to complement at least, challenge at best, the enlightenment style theological rationalism that had purged much "enthusiasm" from the church. Converts had a new found freedom from "the slavery of sin" (John 8:31-36), and were naturally inclined to want to share this new freedom with those seen yet to be in bondage. Like casting out lines to drowning others after having been rescued themselves, evangelical Christians turned first to their own locales, then to their regions, and then "to the ends of the earth" (Acts 1:8).

The second result, paradoxically, was a renewed interest in scholarship. As missionaries encountered other cultures and struggled to learn languages, they wrote prolifically of their experiences and observations. Efforts to translate the Bible into vernaculars in particular produced much scholarly work. At the beginning of the 19th century, the Bible had been translated into only 70 languages, either in part or the whole. By the end of the same century, that number was 520, a gain of 450 new translations in only 100 years (Neill, 1971: 254). Along the way, translators also produced grammars and dictionaries for languages with and without written forms. In India, William Carey et al. translated the entire Bible into six languages, parts of it into 29 more languages, composed three dictionaries and six grammars, and translated the Ramayana into English, among other works.

The third result of the emphasis on religious experience and inner transformation was, perhaps, unexpected to some degree. Concern for reaching
others for Christ quickly became concern for others' circumstances, producing challenges to systems perceived to be unjust. A case in point was the anti-
slavery movement, birthed in England by two evangelicals, Granville Sharp
and William Wilberforce. The abolition of slavery in 1843 was, in fact, the
first significant change in the circumstances of untouchables, many of whom
had been slaves (Mendelsohn and Vicziany, 2000: 83ff). In the end, even the
colonial structures themselves came under scrutiny, as converts embraced nationalism out of a renewed sense of self-respect. Lamin Sanneh explains the
role of Bible translation in this process:

> for many . . . missionaries, the Bible was the greatest authority, and they be-
> lieved that it should for that reason become the living truth for the people to
> whom they brought the message. So they set out to translate it into the mother
> tongue. In doing so, missionaries gave local people a standard by which to ques-
> tion claims of Western cultural superiority . . . Whatever linguistic distortions,
> compromises, egregious inventions and other forms of invasive interference
> missionaries may have introduced, the shift into the vernacular paradigm in the
> long run, if not immediately, would excite local ambition and fuel national feel-
> ing. (1993: 17)

Evangelical and pietist missions, then, brought not only conversion to Christianity, but critique of indigenous institutions, and ultimately denunciation of
the whole colonial enterprise.

In India, Protestant missionaries initially attempted to be tolerant of caste
practices. The very first of them were German pietists who arrived in Tamil
Nadu in 1706, and who viewed conversion as a matter of inward experience,
and caste as a secular concern (Hudson, 2000: 10). Anglican missions, including the Society for the Propagation of the Gospel and the Society for Promoting Christian Knowledge, initially treated caste as promoting individual
morality and enhancing social order. Even the first Baptists failed to realize
the significance of caste for their missionary efforts (Dirks, 2001: 26). Caste
was seen as a matter of civil society, detachable from Hinduism as a religion,
and not necessarily relevant to church life. Caste might remain a source of
morality outside of the Church as long as it did not enter the arena of full
Christian "fellowship."

Still, Protestant missionaries took few pains to accommodate caste sensitivities in their efforts to evangelize. They invited any and all into the Church,
and expected new converts to participate fully with one another as "brothers
and sisters in Christ" (Webster, 1992: 35). A central symbol of this solidarity
was the Eucharist, or Lord's Supper, which is taken together with the entire

congregation. When high caste converts refused to eat and drink with low caste converts, the fundamental clash of values between Hinduism and Christianity was revealed. Significantly, the symbolic meaning of commensality is the same in the two religions: eating together marks a fundamental equality. In Christianity, a refusal to do so implies a break in fellowship, and in Hinduism, it marks hierarchy. Hence, high caste converts understood correctly that they were being required to give up their superior rank in accepting the bread and wine together with low caste converts. Christianity was putting them on the same plane as untouchables.

Of course, it is not that Christians were entirely without concepts of hierarchy and authority. These were present in missionary thinking, but only as regards temporal structures in the Church, not as matters of difference in essential worthiness. In fact, Forrester suggests that historically:

> The strong hierarchical dimension in Christian thought derives largely from philosophies such as Neo-platonism and Aristotelianism which, although not of Christian origin, were used for the undergirding and development of Christian thought. The continuing radical egalitarian emphasis of Christianity is demonstrated by the remarkable proliferation of egalitarian protest movements which arose within a Christian context and regularly relied upon biblical and theological arguments to present equality as a Christian thing, and rank, status, and disparities of wealth as having no Christian sanction or justification. (1980: 10)

Claims to human authority have always been seen in Christianity as potential threats to divine authority (Van Leeuwen, 1964). In the Old Testament account, it was with reluctance that God granted kings to the Israelites, chiding them for their rejection of divine rule through the judges and warning them of the abuses of human power (I Sam. 8). In the New Testament, the Church as "the body of Christ" is represented as having but one head, Jesus himself, joining all of its members into a single corporal entity (Ephes. 4:15). Thus, human authority is always temporal and subject to divine judgment. And the idea of a church tiered by inherent differences is fundamentally alien to the Christian worldview.

By the mid-nineteenth century, as caste interfered progressively with conversion and with church life, missionaries took an increasingly dim view of it and began to identify its rootedness in Hinduism. Some began requiring converts to renounce *jati* membership entirely in order to join the church. In 1833, Daniel Wilson, the Anglican bishop of Calcutta, wrote in a pastoral letter:

> The Gospel recognizes no distinctions such as those of castes, . . . condemning those in the lower ranks to perpetual abasement, placing an immovable barrier against all general advance and improvement in society, cutting asunder the

bonds of human fellowship on the one hand, and preventing those of Christian love on the other. (Forrester, 1980: 38)

In 1845, the bishop of Madras declared caste distinctions to be "unquestionably religious" in nature, and hence incompatible with Christian conversion. And, in 1850, the Madras Missionary Conference passed a resolution against caste practice in the Church (Forrester, 1980: 39). Slowly, protestants began to identify caste with Hinduism and to require its removal from the Church.

Missionary refusal to allow caste to dictate the terms of church life cost them high caste converts, but it won them an explosion of low caste and untouchable converts. Between 1880 and 1940, the Indian church tripled in size (Harper, 2000: 182). An average of over 12,000 people converted to Christianity *each month* between 1921 and 1931, yielding a church that was 80% low caste or untouchable (p. 184). The movement in Andhra, one of the largest, was spawned by the itinerant preaching of an untouchable convert, Verragunthla Periah. Periah's ministry was supported by a Baptist missionary, Rev. John E. Clough, who decided to welcome low caste people into the church despite the objections of higher caste converts based on the following Bible verses:

> For consider your call, brethren: not many of you were wise according to worldly standards, not many were powerful, not many were of noble birth; but God chose what is foolish in the world to shame the wise, God chose what is weak in the world to shame the strong, God chose what is low and despised in the world, even things that are not, to bring to nothing things that are, so that no human being might boast in the presence of God. [I Cor. 1:26-29] (Webster, 1992: 40-41)

Webster cites one convert as having commented, "Christ gave me a *pagri* (turban, symbol of respect) in place of dust" (1992:53). By 1912, the Andhra church numbered over 60,000, nearly all of untouchable background, and as late as 1936, a single district in Andhra was still baptizing 200 converts per week (Harper, 2000: 185).

EDUCATION AND ECONOMIC MOBILITY

In the long run, converts were socially and economically better off, but in the short run, most faced real persecution for having converted. High caste Hindus saw conversion not as a personal religious decision, but as a threat to the social and economic fabric of the village. Backlashes to converts ranged from the refusal of ordinary services and rights to work, to "physical abuse, burning chapels, and getting converts arrested on false charges" (Webster 1992: 61). Hence, churches had to step in simply to sustain converts through the first years. Education, medical help, legal defense, job training, and better hygiene all became part of the mission agenda.[7]

In the middle of the 19th century, the Young Men's Christian Association came to India. The YMCA had begun in England as one of the "socioreligious movements that arose to counteract the disruptive effects of industrial society on young men" (Harper, 2000: 37). Initially, branches were established in cities in India to provide expatriate young men with the kinds of athletic and spiritual activities that would keep them out of trouble. But as the movement expanded, it developed into a truly ecumenical, inter-ethnic, and multi-national organization. Its focus on the expansion of the Christian mission in holistic terms caused it to open its doors early, not only to Indians, but to low caste and untouchable members.

V. S. Azariah, a low caste convert who later became the first Indian Anglican bishop, was secretary of the YMCA in Madras from 1895 to 1909. Azariah combined enthusiastic evangelism with encouragement of improved standards of living and morality. As regards untouchables, Azariah's objective was to drive out the "four demons: dirt, disease, debt, and drink." To that end, he involved the church in the founding of schools, medical dispensaries, cooperative societies, banks, printing presses, agricultural settlements, and industrial projects, and wrote in a bishop's letter to pastors, "Educate, educate and educate every child and adult that you can get hold of" (Harper, 2000: 263). Christian conversion became associated with a total conversion of community and lifestyle.

Such transformation had the effect of enhancing the self-respect of low caste and untouchable converts by challenging high caste depictions of them. Ultimately it resulted in the raising of Dalit consciousness and an anti-caste political agenda. Jayakumar (1999: 151-221) credits the following things with producing the Dalit movement: missionary linguistic scholarship, preaching in the vernacular, general education (including women) leading to occupational mobility, teacher training of low caste and untouchable people, lay leadership in the church (though higher level posts were retained by Europeans), and direct provision for needs, such as medical help, orphanages, etc. In addition, missionaries frequently supported lower caste court claims against abusive landlords. As a result, "the change of the mental and spiritual climate in the attitudes or consciousness of the poor and the oppressed was an important contribution to their social mobility" (Jayakumar, 1999: 285).

The Nadars (or Shanars) of Tamilnadu, for instance, had been low caste toddy tappers of the southern palmyra forests. Anglican missions to the group included economic development projects such as digging wells, planting trees, and improving sanitation, and the encouragement of education. By 1820, twelve Nadars had enrolled in teacher training. By the 1840s, a mass movement of Nadars into Christianity was taking place. And by the 1870's most Christian Nadars had left the stigmatized toddy tapping behind and taken up shop keeping and agriculture (Hardgrave, 1969).

As they moved up economically, Nadars began to reject their untouchability and to adopt symbols of higher caste status such as the right to wear shirts. Most significantly, Nadar women began to wear the blouses under their saris that had been previously forbidden them. Higher caste resistance to this move included beating women in markets, disrupting schools, and even riots in the 1820's over what came to be called "the breast-cloth controversy." The raja of Travancore, in an effort to settle the matter, issued a royal proclamation in 1829 stating that,

> . . . as it is not reasonable on the part of the Shanar women to wear cloths over their breasts, such custom being prohibited, they are required to abstain in future from covering the upper part of their body. (Hardgrave, 1969: 62).

Nadar women were not dissuaded, however, and attacks on women resulting in rioting reoccurred even more dramatically in the late 1850's. Finally, the king reversed his decision and the Nadars succeeded in their bid for respect. Hardgrave explains the Christian Nadars' success as follows:

> [Compared to Hindu Nadars,] the Christians [Nadars] enjoyed a substantially improved position. Through education and migration, they enjoyed a slightly higher economic position, and through their unity in the mission organization they had been able to improve their standard of living. Where the Hindu Nadars were divided, often without a single village authority, into client groups dominated by influential and powerful [high caste] Nadans, each in a constant dispute and litigation with the other, the Christians, under the direction of the missionaries, sought to achieve unity among themselves for the discipline and well-being of all.[8] (1969: 54)

In this case, the incorporation of a mass movement of low caste people into the Church produced a political power bloc that could not be matched by *jati* solidarity within Hinduism.

In sum, conversion to Christianity produced more than reform. It produced revolution. The fundamental values of hierarchy and social conservatism were challenged, and new values associated with loving God and loving one's neighbor as one's self were adopted. The result was communities of self-respect and advancement. Bishop Azariah, himself a Nadar, compared Hindu and Christian notions of community:

> Hinduism has never set forth a body of doctrines which every follower of that religion should more or less accept; it presents a scheme of life. A Hindu may believe in anything and everything, or nothing; he will still be a Hindu if only he does not transgress the social restrictions of that particular caste in which he was born, to which he belongs through life, and in which he must die. In this limited sense, caste is Hinduism and Hinduism is caste. . . .
>
> But what is Christianity? . . . it is a scheme of life in a society; it is an organism, a family; a fellowship, a brotherhood – whose center, radius and circumference is Christ. In fellowship with all others who are attached to the Lord, bound together by outward rules and rites and throbbing with one inward pulse and purpose, men and women of all ages, races, tongues, colours and nationalities have accepted this scheme of life, and separated from all others are more and more experiencing in this fellowship the impetus and power issuing from the Spirit who is its indweller and life-giver. (Harper, 2000: 248)

This ideal for Christian community was not always fully realized as we shall see. But in the main, low caste and untouchable communities benefited tremendously from adopting Christianity then, and continue to do so when they convert today.

HINDU REFORM AND RESISTANCE

Not a few social scientists have remarked on India's caste-based village society's ability to withstand, not merely criticism, but invading armies over the centuries. The early 19th century East India Company collector, Thomas Metcalf, commented:

> The village communities are little republics, having nearly every thing they can want within themselves, and almost independent of any foreign relations . . . Dynasty after dynasty tumbles down; revolution succeeds to revolution; . . . but the village community remains the same. (Dirks, 2001: 28)

The usual means of absorbing the shock of new peoples and new ideas is to subsume them within the existing values and structure as simply another part of the whole. Not a few new religions have found themselves transformed over time into yet another caste.[9]

In the 19th century, however, there were thoughtful and well-educated Hindus who, from within their religion, attempted to respond seriously to the Christian critique of caste. Typically they did this by accepting Jesus' social ethic, while rejecting his claims to uniqueness of divinity.[10] For instance, Rammohan Roy (1772-1833), who is now remembered as "the father of modern India," wrote:

> I feel persuaded that by separating from the other matters contained in the New Testament, the moral precepts found in that book, these will be more likely to produce the desirable effect of improving the hearts and minds of men of different persuasions and degrees of understanding. . . . This simple code of religion and morality is so admirably calculated to elevate men's ideas to high and liberal notions of one GOD, who has equally subjected all living creatures, without distinction of cast[e], rank, or wealth, to change, disappointment, pain, and death, and has equally admitted all to be partakers of the bountiful mercies which he has lavished over nature, and is also so well fitted to regulate the conduct of the human race in the discharge of their various duties to GOD, to themselves, and to society, that I cannot but hope the best effects from its promulgation in the present form. (Hay, 1988:25)

Roy rejected personal conversion to Christianity, but he worked collaboratively with William Carey as a tireless campaigner for social reform. He was not persuaded of Jesus' divinity, nor of his miracles (which he compared disparagingly with Hindu mythology), but he was so persuaded of the value of Jesus' ethical teachings that he published a number of pamphlets promoting them as, "more conducive to moral principles, and better adapted for the use of rational beings, than any others which have come to my knowledge" (Hay, 1988:16).

In 1828, Roy founded a Hindu reform society, the Brahmo Samaj (Society of God), which attempted to marry Christian ethics, along with Western education, science, and humanism, to Hindu philosophy. The Brahmo Samaj was part of a larger movement of intelligentsia trying to respond to Christian critique by combining a pride in India's long history of religious thinking with a passion for the reform of contemporary Hindu society. The agenda included promotion of education; discouragement of child labor and slavery; protection of women from early marriages, illiteracy, and the practice of *sati*; and anti-untouchability. The Brahmo Samaj advocated reform through pamphlets and speeches, did some relief work, and even built its own schools.

Yet, the Brahmo Samaj's approach to caste was always somewhat ambivalent, and Roy himself never broke caste practice. His reform consisted primarily in the promotion of good treatment of untouchables and of their education. The idea was to retain caste as an organizing principle, but to purge it of its more objectionable features, such as untouchability. Later, the internationally renown publicist of Hinduism to the West, Vivekannanda, exegeted this view of caste by suggesting that "Men must form themselves into groups

. . . [though] there is no reason you should trample on my head" (Forrester, 1980: 159).

More extreme proponents of Hindu pride, however, were willing to justify the whole of the caste system unequivocally. The nationalist leader Bal Gangadhar Tilak (1856-1920) defended Hindu society by rooting his argument in the Bhagavad Gita and its admonition to perform one's duty selflessly and without passion. He identified himself with a 17th century Marata military leader, Shivaji, who was remembered for defeating the Mughal Empire, resurrected Hindu holidays by turning them into popular religio-political events, and openly rejected the social programs of the mainstream nationalist leaders. In 1891, for instance, he vigorously opposed the latest in a series of reforms for women raising the age of statutory rape from 10 to 12 years old (Wolpert, 2004:257). For Tilak, and other "extremists," nationalism and Hinduism were welded together to create a powerful, and sometimes violent, rejection of all ideas or practices perceived to be foreign in origin.

An even more zealous form of resistance was advocated by the Arya Samaj (Society of Aryans) founded by Dayananda Saraswati (1824-1883) in 1875. Dayananda was ascetic, argumentative, and militant. Hay (1988: 53) remarks:

Dayananda's energetic and sometimes acrimonious method of disputation signaled the shift among those Hindu religious leaders who were aware of the challenge of Christianity from an assimilative or defensive attitude to an active, aggressive one.

He accused the more moderate reformers of being sycophants of the Europeans and of failing to educate themselves in ancient Indian texts. The Brahmo Samaj, for instance, had "saved many persons from the clutches of Christianity," but was inclined nonetheless to "eulogize Christians" (Hay, 1988: 59). While he advocated the elimination of untouchability, citing the lack of references to it in the Vedas, he clearly had not given up caste sensibilities. He complained that the moderate Hindu reformers were so rude as to "observe no restrictions on interdining with Englishmen, Moslems, and low class people" (p. 60). On the whole, observance of caste practices and pollution restrictions made the Arya Samaj's purported commitment to improving the status of untouchables appear "less than whole-hearted" (Mendelsohn and Vicziany, 2000: 93).

As an antidote to Christian conversion, Dayananda adapted a purification rite for temporarily polluted high caste people, *shuddhi,* to be a ceremony for readmitting people into Hinduism. Subjects were cleansed of the polluting contact they had had with other religions and thereby made fit to become Hindus once more. This was significant for formerly low caste and untouchable people because, via *shuddhi,* they were able to be "purified" in a manner previously denied to them, and incorporated back into Hinduism with a degree of respect. Throughout the 20th century, *shuddhi* campaigns waxed and waned in response to perceived "forced" conversions of untouchables to Christianity and Islam.

Yet the protection of purity was not the only concern. Central to high caste Hindu resistance to untouchable conversion was the matter of the agricultural labor supply. Landowners were invariably of middle or high castes, and Brahmins were forbidden to do manual labor (literally, "plough the earth") by the Laws of Manu (X: 84). Under the traditional system, untouchables were excluded from most important Hindu temples and only given restricted roles in religious ceremonies - those considered supernaturally dangerous, such as playing the drums at funerals or appeasing the goddesses of disease. But, their labor in the fields was vital to the village economy. At this level, they were completely incorporated into Hindu society. And conversion to Christianity, or for that matter to Islam, threatened the religious sanction given to that role.

Webster (1995: 42) illustrates the impact that Christian conversion had on the village economy by noting the full implications of the three mandates Rev. Clough gave to his new converts: 1) not to work on Sundays, 2) not to eat carrion, and 3) not to worship idols. The first of these introduced a weekly day of reprieve from work that had not been previously given, the second removed a form of payment in kind and thereby increased the need for direct payment, and the third removed converts from their ritually polluting roles in ceremonies such as funerals. The change was real enough, and the result was a backlash against Christian religious, social, and cultural influences that developed in time and deepened into a conservative high caste reaction to change.

Even among the "moderates," attempts to defend Hinduism inevitably compromised the more radical change needed to truly free the untouchables. This compromise could be seen, for instance, in the highly celebrated debate that occurred in the 1930s between Mahatma Gandhi (1869-1948) and Bhim Rao Ambedkar (1891-1956). Gandhi was an ardent Hindu, and as such, never rejected caste *per se*. His political philosophy was centered on the autonomous village republic, which he saw as being held in orderly stability by the division of labor inherent in the caste system. What he hoped for and advocated in speeches and writings was a harmonious community, one which incorporated everyone, and which had humility and service as its central values. The practice of excluding untouchables and the lack of appreciation for the work that they had traditionally done were incompatible with such a notion of community. Hence, Gandhi tried, not so much to change the social position of untouchables, as to present it to society in a new light.

In order to make his point, Gandhi called untouchables "Harijans," or God's children, and declared that they were above all others the most righteous because they were doing the most humble, and therefore the most spiritually valuable, work. Other castes ought, in fact, to imitate them. Gandhi required all of the members of his ashram to clean the common latrines, and took his own turn along with them. For his higher caste followers, raised in a society that spurned all manual labor, much less such polluting work, the requirement made a powerful point: God values the work of a humble servant; if you wish to know God you must give up your pride and become an untouchable.[11] Hence, Gandhi's effort to reform the caste system consisted primarily in appealing to the conscience of higher caste people to take better care of those beneath them. He certainly did not lack vigor in making this point. He wrote:

> So far as I am concerned, the untouchability question is one of life and death for Hinduism. As I have said repeatedly, if untouchability lives, Hinduism perishes, and even India perishes. . . . What I am aiming at is not every Hindu touching an 'untouchable,' but every touchable Hindu driving untouchability from his heart, going through a complete change of heart" (Manshardt, 1949: 79-80).

But, Gandhi was little interested in anti-untouchability legislation. He wanted the Hindu community to voluntarily reform itself. And, it would have been inconsistent for him to encourage untouchables to leave behind their traditional work for more prestigious or better paying jobs. Poverty and humble service were to be everyone's aims.

Above all else, Gandhi wanted untouchables to be kept within the Hindu fold. He objected vigorously to their conversion to Christianity, suggested that the mass movements were insincere, and even refused to allow untouchables a political autonomy that might have empowered them vis-à-vis the rest of Hindu society. In 1932, he engaged in a high profile fast to protest the creation of separate electorates for untouchables on the grounds that it would divide the Hindu community. In 1941, he revealed a disturbingly patronizing view, while attempting to dissuade a Christian missionary from proselytizing. He asked the missionary:

> Would you preach the Gospel to a cow? Well, some of the untouchables are worse than cows in understanding. I mean they can no more distinguish between the relative merits of Islam and Hinduism and Christianity than a cow. (Webster, 1992: 107)

Clearly, Gandhi was referring to lack of education rather than innate inability. But, certainly in Bhim Rao Ambedkar's mind, his advocacy of higher caste care for the lower castes always contained a patronizing tone.

Ambedkar was himself of untouchable background. He had a Western education, including a Ph.D. from Columbia University in New York where, by his own testimony, he had experienced for the first time the real respect of being viewed as a full colleague. With a background of painful experience of discrimination in India, Ambedkar was less interested in glorifying untouchables than in liberating them. He labeled them "Dalits," or 'oppressed ones,' to highlight their real circumstance. And he campaigned vigorously for legislative reform that would protect them from the rest of Hindu society.

Gandhi and Ambedkar were not enemies. Together they participated in the movement to gain access for untouchables to temples, wells, public roads, and schools. But Ambedkar did not share Gandhi's optimism with regard to the religious reform of high caste minds. In the debate over separate electorates, Ambedkar vigorously asserted that the electorates were necessary to prevent high caste influence over low caste voting. Reserved seats, which require that the candidates for office be untouchables but do not restrict the voters within the district, were granted. But separate electorates, which would have permitted only untouchable voters for untouchable candidates, were not. Hence, in Gandhi's favor, "the principle that Untouchables were Hindus had successfully been defended" at the expense of Dalit empowerment (Mendelsohn & Vicziany, 2000: 105).

Ambedkar subsequently played a central role in the construction of the democracy. At independence in 1947, he was named chair of the drafting committee for the constitution to ensure the establishment of full citizenship rights for Dalits. Under his leadership, Article 17 of the constitution abolished the practice of untouchability, and subsequent acts made discrimination a punishable offense with increasingly severe sanctions. Later legislation also introduced a number of forms of "compensatory discrimination" for untouchables, such as educational scholarships and government job quotas.

But for Ambedkar, the pace of reform was tediously slow. He often made despairing statements about the future and signaled his frustration with highly symbolic, religiously oriented, political acts. In 1927, he led a group of untouchables to "pollute" a high caste water tank by drinking from it, and later he publicly burned a copy of the Laws of Manu. In 1935, he declared "I was born a Hindu, but I will not die a Hindu." And, true to his word, in 1954, he converted to Buddhism along with 50,000 followers in a mass ceremony. In the half century following, more than four million untouchables converted to Buddhism in political protest following his example. Hence, Ambedkar's view that true liberation for untouchables is only possible by leaving Hinduism became the watchword for the more

radical elements of the Dalit movement. (Hay, 1988: 339). Ambedkar
wrote:

> Caste among Non-Hindus has no religious consecration; but among the Hindus
> most decidedly it has. Among the Non-Hindus, caste is only a practice, not a sa-
> cred institution. They did not originate it. With them it is only a survival. They
> do not regard caste as a religious dogma. Religion compels the Hindus to treat
> isolation and segregation of castes as a virtue. Religion does not compel the
> Non-Hindus to take the same attitude towards caste. If Hindus wish to break
> caste, their religions will come in the way. (Shah, 2002: 102)

For Hindus, said Ambedkar, caste is a religious matter, and as such, will not
be eliminated without conversion.

The clash between religious and secular interpretations of caste came to a
head in the matter of compensatory discrimination. According to the secular
view of caste, benefits should be given to all those with a history of socio-
economic disadvantage. But according to the religious, or "sacral," view of
caste, which depicted "the caste group as a component in an overarching
sacral order of Hindu society," benefits should only be given to those who
were within Hinduism and therefore experiencing the particular stigma of untouchability associated with notions of purity and pollution (Galenter, 1970:
300). Were all historically untouchable groups to benefit?, or only those who
had remained Hindus?

The government decided that, for purposes of compensatory discrimination,
only Hindus could be considered untouchables. It had previously established a
list of "scheduled castes," i.e. castes on the schedule, that had included a wide
variety of nonHindu and tribal groups along with traditional untouchables. But
when benefits were established, Christian, Buddhist, Muslim, and even Sikh
untouchables were systematically excluded from the list.[12] In 1935, the Government of India Act stated specifically that "No Indian Christian shall be
deemed a member of a Scheduled Caste." In Madras, the state legislature declared the following in regard to the granting of educational fee remission: "It
is not intended that these concessions should be granted to converts from
scheduled castes to Christianity or any other religion" (Webster, 1992: 113).
When this policy was contested in 1950, the president declared, "no person
who professes a religion different from the Hindu religion shall be deemed to
be a member of a scheduled caste" (p. 128). The result was a strong social and
economic disincentive for untouchables to convert away from Hinduism.[13]

With disincentives to convert, many fewer Dalits became Christians in the
latter half of the 20th century than had in the first. The census reveals that between 1931 and 1951, the number of Christians increased by nearly 40%,
while the general population grew a mere 2.3%. But between 1951 and 1971,

Christians increased by only 30%, while the general population's growth had jumped dramatically to 24%. In the next decade, the percentage of increase of Christians, 14%, dropped well below the increase in general population of 21% (Webster, 1992: 153). The mass movements had come to an end, and the Hindu community was resisting the loss of its lowest ranking members through a mixture of protective legislation and social reform. One Hindu reformer commented, "The fear of the Christian Missionary has been the beginning of much social wisdom among us" (Webster 1992:68).

CASTE IN THE CHURCH

According to Christian theology, the Church is composed of redeemed (i.e. "bought back"), but not yet perfected, followers of Christ. Hence it should not be surprising, though it is certainly disappointing, that the Church throughout history has accommodated itself so easily to the social evils of its day. In India, caste prejudice was not eliminated from the Christian community. Christians of high caste background resisted a common Eucharist, worshipped in separate churches, and refused to intermarry with lower castes. The early 20th century British bishop, Henry Whitehead, commented, "Four sick passions . . . are the curse of the Church in South India – race prejudice, caste feeling, party spirit and personal jealousy . . ." (Harper, 2000:136). His friend and colleague, Bishop Azariah, agreed:

> How sad to find Christians eaten up with pride of caste and wealth, sunk in worldliness and superstition, given in various instances to fashionable forms of vices, and lacking in zeal for the Master's cause. (Harper, 2000: 57)

Caste had penetrated the Church.

But then, race prejudice was also evident in the Church. Expatriot Europeans were retaining positions of leadership long past when it was reasonably necessary. In a 1910 speech to the World Missionary Conference in Edinburg, Azariah commented to a chagrinned and chastened, largely white, audience:

> The problem of race relationships is one of the most serious problems confronting the Church to-day. The bridging of the gulf between East and West, and the attainment of a greater unity and common ground in Christ . . . is one of the deepest needs of our time. (Harper, 2000: 149)

On this point he was joined by the Anglican friend of Gandhi's, C.F. Andrews, who "from the beginning, . . . understood caste discrimination and racial discrimination as essentially the same thing; against both his face was

set implacably. With such intolerable evils no compromise was thinkable"
(Forrester, 1980: 149). Race, like caste, was a deadly accommodation to social conservatism; a failure to embrace the full revolution of Christianity.

NOTES

1. The term "Dravidian" is the one that is popularly used, but it conflates the original inhabitants of the Indus Valley, now in Pakistan, with many other indigenous
groups in central and south India. In modern times, it has functioned as a political tool
for nonBrahmin castes of the south (not untouchables) to improve their political and
economic circumstances (see Irschick, 1969).

2. Both poems reflect the period of medieval Aryan kingdoms in the north. In the
Ramayana, Rama, a prince from the north, defeats Ravana, a demon from the south,
in what is probably an allegory of the Aryan conquering of the subcontinent. Recognizing this, 20th century nonBrahmin activists have attempted to rewrite the story in
favor of the demon!

3. There has always been regional variation in the specifics of the caste structure.
Still, the existence of *jatis* as birth-based groups that exchange services, their organization into the hierarchical structure of *varna*, and the use of Hindu pollution
metaphors to legitimize that hierarchy have been India-wide phenomena.

4. I have collected this list of practices over the years from a wide variety of references.

5. Lamartine has said, "Man never fastened one end of a chain around the neck of
his brother, that God did not fasten the other end around the oppressor."

6. For a biography of one such woman, remarkable for both her adaptation to Indian culture and her challenge of caste practices, see Elliott's (1987) account of the
life of Amy Carmichael.

7. Webster (1995:67) remarks, "Neither the government nor the Hindu reformers
took much interest in the uplift of the Dalits until after the mass movements [of untouchables into Christianity] were in progress. The government took minimal steps
towards providing land or education for the Dalits, and then only under provocation.
Throughout India it was invariably the mission schools rather than in government or
other private schools that the first battles over the admission of Dalit students on a par
with others were fought and won."

8. Webster (1992:66) says, "the mass movements initiated a process of primarily
cultural change which included alterations in perceptions of self and the world, in lifestyle, as well as the acquisition of enhanced resources for self-improvement and self-
empowerment."

9. Examples would include Jainism, Sikhism, and even Christianity in its Syrian
form on the Kerala coast. Islam has remained outside of, and polluting to, Hinduism,
but even Muslims in India have adopted a four-fold caste structure in their own communities.

10. Of course, everyone has an element of divinity within them in Hindusim (the soul). But the Hindu reform movement was centrally focused on the elimination of idolatry and the promotion of monotheism. Hence, its proponents rejected Christ's claim to be uniquely God's Son.

11. In comparing Gandhi's religious convictions to Christianity, it is important to remember that Gandhi did not believe in a personal God. He believed that God and Truth were entirely synonymous, a pantheistic point of view. Like other moderate reformers, he admired Jesus' ethic, but placed it within a fundamentally Hindu worldview (see Hay, 1988: 270-3).

12. Buddhists and Sikhs were subsequently added, but Muslims and Christians remain excluded to this day.

13. As late as 1990, over 100,000 Christian Dalits gathered in New Delhi to campaign for the benefits of Scheduled Caste status, to no avail.

Chapter Seven

Women in Hindu Society

Market women are painstakingly saving money for dowries for their daughters. The going rate for a dowry is Rs. 20,000 (equivalent to US $400), a fabulous sum for women earning less than Rs. 50 (U.S. $1) per day. For most such women, years of careful accumulation are necessary to marry off just one daughter, let alone a number of them. These mothers were not given dowries at all when they were married. Some had, in fact, brought bridewealth into their natal families. In the lower caste and untouchable communities, bridewealth has traditionally been paid to the bride's family in compensation for the income expected of her labor. But higher caste communities have traditionally restricted women's labor outside the home, making them a financial liability and encouraging the payment of dowry for their upkeep. As a result, dowry is a symbol of high rank. Market women marry their daughters within their own "ex-untouchable" communities. But these communities are upwardly mobile. They are adopting dowry as part of the sanskritising process. So, market women are preparing to purchase a life of higher prestige and less labor, but more restriction, for their daughters.

At the same time, market women are trying to keep their daughters in school. When necessary, they bring one daughter, or perhaps a son, to work with them. But they do this with regret, and only to make it financially possible for their other children to stay in school. On this score, it would seem that rather than sanskritising, they are modernizing or "Westernizing" (Srinivas, 1969). Yet the education of their sons produces little hope for them in terms of future support, and the education of their daughters is seen partly as an investment in marriage possibilities. On the whole, grooms' families want educated brides for two reasons: 1) because grooms themselves prefer an educated wife as a companion, and 2) because educated wives can bring an income to the family if they find employment that a "respectable" woman can do, such as clerical work. In fact, an educated woman needs less dowry than an uneducated one, making education itself a kind of dowry savings. Thus, in this matter too, market women are opting for a reformed Hindu view of upward mobility rather than a fully revolutionary one.

TRADITIONAL VIEWS OF WOMEN

The conservative ideal for womanhood depicted in the Laws of Manu centers on the domestic roles of wife and mother, and stresses women's subordination to men:

> No act is to be done according to her own will by a young girl, a young woman, or even an old woman, though in their own houses. In her childhood a girl should be under the will of her father; in her youth, of her husband; her husband being dead, of her sons; a woman should never enjoy her own will. (Hopkins, 1995: 130)

Earlier sacred writings about women were not as restrictive. Women in the Rig Veda were depicted as lovers, as wives, and as mothers, but were never instructed in these roles, nor given ideal images of the feminine. The Vedas were written by and for men, and hence were not intended to be prescriptive for women (O'Flaherty, 1981: 245). But, during its long medieval period, Indian society was codified into more rigid structures of caste and gender, such that by the time of the arrival of the Europeans the following kind of texts had become canonical:

> There is no other god on earth for a woman than her husband. The most excellent of all the good works that she can do is to seek to please him by manifesting perfect obedience to him. Therein should lie her sole rule of life.
>
> Be her husband deformed, aged, infirm, offensive in his manners; let him also be choleric, debauched, immoral, a drunkard, a gambler; let him frequent places of ill-repute, live in open sin with other women, have no affection whatever for his home; let him rave like a lunatic; let him live without honour; let him be blind, deaf, dumb, or crippled; in a word, let his defects be what they may, let his wickedness be what it may, a wife should always look upon him as her god, should lavish on him all her attention and care, paying no heed whatsoever to his character and giving him no cause whatsoever for displeasure. (Abbe Dubois, 1999: 345)

The full text describes a woman's complete devotion to her husband by serving his every need, sharing his every emotion, and meekly enduring his every abuse. In the end, if widowed, she is to commit *sati*: "She must, on the death of her husband, allow herself to be burnt alive on the same funeral pyre; then everybody will praise her virtue" (p. 349). A woman's life is in her husband's life, and if he is gone, she must go with him.

Of course, such prescriptive religious texts may say little about how women have actually functioned in Hindu homes. The power exercised behind the scenes, especially in family life, can be very real. But writing in the 19th century, the missionary Abbe Dubois commented regarding the prescriptions in the Laws of Manu: "These rules of conduct may seem extremely severe, yet they are faithfully observed, especially among the Brahmins" (1999: 352), and, "The Hindu wife finds in her husband only a proud and overbearing master who regards her as a fortunate woman to be allowed the honour of sharing his bed and board" (p. 233).[1] The power of religion and of men was securely established, and it surely would have been difficult for women to effectively challenge their circumstances.

In a contemporary study, *Dangerous Wives and Sacred Sisters*, Lynn Bennett (1983) describes how high caste Hindu women's lives are circumscribed by restricted roles and ideal images even now. Women grow up in one patrilineal joint household and marry into another. After marriage, they return frequently to their own homes for visits as long as three to nine months at a time, especially when children are born. Hence, women experience their lives as an alternation between two families, natal and affinal, in which they play very different roles and receive very different treatment.

Patrilineal joint families potentially have the following members in a household: the patrilineal grandparents, all adult sons, these sons' wives (daughters-in-law), the sons' and their wives' children, and unmarried or visiting adult daughters (sisters). Visiting sisters are honored by their brothers with ritual worship, given little if any work to do, and generally showered with love and affection. Daughters-in-law are greeted on the wedding day with ritual abuse, expected to do the worst family chores without complaint, and blamed for their husbands' quarrels. Women are idealized as sisters, but restricted and enslaved to work as daughters-in-law.

In the affinal home, a woman's status is lowest when she first enters as a bride. She is to obey her mother-in-law implicitly, avoid speaking to her husband when his parents are in the room, massage the legs of her father-in-law in the evenings, and generally exhibit demureness with silence and downcast eyes. The birth of her first child elevates her position, especially if it is a son. By producing a son, she extends the family lineage and thereby proves her value to it (Bennett, 1983: ix). Age also gradually empowers her as she prepares to take on the role of mother-in-law herself. Finally, due to the high value placed on motherhood, she receives a good deal of devotion and honor from her adult sons as an elderly woman.

Yet, any married women is to serve and worship her husband as a personal god.[2] Ritual acknowledgement of this arrangement takes the form of washing his feet and drinking some of the water, eating the polluted leftovers from his dinner plate, walking behind him and carrying his burdens, and addressing him with highly honorific terms, such as "Lord" (Bennett, 1983: 174-5). Furthermore, while motherhood is deemed unequivocally good in Indian culture, the role of the wife is viewed with ambivalence. The Goddess, Devi, to whom women across India are compared, is alternately depicted in the form of the good and pure Parvati, and the dark and dangerous Kali. She is, says Bennett (1983: x), a "core symbol that expresses key oppositions within Hindu culture and reinforces the social roles of actual women." Parvati is sensual and yet chaste, flirtatious and yet faithful, fertile and yet utterly pure. Kali is bloodthirsty and violent, yet powerful to help in a time of need.

Perhaps the ambivalence toward women as wives can best be seen in Hindu views of sexuality (Carstairs, 1975: 163ff). Sex is thought to deplete a man's *tapas*, i.e. "heat" or energy, and generally to pollute him. A man begins adult life as a *brahmacarya*, a pure premarital celibate. After he has married, he observes periods of abstinence to cleanse himself for important rituals.[3] Finally, in his senior years, he is expected to renounce sex altogether for spiritual purpose, i.e. to gain *tapas* (as, for instance, did Gandhi). So for men, wives are a distraction at best, a danger at worst, to religious life.[4] Allen (1990: 2) suggests:

> For the typically male renouncer woman, with one foot planted firmly in the physical world of reproduction and sexuality, and the other in the social world of the family, is the principle obstacle to the goal of spiritual salvation.

Furthermore, all of women's sexual functions are believed to be polluting. Women must observe periods of confinement at menarche, during all subsequent menstruation, and at childbirth, to avoid contaminating others. Bennett (1983: 215) describes the circumstances thus:

> During the first three days of every menses, women become polluted and *untouchable*. As one woman explained, " . . . We become like female dogs." For these three days a woman must not enter the kitchen, touch food or water that others will eat or drink, or even worship the gods or ancestor spirits. She may not comb her hair or oil it, and she sleeps separately in a downstairs room. Also she may not touch an adult man. Some very orthodox women also avoid touching other women or children. [emphasis mine]

In previous times, full seclusion in a dark room was practiced, and even speaking was forbidden. A woman's most polluted stage of life is as a widow, when her very presence, especially at weddings or other celebrations, is considered

Figure 7.1.   Parvati, the Goddess as Dutiful Wife. Parvati is ornately dressed, stands beside her husband Shiva, and offers a blessing with her right hand. She is light complexioned and wears a peaceful smile. The many myths about her stress her responsible character and her devotion to her husband.

Figure 7.2. Kali, the Goddess as World Conqueror. As Kali, the same goddess is clothed in the severed parts of demons she has killed, is dark complexioned, and has her tongue hanging out. Myths about her stress her power in defeating dangerous enemies, thereby saving the world. Here, she is standing triumphantly on the dead body of her husband.

exceedingly bad luck. Hence, all women experience at least temporary, and sometimes more permanent, levels of untouchability by virtue of their status as women.[5]

In sum, women are sacred in some contexts, polluted in others, but dangerous to men in any case. When their power is directed toward culturally conservative ends it is valuable. When not, it threatens to destroy the social order. Part of the solution is in restrictions on women's roles outside the home, and part in a worship of women in their roles as wives and mothers that is disempowering of them as people. Allen (1990:10) remarks:

> Just as the veneration of women as pure beings yet further guarantees their rigorous control by men, so too does an exaggerated value given to their maternal capabilities lead to their worship, and hence substantial removal from the worldly arena of power and wealth.

Idealized and restricted roles force women to sacrifice their own full development as persons, and allow society to ignore their needs. Most importantly, women's intrinsic value is denied in favor of their utilitarian value to the male order (Nussbaum, 2000). Women experience themselves as valuable only insofar as they serve others.

Hence, it is not surprising that most women try to channel their energies in socially conservative directions. Hindu women are presented with a split image of themselves: good, if subservient like Parvati, but evil, polluting, and dangerous—even untouchable—if powerful like Kali. According to Bennett, most high caste Hindu women attempt to demonstrate their value by identifying with Parvati, and by scrupulously observing family religious duties such as worshipping household gods and maintaining a pure kitchen:

> It is in this context that . . . women's specific responsibility for and frequent personal preoccupation with dharma—with the honoring of household gods, the maintenance of strict ritual purity in the kitchen, and the observance of frequent fasts and religious vows—becomes so understandable . . . Even women who have rebelled against the restrictions of the patrifocal model by pushing for partition [of the household] continue to share its values and seek to define themselves as dutiful and obedient. (Bennett, 1983: 313-14)

Such a conservative response can be found in women of other times and places as well. Muslim women have enforced the restrictions placed on their own sex in their own communities. Conservative Christian women have been opponents of the feminist movement in the West. Regardless of the religion, the strength of women's loyalties to family, caste, and class can cause them to work hard for systems that are oppressive, even to themselves.

REFORMERS FOR WOMEN

As with untouchability, in the 19th and early 20th centuries, Christian missionaries engaged reform-minded Hindus and liberal colonialists in common cause to bring about change for women. Among their concerns were the practices of female infanticide, child marriage, the treatment of widows, and *sati*. Later, concerns for women's illiteracy and poverty were added to the list.

At the start, William Carey and Rammohan Roy worked cooperatively to lobby the initially uninterested East India Company for bans on infanticide and *sati*. Infanticide had been practiced for three reasons: medical purposes, annual sacrifices to Mother Ganges, and getting rid of unwanted girls (Walker, 1960: 197ff). Girls, then as now, were expensive to have due to dowry, and were subsequently lost to their families due to the practice of patrilocal postmarital residence. The temptation was (and is) strong to permit girls to die, either intentionally or unintentionally through neglect of food and medical care. A proverb from Haryana states, "The unfortunate one's son dies; the fortunate [literally, "God blessed"] one's daughter dies" (Chowdhry, 1997: 305-6).

Governor General Lord Wellesley was sympathetic to the liberal social agenda, and as a first step, appointed Carey to investigate the Hindu scriptures to see whether female infanticide was permitted there. Carey, who was proficient in Sanskrit, reported with enthusiasm that Hindu texts did not in fact sanction it. Wellesley moved quickly to ban infanticide in 1870. Enforcement of the ban was not only by witness to the act itself, but by indirect evidence attained through censuses, birth registrations, and investigations of all child deaths. The government declared communities with less than 40% girls in the under 12 age group automatically "guilty" of infanticide, and those with less than 25%, "very guilty" (Nair, 2000: 84). Punishments included fines and imprisonment. The result was dramatic, with infanticide dropping out of common practice within a few short years.[6]

With this initial success, Carey and Roy turned to the matter of *sati*. Carey recalled his horror on directly encountering the practice of *sati* for the first time in 1799. Walking by a riverside one evening, he chanced upon the ceremony in progress, and attempted to stop it:

> I talked till reasoning was of no use, and then began to exclaim with all my might against what they were doing, telling them that it was a shocking murder. They told me it was a great act of holiness, and added in a very surly manner, that if I did not like to see it I might go farther off. . . . I told them that I would not go, that I was determined to stay and see the murder, and that I should certainly bear witness of it at the tribunal of God. I exhorted the woman not to

throw away her life; to fear nothing, for no evil would follow her refusal to burn. But she in the most calm manner mounted the pile, and danced on it with her hands extended as if in the utmost tranquility of spirit . . . Two bamboos were then put over them [husband and wife] and held fast down, and the fire put to the pile which immediately blazed very fiercely. . . . It was impossible to have heard the woman had she groaned or even cried aloud, on account of the mad noise of the people, and it was impossible for her to stir or struggle on account of the bamboos which were held down on her like the levers of a press. We made much objection to their using these bamboos, and insisted that it was using force to prevent the woman from getting up when the fire burned her. But they declared that it was only done to keep the pile from falling down. We could not bear to see more, but left them, exclaiming loudly against the murder, and full of horror at what we had seen. (Walker, 1960: 199-200)

In 1805, Carey began presenting evidence against *sati* to the government, initiating a public debate. The practice was legal at the time, but government records of all such deaths were being kept. According to these records, at least 6,632 *satis* had occurred between 1815 and 1824 (Nair, 2000, 54), and 8,134 during the record keeping period (Mani, 1997: 88). Not a few women were dying! Furthermore, Rammohan Roy described *sati* as a natural consequence of the whole treatment of women in Hindu society:

At marriage the wife is recognized as half of her husband, but in after-conduct they are treated worse than inferior animals. For the woman is employed to do the work of a slave in the house, such as, in her turn, to clean the place very early in the morning, whether cold or wet, to scour the dishes, to wash the floor, to cook night and day, to prepare and serve food for her husband, father, mother-in-law, sisters-in-law, brothers-in-law, and friends and connections! . . . If in the preparation or serving up of the victuals they commit the smallest fault, what insult do they not receive from their husband, their mother-in-law, and the younger brothers of their husband? . . . If unable to bear such cruel usage, a wife leaves her husband's house to live separately from him, then the influence of the husband with the magisterial authority is generally sufficient to place her again in his hands; when, in revenge for her quitting him, he seizes every pretext to torment her in various ways, and sometimes even puts her privately to death. These are facts occurring every day, and not to be denied. What I lament is, that, seeing the women thus dependent and exposed to every misery, you feel for them no compassion that might exempt them from being tied down and burnt to death. (Hays, 1988: 28-9)

In 1829, Roy presented a petition to ban *sati* with over 300 signatures, and the government acquiesced shortly thereafter (van der Veer, 43).

Traditional marriage practices came under scrutiny next. The higher castes were marrying off daughters in childhood in order to avoid the social stigma of an unmarried woman in the house. Marriages were sometimes consummated as early as eight years old. Such young brides were at risk for becoming widows, with no possibility of remarriage. In 1860, the government responded to reformist lobbying by setting the age of "consent" for girls at 10 years old. In 1891, due in part to the rape death of an eleven year-old wife, the government raised that age to 12, spawning a massive protest from conservative Hindus who complained of government interference in family and religious life (Borthwick, 1990: 116). Yet reformist pressures prevailed again, and by 1925, the age of consent for girls had been raised to 14 years (Nair, 2000: 71). Currently, the law requires 18 years for girls and 21 for boys to marry, though this law is commonly ignored. According to the census, in 1991, 18% of married women in the conservative state of Rajasthan had been wed between the ages of ten and fourteen years old (Nair, 2000: 5).

Influence from the West was also altering views on the very nature and purpose of marriage in India under colonialism. In educated families, ideals of monogamy and companionship were taking hold, threatening the traditional practices of polygamy, dowry, the ban on widow remarriage, and even the joint family (Gupta, 2002: 23). Roy's reformist Hindu organization, the Brahmo Samaj, defended widow remarriage vigorously, with the result that it was formally sanctioned by the government in 1856 (Nair, 1996: 62). In literature campaigns, Brahmos promoted the model of a full and equal partnership in marriage. The "new marriage" was to be better for both women and men.

Reform of marriage practices, however, soon became entangled in the rising tension between religious communities as the government moved to codify civil society into law. Reformed Hindus were encouraging monogamy and restriction on divorce, marriage being a sacrament in Hinduism. Muslims, afraid of Hindu influence, began to demand a "gradual Islamisation" of the law for themselves to bring it in line with the Shari'a (Nair, 2000: 192). With marriage a civil contract in Islam, they defended polygamy (as sanctioned in the Qu'ran) and divorce. In the end, the government was forced to design separate legal structures based on religious affiliation for marriage age, dowry, divorce, parents' rights, adoption, legitimacy, wills, and inheritance.[7] To this day, the "personal law" differs by religion in India.

Reform of legislation pertaining to women's property rights and working conditions progressed slowly. Initially, colonial concern for land fragmentation and poverty had caused the government to discourage partition of property between sons and daughters, to support the levirate as a means of caring for widows, and to encourage women's continued unregulated labor in agricultural fields (Chowdhry, 1997: 315ff). But reformers were campaigning for equal inheritance and restrictions on working hours. Hence, the Hindu Women's Right to Property Act of 1937 gave widows inheritance of a share of their husbands' property for the first time (Nair, 2000: 64), and later, the Hindu Succession Act of 1956 gave daughters nearly equal inheritance with sons (Antony, 1989: 132). Much of this legislation, however, is commonly ignored even today.

Labor regulation under colonialism was most needed for poor women. While high ranking women, Hindu and Muslim, were cloistered in the joint family home by the practice of *purdah*, low ranking women worked long hours at strenuous, poorly paid, or unpaid, jobs. The most common such work was agricultural labor, which involved back-breaking hours transplanting rice and threshing wheat. But, industrialization and the capitalist market brought new forms of monotony. Women worked on coffee and tea plantations (where they made up 40% of the workforce), in coal mines (34%), and in factories of various types (10-20%) (Nair, 2000: 99ff). In 1911, women's working hours in industry were limited to eleven hours per day, with night shifts forbidden. In 1929, employers were restricted to hiring adult men to work in mines after decades of pressure from the International Labour Organization. And in 1948, the factory work week was restricted to 48 hours, with a maximum of nine hours per day and a day of rest per week (Antony 1989: 24). Hence, progress was made in regulating the industrial sector. But no such protections exist for market women now. Nearly 90% of working women currently are found in the informal economy, where "sexual harassment, arbitrary laying off of workers, wage discrimination and working long beyond the stipulated eight hours a day" yet occur (Karlekar, 1982: 51).

The reformers' insistence on educational benefits improved women's circumstances more significantly than did their legal accomplishments during the colonial period. Traditionally, only high caste men had been given formal education. Untouchables and women were forbidden to read the Vedas or worship Vedic gods (Krygier, 1990: 79). Hence, no single thing transformed Indian society during this period more dramatically than the provision of basic education to an increasingly broad circle:

> Being based on the principle of equality of opportunity, [Western education] threw open for the first time, in theory at least, the doors of education at all levels and in all branches of learning to all, irrespective of caste, class, religion and sex: a far cry from the pre-British period when education, especially Sanskritic education (equated with higher learning), was viewed as the main prerogative of male members of upper castes . . . (Shivakumar, 1982: 7)

Education empowered women in the home by making them able to converse on a par with their husbands, prepared them for higher levels of employment outside of the home, and ultimately engaged them in the political movement for their own defense.

Protestant missionaries began teaching women to read almost immediately, and were first to set up western style schools in vernacular languages. Jayakumar remarks, they undertook this work with such passion that "some critics exclaimed, 'Dear me! Missionaries will teach the cows next.'" (1999: 200). Mukherjee (1990: 167) describes the impact in the Calcutta area:

> The missionaries started a debate on the status of women during the second decade of the nineteenth century. They also took the initiative in promoting female education. In 1819 the Juvenile Society for the Establishment of Female Schools was established by the missionaries with the support of a group of *bhadralok* [Hindu intelligentsia]. By 1824 they had some fifty female schools in and around Calcutta.

In Bangalore, the city adjacent to Mysore, girls' schools were started in the 1840's, and made rapid progress in enrollment between 1890 and 1920 (Shivakumar, 1982: 9-13). These schools were far from reaching all girls. As late as 1951, women's literacy was still at only 8% nationwide (Devadas, et. al: 1990). Yet a profound conceptual shift had occurred, permitting women to begin to expect a right to education.

For Hindu reformers, the benefits of women's education included the enhancement of the image of Indian society in the West (Borthwick, 1990: 109), and in general, a modernizing influence. The new marriage, based on companionship between intellectual equals, would be the vehicle for opening up women's very closed and traditional world (Chakravarti, 2000: 206). Pearson (1990: 138) comments:

> Education was seen by the social reformers as the means to equip some women as intermediaries between the new ideals of the male world and the separate female world. The first women groomed for this role received their instruction within the household. Subsequently, girls' schools were established within which the next generation were trained and women's associations founded to foster a wider world view in a less formal manner. This process occurred within the upper echelons of different communities in close contact with the colonial state within which a reform tradition was well established.

As education expanded, the government became increasingly involved, with the result that a comprehensive nationwide public school system was established for all children by the time of independence in 1947.

Receiving an education has brought women into professions quickly. In 1870, there were 218 girls' schools with over 9,000 students in them in the Bombay Presidency. By 1921, there were 536 professors and teachers, 67 medical practitioners, and 24 lawyers who were women (Pearson, 1990: 139-40). Nationwide, women's literacy has increased from 8% in 1951 to 25% in

1981 (Devadas, et. al: 1990) and to 50% in 1997 (as against 73% for men in the same year) (World Bank, 2000: 22). And, currently, the proportion of girls attending primary schools in cities is 80% (84.5% for boys), and in villages it is 55.4% (70.3% for boys) (Parikh, 1999: 70).

THE WOMEN'S MOVEMENT

In the initial stages, the movement for women in India was composed entirely of concerned men.[8] Men were first to advocate for women's literacy, for instance, with a number of prominent men publicizing their case by teaching their own wives and daughters to read (Pearson, 1990: 138; Shivakumar, 1982: 12). Later, educated women began to speak out for themselves. Tarabai Shinde (1850-1910), for instance, wrote for the press, called into question the sexual double standard, and advocated for a wide variety of women's concerns. Pandita Ramabai Saraswati (1858-1922) converted to Christianity, campaigned for women's education, and started a home for widows (Nair, 2000: 68ff). By the 1920's the first women's organizations were founded, including the Women's India Association in 1917, the National Council of Women in India in 1926, and the All India Women's Conference in 1927 (Satyamurthy, 1996: 445). All three of these organizations have continued their advocacy work to today, along with newer organizations focusing on special concerns such as micro-business, represented by the Self-Employed Women's Association, or the protection of the environment, represented by the Chipko Movement (Omvedt, 1993: 76-8; Sen, 1996: 450).

Women's participation in public life turned out to be most valuable in the nationalist campaign. Donning white saris, women marched as "freedom fighters" in big numbers behind Gandhi, earning national respect for their commitment and sacrifice. The women's movement itself gained credibility due to this association. Women were joining men in common cause for the nation, campaigning for rights for the whole. Certainly, "appeals (rather than demands) made in the name of nationalism and in recognition of the sacrifices women were making in their daily lives, were . . . more likely to be entertained by male nationalists than strident demands for women's rights" (Nair, 2000: 127). As a result, unlike in the West, women's political involvement was perceived as uniting, rather than dividing, the community. Women were supporting men in the nationalist campaign, and (educated) men were encouraging women to take up new roles in society.

Additionally, the benign nature of the campaign for women at this stage was facilitated by the fact that much of the battle, especially for the franchise, had already been fought for and won by women in the West (Antony, 1989:9).

Both Gandhi and Nehru vigorously supported women's suffrage. When the constitution was drafted, awarding women the vote was never questioned. Article 15 stated: "The State shall not discriminate against any citizen on the grounds only of religion, race, caste, sex, place of birth, or any of them." Women were to have the rights and responsibilities of full citizens in the new democracy.

Yet, after independence was gained, the need for women's political participation diminished (Sen, 1996: 448), and the contradiction between the promotion of the individual rights inherent in full citizenship and the protection of religious communities through separate personal law became evident. In the Muslim community, a man's right to four wives was upheld in accordance with the Shari'a, as was his ability to easily divorce, leaving his ex-wife with no financial recourse. In the Hindu community, traditional practices such as dowry, disinheritance of daughters, and the ban on widow remarriage were permitted to continue unabated for fear of arousing religious tensions. Women's participation in politics dropped, with the proportion of women in parliament falling from 11% in 1956 to 5% in 1991 (Nair, 2000: 5), and women returned to the home as they had done in the West after World War II. Martha Nussbaum (2000: 168) describes the critical nature of the religious problem:

Modern liberal democracies typically hold that religious liberty is an extremely important value, and that its protection is among the most important functions of government. These democracies also typically defend as central a wide range of other human interests, liberties, and opportunities. . . . Sometimes, however, the religions do not support these other liberties. Sometimes, indeed, they deny such liberties to classes of people in accordance with a morally irrelevant characteristic, such as race or caste or sex. Such denials may not mean much in nations where religions do not wield much legal power. But in nations such as India, where religions run large parts of the legal system, they are fundamental determinants of many lives.

In the case of Hinduism, with its values on hierarchy and conformity, the tension between religious interests and the democracy was particularly acute (Baird, 2001: 148). And for women, whose lives yet revolved more around home than public arena, religion had priority. Seema Midha (1990: 76) has remarked "it is religion rather than law which controls the lives of women in India."

In fact, since the 1980's, rightist women in India have been increasingly vigorous in their public defense of traditional Hindu social practice (Sarkar, 1995: 3). The fundamentalist Hindu organization, Shiv Sena, has recruited more women to its causes than has the feminist movement. Comparing women to

Durga (Kali) as "the destroyer of evil, an angry and rebellious woman," the Shiv Sena has harnessed women's energies to conservative religious ends, including "a systematic hate campaign" against Muslims (Agnes, 1995: 140). Nussbaum (2000: 179) reminds us that if women are to be given liberty, such must include "the liberty of religious belief, membership, and activity." The choice to defend tradition is women's own to make. But, the decision to contest reform is not without its reasons. While religion commonly demands sacrifice, it promises at the same time to provide both personal and social security. For women, whose moral status is already in question, the temptation is strong to accept security and social recognition in the place of justice.

On September 4, 1987, Roop Kanwar, an 18 year-old, educated, high caste woman of Rajasthan, climbed the funeral pyre of her husband and immolated herself to the hysterical screaming of several hundred onlookers. Reports varied tremendously as to whether the act was coerced or voluntary. Remarkably, the event:

> occurred in a fairly well developed small town, and in a family that was quite 'modern' whether in terms of educational levels or levels of consumption. The celebrations that followed the immolation, similarly were well organized, high-tech affairs hardly commensurate with any 'traditional' deification of sati. Yet the Rajput community defended the immolation and the commemoration of it as in keeping with Rajput tradition: as such, they went on to claim that it lay beyond the scope of the law. (Nair, 2000:14)

There had been an estimated 40 such *satis* since independence (Nair, 2000:239). Kanwar's act revived the national debate on the matter. Demonstrations were held across the country demanding women's "right" to commit *sati*. The site of the immolation quickly became sacred, with devotees gathering to worship the new goddess (Kanwar). And a national organization, the Committee for the Defense of the Religion of Sati, was founded. The government tried to make a case that *sati* "is nowhere enjoined by any of the religions of India" (Pariwala and Agnihotri, 1996: 521). But neither fundamentalists nor feminists were persuaded of one another's causes in the ensuing dispute over religious freedom and human rights.

For ordinary women, such national debates can obscure much deeper issues. Women in villages tend to be completely ignorant of the law in their favor regarding minimum age for marriage, prohibitions on dowry, grounds for divorce, rights to inheritance, etc. (Baird, 2001: 147). Their lives reflect little of the efforts made in the last century to improve women's circumstances. Sen's "missing women" are a case in point. The drop in the female to male ratio, due to abortions, infanticide, and neglect, means that many millions of ordinary women in India are simply not surviving childhood.

Since independence, the government has made a real effort to empower ordinary women. In 1992, the Panchayati Raj amendments to the constitution (#'s 73 & 74) were passed and enacted. The purpose was to devolve power and responsibility for "economic development and social justice" from the central government to village and district *panchayats,* or councils. Seats on *panchayats,* which had traditionally been hereditary, were mandated to be elected every five years. Women and Dalits were guaranteed voice in the new government structure. The amendments reserved 33% of all seats for women, seats proportional to their population for Scheduled Castes and Tribes, and 33% of these latter seats for women as well, guaranteeing that low caste, as well as high caste, women would be represented. Additionally, *sarpanch,* or chair, positions were reserved for women and Dalits on a rotating basis. Consequently, the 1993-4 elections put 800,000 women into local government for the first time (Vyasulu, 1999: 1).

Resistance to these changes has taken the predictable route of men electing their wives to position and then expecting to make the real decisions themselves. Helen Lambert (Fuller, 1997: 98) describes her visit to a high caste, female *sarpanch:*

> Any intention that the reservation of such seats would have an impact on women's social and political status seemed unlikely to be fulfilled . . . since it was universally assumed that the new *sarpanch's* husband would in fact perform the relevant duties, while the *sarpanch* herself told me that while she would attend public meetings as necessary in order to be adequately informed, her role would be confined to listening as she would naturally remain veiled and silent.

In one case, the president of a district level council was not permitted by her male Vice-President to speak in meetings at all (Vyasulu, 1999: 8). Yet, it appears that some women are demonstrating a willingness to counter undue influence. One low caste *sarpanch* has refused the suggestion that she resign, contested her position to the state high court and won, and proceeded to conduct meetings without the boycotting male members. During her tenure, she has successfully administered the building of a bus stand for her village.

It is high caste women who are reluctant to challenge the status quo. Typically they share the caste prejudices of men in their communities, and, unlike their low caste counterparts, stand to lose benefits such as protection and prestige. Vyasulu (1999: 5) comments:

> To the extent that there is an overlap between caste and gender, the representation given to women has done little to change the caste hold on power. For example, in a given situation, do women align themselves with their caste or along gender lines? Experience has shown that it is often on caste lines. Thus, while

the representation of women in these bodies is a welcome move, it is not reasonable to expect that it will change the caste balance of power in favour of the most disadvantaged groups.

Of course, there are exceptions even here. Vyasulu reports of a high caste, female *panchayat* member who insisted on getting the low caste water pipeline fixed (ibid). But on the whole, high caste women placed in local government are susceptible to conservative pressures. Low caste women have less to lose, though they too may aspire to the prestige awarded to women who conform in Hindu society.

SANSKRITISATION AND WOMEN'S DISEMPOWERMENT

Nineteenth century reformers made significant and irreversible advances in the circumstances for women. Yet, the conservatism that has reasserted itself since independence has also had an impact. The shift from bridewealth to dowry payments among Dalits signals a move to reestablish the Hindu social order. Remarkably, despite opposition from the women's movement, and despite the fact that it is now illegal,[9] the practice of dowry has *increased* substantially not only in India but throughout South Asia, including Bangladesh and Pakistan. White (1992: 102) writes of Bangladesh, "dowry is now common amongst virtually all groups, and the amounts payable have risen dramatically." In a village in Maharashtra, Vlassoff (1994: 713) finds that while women are eating more freely with their husbands (rather than apart, as is traditional), the practice of dowry, which had not been obligatory previously, is "no longer viewed as optional." Since the 1970's, skyrocketing demands for dowry have produced a new form of murder, the "dowry death." Typically, the groom's family tries to extort further payments from the bride's family after the wedding. The bride is held hostage, first with threats, and then with attempts on her life, if payment is not forthcoming. A bride who escapes is most likely to be returned to the conjugal home by her natal family for fear of shame. If she is murdered, she is set on fire, a possible reference to *sati*. Police action is rare, and the groom is subsequently able to remarry, anticipating another dowry. There were 690 dowry deaths in 1983 alone (Nair, 2000: 237).

Dowry extortion would not be possible if brides' families were not sanskritising. In the 19th century, the practices of dowry, sacred marriage, and celibacy for widows were *privileges* of the upper castes, with the latter custom being practiced by a mere 20% of the population (Chakravarti, 2000: 130). Among middle castes, rank could be gained or lost depending on the success with which such practices were, or were not, upheld (p. 17). The lower castes were not encouraged, and untouchables not permitted, to adopt them. Hence, dowry, *sati,* and widows' celibacy marked prestige, while bridewealth and widow remarriage marked degradation (Chowdhry, 1997: 311). Even now, institutions that disempower women are means of establishing and maintaining high rank: child marriage, *purdah*, financial dependency, stigmatization of widows, and *sati*. Institutions that are "indicative of women's more equal status" are taken as evidence of low rank: work outside the home, the giving of bridewealth or no exchange, the ability to divorce, and the remarriage of widows (Webster 1997: 29, 20-21). Hence sanskritising castes are bartering off women's empowerment for higher prestige. "Every move of Sankritisation by a caste . . . [is] predicated upon establishing the purity of women" (Chakravarthi, 2000: 56), and the purity of women is established by their disempowerment.

Market women of Mysore, by denying widow remarriage and saving to accumulate dowries for their daughters, are assisting in the sanskritisation of their communities. They are anticipating opportunities for their daughters to achieve the prestige of higher caste women at the expense of freedoms they themselves take for granted: freedoms such as the ability to move about and work outside the home, the ability to divorce abusive husbands, and the ability to remarry as widows and as divorcees. Chakravarthi (2000: 57) comments:

An analysis of the ideological underpinning of sanskritisation can be sharpened by arguing that hegemonic ideology works to limit the cultural imagination of the lower orders and makes it difficult to radically reconceptualise society.

A less limited imagination might envision a broader future for daughters than merely to take on the restrictions of the higher castes.

In point of fact, Mysore was one of the first parts of the country to make significant changes in women's circumstances, due largely to the progressive kings, the Wodeyars, who ruled there under late colonialism. The Wodeyars ended the *devadasi,* or temple prostitution, system as early as 1892, and gave women inheritance and marriage rights as early as 1933 (Nair, 2000: 204, 167). In the neighboring state of Kerala, women's circumstances rose with the tide of economic development. Kerala currently has low birth rates, high child survival, high income, high literacy, high life expectancy, and a good sex ratio, with daughters actually outnumbering sons. Women in Kerala are educated, married late, and given paid employment, though they remain underrepresented in politics (Jeffrey, 1992: 7-17).

There are multiple reasons for these regional advances, including, in Kerala, a pre-colonial history of matriliny and over forty years of benevolent Marxist government. But a key factor in the improvement of women's circumstances throughout the south has been the greater influence of Protestant missions there than in the north. Jeffrey (1992:10) comments that in Kerala, change for women "began with the Christian churches, which often used their parish priests or missionaries as political 'branch managers' to lobby governments." The Hindu community, deeply divided by caste, was unable to match such organization and influence. Later, it emulated the Church's political methods for its own purposes, as " . . . non-Christians had come to see in Christian institutions a solution to problems of competition and disorganization" (Jeffrey, 1992: 99). Christians, then, both European and Indian, were catalysts for social reform, challenging the government to empower the marginalized with a vision of unity that emerged from the institution of the Church.

All this contests the usual depiction of Christian influence in India as having been merely ideological support for colonial objectives. Chakravarti contrasts the portrayals in history of the activist Annie Besant, a western woman who embraced philosophical Hinduism, with Ramabai Saraswati, an Indian woman who embraced Christianity:

> The difference in the way in which Ramabai and Annie Besant have figured in historical writing in both the late nineteenth and early twentieth centuries as well as now indicates that there has been an easy conflation not only of nationalism with Hinduism but more importantly of Christianity with colonialism. There is a latent assumption that in opting for Christianity Ramabai and others had accepted the religion of the rulers and had therefore become 'compradors' and were complicit with the colonial presence. Such an assumption is both simplistic and motivated. The mere existence of a relationship between Christianity and colonialism is not enough to treat Christianity automatically as the handmaiden of colonialism . . . such a view ties in with the agenda of Hindu nationalists both in the past and in the present. (Chakravarti, 2000: ix)

No doubt many missionaries were ethnocentric, and some were even imperialist. But, the complete and easy conflation of Christianity with the colonial project is simply not born out by the facts (Stokes, 1963).

Then as now, Christians have held a value on human life that refuses the involuntary sacrifice of one group for another. In fact, Christian history reveals a constant and pervasive concern for the disadvantaged and the marginalized. The Christian community under colonialism did not have modern conceptions of women's roles, nor did it involve itself as much as it might have in the nationalist political movement. But, by its social activism, as well as by its example of female missionaries and indigenous teachers (Jayakumar,1999: 201),[10] it challenged the Hindu devaluation of women. The impact of that challenge can be discerned now in the better sex ratio found in the Christian community in India. In 1971, the ratio of women to men was 986:1000 for Christians, while it was 931:1000 for the country, a difference of 55/1000. By 1991, it had *increased* to 994:1000 for Christians, while at the same time it had *decreased* to 927:1000 for the country, a difference of 67/1000 (Webster, 1997: 28). In a recent study, Webster (1997) compared Christian to Hindu Dalit women's lives in a Tamil village. He found that while Christian families gave dowry and had a traditional domestic sexual division of labor (p. 78), Christian women's participation in public life was high, particularly in church and politics. He attributed this to the regular preaching of "Christ as a liberating God, the basic tenet of the faith" (p. 58).

Yet, the gains of the social reforms of the past are under attack now like never before. *Hindutva,* a Hindu reactionary movement bearing the motto "Hindustan [India] is for the Hindus," is challenging the secular democracy; lobbying to alter the constitution in favor Hindus over Muslims, Christians and others; and attempting to lure women and Dalits back to traditional roles with promises of better treatment. The conflict between democracy and freedom of religion that Nussbaum identified has intensified.

NOTES

1. The Abbe Dubois' sympathy for women was plain. In attempting to record a *sati* he had observed, he remarked, "It is impossible for me to describe the finishing scenes of this dreadful ceremony without feelings of distress" (p. 363).

2. Dhruvarajan (1990) confirms that this practice is widespread even today, and suggests that *pativratya*, or husband worship, inhibits efforts to empower women through economic development.

3. I have observed a light hearted acknowledgement of the conflict between a man's religious and familial duties ritually depicted in the Hindu marriage ceremony. Prior to the actual union, the groom picks up an umbrella and a book, and declares to all his intent not to marry. He says that he has decided to go to Varanasi and become a monk. As he steps out the door, the father of the bride follows him and pleads with him to come back and marry his daughter. Amidst much joking and laughter, the groom reluctantly returns and the ceremony proceeds.

4. Murthy (1978) explores the themes and contradictions this creates for a Brahman man desiring to be religiously pure in the novel, *Samkara.*

5. Allen (1990: 5) agrees that "they are, especially during menstruation and childbirth, a source of pollution as great as that associated with untouchables." He goes on to comment that a woman's impurity has "connotations of power," while her purity indicates "a total absence of power" (p. 6). This paradox is particularly evident with untouchable women, who are doubly polluted, and explains the ease with which market women verbally attack their higher caste moneylenders over financial problems.

6. Still, F. G. Bailey (pers. com.) reports that as late as the 1950s in Orissa, "infanticide in the form of not quickening a girl-child was not uncommon," i.e., the child was simply put aside to die.

7. For Hindus, the Hindu Marriage Act of 1955 mandated monogamy and established the current ages for marriages (Antony 1989: 40). Shortly thereafter, the Hindu Code Bill restricted divorce to grounds of desertion, cruelty, and adultery (Nair, 2000: 199, 223).

8. In fact, not all women supported the new social program. Pearson comments (1990: 137), "In many cases, the most vigorous opponents of change were women themselves who had reached a stage of life when they could exercise their powerfulness and brooked no interference in their domain."

9. In 1961, the Dowry Prohibition Act was passed, prohibiting the "giving, taking, or abetting" of dowry, with a potential fine of Rs. 5000 and six months in prison. Unquestionably, the law was a "paper tiger" (Antony, 1989: 98). Dowry protests began in 1978 due to the onset of a rash of dowry deaths, with the result that the law was strengthened in the 1980's (Palriwala and Agnihotri, 1996: 505). Still, enforcement of the law is essentially nonexistent.

10. Protestant missionaries trained "Bible women" to be teachers who were sent to villages on foot to instruct new converts. Catholic orders, such as the Sisters of Charity, also provided new models for women, empowering them for service to a community wider than their families.

Chapter Eight

Religion and the State

In 1947, British rule ended and India became a democracy. The constitution declared India to be a "sovereign socialist secular democratic republic," espousing the values "justice," "liberty," "equality," and "fraternity." The resemblance to the American constitution was not accidental. Ambedkar, whose experience as a graduate student at Columbia University in New York had been a good one, had been named chair of the constitution committee. As an ex-untouchable, it was his task to ensure that India be established as a full democracy, not only with voting rights, but also with structural support such as compensatory discrimination, for women, untouchables, religious minorities, and other disadvantaged groups.

In the more than fifty years following, unlike many other post-colonial nations, India has maintained democratic rule (with a brief exception to be described below). Power in government is separated between legislative and judicial functions; elections regularly produce a turnout of 60% or more; multiple parties exist; local, state, and central governments change party hands; and there is a free press (Jaffrelot, 2003: 1-2). Currently, despite its tremendous regional, religious, linguistic, and social diversity, India is the largest democracy in the world.

Furthermore, the socialism that has been espoused in India has been of the benign variety. Governed by the Indian National Congress, the party that led the country to freedom, public discourse has been characterized by a strong sense of responsibility of government to people, a commitment to the marginalized, and a vision of social and economic equality. In certain regions (most notably Kerala and Bengal), popular and effective communist parties have raised literacy rates, improved women's conditions, and nearly eradicated the lowest levels of poverty. Though the failure to control population growth has significantly diminished the results, on the whole India has successfully constructed a stable political economy, providing the means to a viable life for most of its constituents.

Yet the Indian democracy has its own way of functioning. Most notably, its political discourse is infused with religious symbolism and debate. There is an honesty in this. Modern thought has it that a truly democratic state rests upon the creation of a public sphere free of religion. Even Nussbaum (2000), in her defense of the rights of conservative religious women, presumes a wider secular order encompassing religious beliefs at a subordinate level. But I see two fictions: 1) that an order *can* be constructed apart from deeply held religious propositions and values, and 2) that such an order would best protect human freedom. Van der Veer (2001: 53) reminds us that " . . . religion is a major source of rational, moral subjects and *a central organizational aspect* of the public spheres they create . . ." (emphasis added). For better or for worse, religion is necessary to the construction of the socio-political order, with the *content* of the religion chosen affecting the *nature* of the order constructed.

India's public arena, I would suggest, has been constructed in part by a Christian conception of the community of love: love for God and love for neighbor (as against merely kin). This is despite the fact that India is even now over 80% Hindu, 12% Muslim, and less than 3% Christian. The central values of Christianity were imparted to nationalist leaders through the educational system, and then were adopted, along with social reforms, in the construction of the state. Values such as justice, liberty, equality, and fraternity are means of providing space for all people to grow to full capability, including the socio-politically, and even the religiously, marginalized. In fact, arguably, secularism itself is a product of the Christian doctrine of human freedom (Van Leeuwen, 1964; Troeltsch, 1992). If so, the Indian public arena has rested thus far more on Christian than on Hindu values.

Now, however, for the first time since Independence, the "central organizational aspect" of India's public arena, is being challenged. The *Hindutva* movement openly proclaims India to be a Hindu, rather than a secular, nation: "Hindustan is for the Hindus." While it has promised to preserve democracy, it is socially conservative and balks at legislation designed to protect minorities or the disadvantaged. Violence against the lower castes and nonHindus, especially Muslims, has escalated alarmingly, and women are being encouraged back to traditional roles. So, for poor, untouchable, market women, some of the social and political opportunities of the post-independence period may be fading away. In this chapter, I will trace the history of this shift from social reform to religious reaction.

THE CONGRESS PARTY RAJ

India's "freedom at midnight" was painfully bought. After a half century of struggle with the colonial government to achieve political autonomy, the country tore itself in two with religious fear. Three-quarters of a million people died in the largest refugee movement in history, as Muslims headed for the newly formed Islamic state of Pakistan, and Hindus fled into what was to remain India. Gandhi called it the "vivisection" of the country, and was assassinated for his bold attempts to make peace between the two communities. The Congress Party had worked hard to convince Muslim leadership that coexistence in a plural, democratic state was a viable option. But, Muhammad Ali Jinnah (1875-1948), founder and first prime minister of Pakistan, filed for divorce on grounds of incompatibility. He wrote:

> It is extremely difficult to appreciate why our Hindu friends fail to understand the real nature of Islam and Hinduism. They are not religions in the strict sense of the word, but are, in fact, different and distinct social orders, and it is a dream that the Hindus and Muslims can ever evolve a common nationality. (Hay, 1988: 230)

A common nationality is an "*imagined* political community" (Anderson, 1991: 6) [emphasis added] constructed with the threat of an equally imagined other as "adversary of the common interests" (Lieten, 1996: 238). And Jinnah, drawing on Islamic views of the state, chose to imagine a separate nation for Muslims, and to justify the need for it with a depiction of Hindus as the adversarial others. The result was rioting, bloodshed and dislocation in the immediate, followed by wars between the two new countries in 1948, 1965 and 1971, and a threatened nuclear war in 1998.

In India, the matter of incorporating diverse communities into a single state was addressed by "the institutionalization of difference" (van der Veer, 1994: 200). To protect religious freedom, the Congress Party supported separate codes of personal law, educational systems, and reservation schemes; a policy that won over the remaining Indian Muslim leadership (Brass, 1997: 233). To eliminate caste liabilities, untouchables and tribals, the "Scheduled Castes and Tribes" (SC/Ts), were awarded compensatory discrimination. Based on their proportion of the population in the 1951 census, 15% of all seats in institutions of higher education, public sector employment, and legislative bodies were reserved for SC/Ts. Caste integration in primary and secondary schools was mandated. And, to eliminate gender liabilities, girls' education was promoted and women were given full citizenship.

At the forefront of the establishment of a secular, democratic, and socialist public arena, replete with legal protections for the disadvantaged, was India's

first prime minister, Jawaharlal Nehru (1889-1964). Educated as a barrister in
England, Nehru had been a close associate of Gandhi's and a dedicated laborer in the independence movement, with nine years experience in British
prisons as reward for his leadership role in the Congress Party. Nehru was
himself of Kashmiri Brahman background, but like his educated rebel father
before him, rejected not only colonialism but the social and ritual prejudices
of his own caste. In a letter regarding his sister's impending marriage, he
wrote:

> The Kashmiri community, as a whole (there are exceptions of course in it) dis-
> gusts me; it is the very epitome of the petty bourgeois which I detest. I am not
> particularly interested in a person being a Brahman or a Non-Brahman or any-
> thing else. As a matter of fact I fail to see the relevance of all this; one marries
> an individual not a community. (Nanda, 1998: 97)

Nehru broke with caste and with Hinduism, rejecting even his own religious
funeral rites, and chose socialism as a personal, as well as a political, philosophy. It was the socialist project, he declared, that was the reason "the future
is full of hope" (Hay, 1988: 318).

As prime minister, Nehru built the nation by resisting communal divisions
and promoting civil rights. He refused all attempts to institute a Hindu state
parallel to Muslim Pakistan, declaring in a 1948 speech to the Constituent Assembly, "the alliance of religion and politics in the shape of communalism is
a most dangerous alliance, and yields a most abnormal kind of illegitimate
brood" (Lamb, 1967: 189). He appointed Muslims to head high level min-
istries, and rejected a proposal sponsored by conservative Hindus to ban cow
slaughter and to encourage repatriation of Muslims and Hindus to "their" re-
spective countries. For untouchables, Nehru backed Ambedkar's constitu-
tional protections and compensatory discrimination. And for women, he
sponsored the new Hindu Code bill which prohibited bigamy, mandated
women's inheritance, allowed divorce, and permitted intercaste marriage.
"Our [current] laws, our customs fall heavily on womenfolk," he said, "and
the new laws would bring about certain equality between men and women"
(Nanda, 1998: 109).[1]

Yet, to the degree that he was successful, Nehru's establishment of the new
nation was made possible by his willingness to compromise with vested interests and political realities. The more conservative elements of the Congress
Party did not care either for socialism or for secularism. They were forced to
support Nehru by his unparalleled ability to draw the popular vote. Hence,
party politics consisted, particularly at the local level, of a social democratic
rhetoric overlaid upon entrenched traditional power structures. The Congress
"machine" was composed of networks of landed elite turned party bosses,

who promised to exchange favors for support. Resources from water rights to
electric lines were negotiated down from center to region to village, with political support flowing upward accordingly. At the national level, the central
members of Congress leadership were even referred to as "the Syndicate."

Furthermore, caste-based political associations, formed in the time of
British rule to influence census findings, increased in strength under the democracy, creating power blocs that represented vested caste interests. This
was particularly true of the middle range castes, for whom there was no guaranteed protection in the constitution. The result was a democracy of "vote
banks," rather than of citizens *per se* (Jaffrelot, 2003: 86), with local elite
shoring up their own power bases and negotiating for a larger share of the
benefits. Omvedt's critique (1993: 289) is severe, but makes the point:

> Its bloated bureaucracies were inefficient and parasitical; its scientists, engi-
> neers, and technicians were living off the people rather than trying to create any-
> thing new or engage themselves in renovating the dusty world of village life;
> 'socialism' was only its legitimizing myth.

In the end, Nehru's compromise with entrenched leadership did much to un-
dermine his effectiveness in bringing about real change.

At Nehru's death in 1964, his daughter, Indira Gandhi, succeeded him.
Gandhi had her father's vision for India's future, but not his willingness to
share power, nor his patience with the pace of change. Soon after her election,
Indira challenged the "Syndicate," producing a party split. She instituted a
policy of appointing regional representatives from the center, alienating herself from the landed elite, and putting into place leadership that was sometimes inept and ineffective (Kohli, 1992: 152, 190). To retain the support of
the populace, she established her own control over vote counting by shifting
it from local sites to district headquarters, a move that further alienated the
former members of the "machine." And then, in 1975, when threatened with
being removed from office on charges of campaign malpractice, she declared
a state of emergency, closed the press, arrested thousands, and took central
control of states not already under Congress leadership. The "Emergency"
only lasted two years, and was not without its benefits. Inflation was brought
under control, corruption nearly eliminated, and by all accounts, "the trains
ran on time" (Wolpert, 2004: 398ff). Yet, the tragedy it revealed was that,
"[Congress Party] could only sustain political democracy at the expense of
social democracy and promote social democracy when political democracy
was not working, . . . It [was] as if political democracy and social democracy
were incompatible" (Jaffrelot, 2003: 143).

In 1977, Indira Gandhi lifted the state of emergency, declared general elections, and was voted out of office. But, following a singularly incompetent

government in the interim, she was returned to office by a landslide popular victory in 1980. During this second term, with lessons learned from her loss of power in the first, Gandhi turned to religion to shore up her political support. Her rhetoric in campaigns developed a new note of communalism. Speeches were laced with "themes of Hindu hegemony that would appeal to India's Hindi heartland" (Kohli, 1992: 310). She began visiting Hindu temples, and attended the 100th anniversary of the Hindu nationalist organization, the Arya Samaj. Gandhi was, in fact, abandoning her father's commitment to secularism in favor of religiously-based political fervor.

In 1984, Indira Gandhi's life was cut short by a Sikh separatist's bullet. She was succeeded by her son, Rajiv Gandhi, who in 1992 was assassinated for supporting the Sinhalese government in Sri Lanka against the Tamils. The assassinations ended a forty-five year "dynasty" of the Nehru family. Furthermore, the Congress Party was experiencing a "declining capacity to govern," as measured by the number of violent political protests per annum (dubbed "riots" by the police). These had nearly tripled between 1955 and 1982, from 60 per million to 160 per million (Kohli, 1992: 7).[2] According to Kohli (1992: 17), Congress was failing to retain its broad-based political support due to 1) its inability to form enduring coalitions with other parties, 2) the perceived ineffectiveness of its policies, and 3) an incapacity to accommodate political conflict without allowing it to turn violent. Hence, by the early 1990s, Nehru's vision for a secular socialist democracy was fading with the populace, and a political vacuum was emerging.

ORIGINS OF HINDU NATIONALISM

As we have seen, historically the Hindu social order has been able to weather a good deal of political upheaval without losing its fundamental values and structure. Waves of invaders over millennia have been absorbed and indigenized by the Brahmin controlled Hindu caste system and cosmology. This strategy is, however, a defensive one resting on a fundamental rejection of change. Jaffrelot (1996: 3) comments:

> Paradoxically, the ability to integrate newcomers also reflected an inability to recognize the Other as such. Brahminical texts assume that the indigenous social order has a homologous relationship to the cosmic order, the Dharma; and it is the preservation of this relationship in equilibrium which tends to demand the assimilation of foreign elements into the social system.

Social change, then, has been effectively resisted by a process of assimilation, i.e. squeezing new elements into old forms and thereby disarming them. The

Brahmin equation of society with the cosmos has made this assimilation both possible and necessary.

Yet, it has not been so easy to absorb the social changes of the 19th and 20th centuries into the old Hindu caste- and gender-based structures. These changes were the result of a profoundly different perspective and set of values. So, the conservative response has been to fight back directly through the *Hindutva* movement. The term was originally the title of a book written in 1923 by a Brahmin activist, V.D. Savarkar. After a period of imprisonment by the British for inciting violence (during which he wrote the book), Savarkar became president of an extreme nationalist organization, the Hindu Mahasabha, and continued his political activities through writings and speeches. He was arrested again just after Independence for having been implicated in the murder of Mahatma Gandhi, but was released due to lack of evidence.[3] He died in 1966, but is remembered to this day especially by intellectuals within the *Hindutva* movement.

The book, *Hindutva*, is built upon notions developed originally by the Arya Samaj that the Aryans are a master race, "lords of the earth," who descended into *Aryavarta* (north India), bearing with them Sanskrit, "the mother of all languages," and establishing the Vedic golden age (Jaffrelot, 1996: 16). Savarkar makes much of the fact that the terms Hindu and India are derivatives of the same root word, *Sindh* ("river"), making India the unique holy land of the Hindus, and Hinduism the only appropriate religion for India (Savarkar, 1999: 1ff).[4] Hindus are declared to have a "common blood" (p. 55) and to be "one because we are a nation, a race and own a common Sanskriti (civilization)" (p. 57). Patnaik and Chalam (1996: 260) suggest that Savarkar has imagined a nation established by a process of "assimilation and elimination;" assimilation of groups perceived to be within the broader Hindu fold, such as Jains, Sikhs, and Buddhists; and elimination of those who are not, such as Muslims, Christians, and Parsis. The nation of Hindustan is to be constructed by a refinement process that eliminates all foreign elements in favor of the religion, culture, race, and land of the Hindus.

Such militant Hinduism first emerged in the 1870s and began to engage in violent communal clashes in the 1920s (Gupta, 2002: 21). The relatively benign Arya Samaj ("Aryan Assembly") had endeavored to protect Hindu culture by incorporating external criticisms into a reformed form of the religion, sanitized of the evils of idol worship, untouchability, and women's subordination, and legitimized by a mythical Vedic past. But, later organizations were less moderate. The Rashtriya Swayamsevak Sangh (RSS, or "National Service Party"),[5] was founded in 1925 as a paramilitary organization, complete with martial arts training camps (Basu, 1995: 161). These camps, which are run all across the country today, train both women and men in the use of easily obtainable weapons such as knives, clubs, and tridents (the familiar symbol of the god, Shiva). At the camps, Hindu unity is promoted by the temporary suspension of sectarian, linguistic, and even caste differences, as participants engage in a rigorous program of physical, mental, and religious exercises. Members take an oath of loyalty "with whole body, heart and money for in it lies the betterment of Hindus and the country" (Jaffrelot, 1996: 37). And, with religious fervor aroused, camp-trained *sevaks* ("volunteers") go out to promote the Hindu cause with literature and recruitment campaigns, stand ready to protect their communities with violence if necessary, and assist in the promotion of Hindu values such as anti-cow slaughter and the reclamation of mosques purported to be the sites of former temples.

In the early 20th century, the RSS often found itself at odds with the broader nationalist movement. The Congress Party was gearing up for the creation of a plural democracy. RSS members were wary of the role to be played in such a democracy by nonHindus. They complained especially of a perceived "policy of appeasement" toward Muslims. K. B. Hedgewar, founder of the RSS, was an avid reader of the extremist Bal Gangadhar Tilak's weekly journal, and later a member of his inner circle. He wrote:

> The Hindu culture is the life breath of Hindusthan. It is therefore clear that if the Hindu is to be protected we should first nourish the Hindu culture. If the Hindu culture perishes, if the Hindu society ceases to exist, it will hardly be appropriate to refer to the mere geographical entity that remains as Hindusthan. Mere geographical lumps do not make a nation. The Sangh will cooperate with the Congress in the efforts to secure freedom so long as these efforts do not come in the way of preserving our national culture. (Thakur and Sharma, 1999: 10)

Hindu nationalists, then, rejected Nehru's "territorial and universalist version of nationalism" in favor of "a variant of ethnic nationalism" (Jaffrelot, 1996: 83).

Post-independence, Hindu nationalists found themselves to be a marginalized group, even a source of embarrassment, to the leadership of the democracy. As a result, they turned their attention to cultural work. In 1964, the RSS formed a new organization, the Vishva Hindu Parishad (VHP, or "World Hindu Council"), to do social work, collect funds, and make contact with Hindus outside of India. The VHP also took up the *shuddhi* (reconversion) campaign, initially begun by the Arya Samaj, to bring Muslims and Christians back into the Hindu fold. A women's organization, Rashtrasevika Samiti, was created, and a youth wing, Bajrang Dal, was formed to train "warriors of the *Hindutva* revolution." Together with regionally based extremist groups such as the Hindu Mahasabha, the RSS and its affiliates assembled themselves into what has come to be called the Sangh Pariwar ("family") of Hindu nationalist organizations.

Of course, not all Hindus subscribe to extreme nationalist views. There have been many, even a majority so far, who, following in the footsteps of leaders such as Ram Mohan Roy and Jawaharlal Nehru, have encouraged and promoted social change. But, on the whole, the *Hindutva* movement has gained, not lost, popular support across the country in the past century. Consequently, it now constitutes the most serious threat to advances already made in improving the circumstances of Dalits and women. "*Hindutva* ideology is essentially Brahminical in character and aims at a reaffirmation of the Hindu caste order," say Patnaik and Chalam (1996: 268), "In other words, *Hindutva* remains an extraneous ideology for the chief victims of Brahminism, namely Dalits and women."

For its part, the RSS has claimed that elimination of untouchability, respect for women, and eradication of poverty, are in fact part of its social agenda. In the 1920's, Hindu nationalists were in favor of untouchable access to wells, roads, and other public spaces. Since then, the RSS has, with the support of high caste financial contributions, built schools and temples for Dalits; encouraged women and Dalits to read the Vedas and participate in festivals; provided free medical care and assistance with sanitation to Dalits; discouraged the consumption of alcohol, meat, and tobacco, a morality formerly considered to be above untouchable station; and performed *kanya puja*, a ritual in which activists wash a Dalit girl's feet as part of worshipping her (Jaffrelot, 2003: 459). In addition, the RSS has encouraged women to be outspoken about their political views and to contribute to the nationalist campaign (Basu, 1995). It has even held rites of apology to acknowledge the sins of abuse from the past.

Yet, the socially conservative purpose of the *Hindutva* movement remains evident. Never is it suggested that Dalits should take up new work, or women new roles, in society. Traditional caste and gender hierarchies are still openly valued as contributing to the organic whole of both community and cosmos. Jaffrelot (1996: 30) reminds us that:

> In the Brahminical world view *jatis* [castes] are species (human, animal and vegetal) which occupy different ranks in the universe in conformity with the Dharma (universal law). Human species are integrated in a hierarchical social order, the caste system . . . Some *jatis* may occupy a very low position, but they are nonetheless part of the system.

The incorporation of oppressed groups is, in fact, vital to the maintenance of the whole. Hindu nationalists are sustaining hierarchy by offering women a voice in the public arena, so long as it promotes traditional women's virtues, and offering Dalits better living circumstances and respect, so long as they are willing to perform traditional services and to acquiesce to Hindu values. An RSS activist has commented:

> We don't call them either Dalit or Harijan; we believe that they were part of the Hindu society who has remained ignored for some reasons, like some part of the body is ignored or hailing [sic]. To serve it is natural *dharma*. If the thumb of the leg [i.e. the big toe] is hurt the hand rushes to it. No need to mistrust it. With this objective we have started our service work. (Jaffrelot, 2003: 460).

Hence, it would appear that the RSS's "ideological purpose is to divert the Dalits, who are naturally appreciative of charitable work, away from egalitarian ideologies and to assimilate them into a 'Hindu nation'" (Jaffrelot 2003: 455).

Furthermore, if Dalits and women are being portrayed as welcome members of the community, now more than ever, Muslims and Christians are being portrayed as adversarial others. Savarakar (1999: 70) wrote at length on the matter:

> . . . our Mohammedan or Christian countrymen, who had originally been forcibly converted to a non-Hindu religion and who consequently have inherited along with Hindus, a common Fatherland and a greater part of the wealth of a common culture – language, law, customs, folklore and history – are not and cannot be recognized as Hindus. For though Hindusthan to them is Fatherland as to any other Hindu yet it is not to them a Holyland too. Their holyland is far off in Arabia or Palestine. Their mythology and Godmen, ideas and heroes are not the children of this soil. Consequently their names and their outlook smack of a foreign origin. Their love is divided. Nay, if some of them be really believing what they profess to do, then there can be no choice – they must, to a man, set their Holyland above their Fatherland in their love and allegiance. That is but natural. We are not condemning nor are we lamenting. We are simply telling facts as they stand. We have tried to determine the essentials of Hindutva and in doing so we have discovered that the . . . Mohammedan or Christian communities possess all the essential qualifications of Hindutva but one and that is that they do not look upon India as their Holyland.

The essence of the argument is that neither Muslims nor Christians can truly be Indians. The complex variety of religious beliefs and practices found in India have been reduced to two: Hindu and nonHindu (especially Muslim). As Patnaik and Chalam (1996: 257) suggest, "Brahminical appropriation is . . . sought by positing a monolithic conception of Muslim communities standing, as it were, in perennial opposition to a monolithic construct of Hinduism." The imagined nation is of Hindus, and the imagined other is of Muslims.

Hindu-Muslim antagonism is centuries old in India, predating the colonial period. When Muslims first entered the subcontinent in the 10th century, they came as invaders, smashing idols, razing temples to the ground, slaughtering and converting, "waging . . . *jihads* at least as much for plunder as for the promise of paradise" (Wolpert, 2004: 107). In north India, more than five centuries of Muslim rule, variously tolerant and despotic, followed. So, as independence from the British approached in 1947, Hindu nationalists were able to ratchet up fears of another era of Muslim hegemony, causing RSS membership to skyrocket from 76,000 in 1943 to 600,000 in 1948 (Jaffrelot, 1996: 75).

Since the partitioning of India and Pakistan, Hindu nationalists have heavily blamed Muslims for the 'unnatural' bifurcation of *Bharatma*, "Mother India," the holy land that was to have become a Hindu state (see figure 8.1). And, they have claimed that the population of Muslims remaining in India are a threat to the Hindu community. A recent issue of *The Organiser*, an RSS publication, states:

> Muslims [in India] are traitors and harbour pro-Pakistan sentiments . . . [they] severed the two arms of Mother India (East and West Pakistan) . . . Muslim polygamous practices means that they have a higher birthrate and Hindus are in danger of being swamped by Muslim. (Abbott, 1999: 243)

Muslims are a mere 12% of the population in India, and are a relatively impoverished and disempowered community there. Yet, they are represented as a dangerous internal threat to the country, in league with the external one of Pakistan. Noting the unrealistic nature of the fear being promoted in the Hindu community, *India Today*, the country's premier news magazine, has declared that: "The Hindu juggernaut has arrived . . . The majority appears to have developed a minority complex" (May 11, 1986).[6]

THE RISE OF THE BJP

At its inception in the early part of the century, the RSS declared itself to be a religious and cultural movement without political intentions. But, in 1951, it organized a separate party, the Jana Sangh, and presented candidates for office. In 1980, a merger with another party formed the Bharatiya Janata Party (BJP, or "Indian People's Party") to voice RSS concerns in the political arena. The BJP ran candidates on a platform that advocated a strong central government, a powerful military, the elimination of corruption, a liberalized economy, a retraction of the "appeasement policy" toward Muslims, and, of

हिमालयं समारभ्य यावादिन्दुसरोवरम् ।
तं देवनिर्मितं देशं हिन्दुस्थानं प्रचक्षते ॥

Figure 8.1.   Bharatma. Mother India presides not only over modern day India, but also Pakistan, Bangladesh, Nepal, and other small countries in the region. Territorial boundaries are obliterated by the "mother's" unifying force (Abbott, 1999: 241).

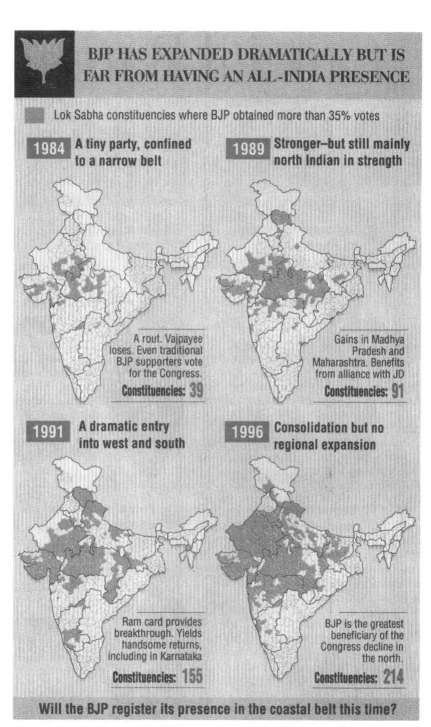

BJP HAS EXPANDED DRAMATICALLY BUT IS FAR FROM HAVING AN ALL-INDIA PRESENCE

Lok Sabha constituencies where BJP obtained more than 35% votes

1984 A tiny party, confined to a narrow belt

1989 Stronger—but still mainly north Indian in strength

A rout. Vajpayee loses. Even traditional BJP supporters vote for the Congress.
Constituencies: 39

Gains in Madhya Pradesh and Maharashtra. Benefits from alliance with JD
Constituencies: 91

1991 A dramatic entry into west and south

1996 Consolidation but no regional expansion

Ram card provides breakthrough. Yields handsome returns, including in Karnataka
Constituencies: 155

BJP is the greatest beneficiary of the Congress decline in the north.
Constituencies: 214

Will the BJP register its presence in the coastal belt this time?

Figure 8.2.   The Rise of the BJP: Electoral Maps. The BJP has steadily gained electoral strength in India's heartland.
Source: India Today (Dec. 15, 1997, p. 38)

course, Hindu nationalism. Few in India's political center would have predicted its success. Yet, over the past twenty-five years, despite setbacks, the
BJP has steadily replaced the Congress Party with the electorate at the local
level (see figure 8.2).

The BJP launched its campaign in the 1980s with characteristically Indian
forms of demonstration. It conducted *satyagrahas* (civil resistances), *bundhs*
(shop closings), and *yatras* (chariot processions modeled on those given annually to Hindu gods), using Hindu symbolism in posters, writings, and
speeches. The modern media was engaged to present images of Hindu pride
rooted in the religio-mythical past. In 1987-8, a television series of the Ramayana, consisting of 78 episodes, aired weekly on Sunday mornings. This
was followed by a 91 episode series of the Mahabharata, with an average audience estimated by India Today magazine at 91% of those owning television
sets.[7] Watching the programs became an act of religious devotion, as viewers
performed *puja* in front of their TVs and claimed they were receiving *darshan*
(blessings from the gods) back (Jaffrelot, 1996: 389). The television series
were not produced directly by the BJP. But, the party was able to capitalize
on them in the 1989 election campaign. It issued campaign posters that depicted the god Ram, of the Ramayana, as an icon of Hindu masculine pride.
Also depicted, were drawings of a temple to be built upon the purported site
of Ram's birthplace, a site occupied at the time by a mosque. The message
was clear:

> Hindus, who were always being described in VHP publications as too tolerant
> and passive, were thus invited to prepare themselves to meet the challenges
> which confronted them; the example of the strong, aggressive Ram was in-
> tended to illustrate the style of forceful action which would be required. In other
> words, Ram was cast in the role of the 'angry Hindu'. (Jaffrelot, 1996: 391)

By the use of pan-Hindu iconography, the BJP was conducting a very successful campaign of "assimilation and elimination."

Much of the BJP's campaign strategy was to make oblique references to
the Muslim "threat." But, external threats were not, in fact, the real problem.
The Hindu community was experiencing serious political disunity at the time,
due to competition between castes. As the full implications of the country's
commitment to justice, liberty, equality, and fraternity had emerged, another
group was demanding equal representation, the "Other Backward Castes," or
OBCs. OBCs were low caste, i.e. Shudra rank, groups that were generally
economically and educationally disadvantaged. Because they were not untouchable, however, they were not directly protected by the reservations and
job quotas awarded to Scheduled Castes and Tribes by the constitution. These
castes had first emerged as a political bloc in Madras in the 1870s when, with

the encouragement of missionaries, they had begun to agitate for access to education. In the south, where some of their members were landed and wealthy, the OBCs had formed political associations that had been successful in significantly reducing Brahmin influence in state government (Irschick, 1969). In the north, however, where OBCs were composed almost entirely of poor servant classes, caste continued to be a barrier to economic and political advancement.[8]

In 1980, the government, led by a liberal socialist party, the Janata Party (later, Janata Dal), had established a commission to address the matter of OBC representation, appointing as its chair a low caste politician by the name of B. P. Mandal. When the work was completed, the Mandal report identified the under-representation of the OBCs in government posts, especially at higher levels, and specifically targeted caste affiliation as having inhibited OBC promotions. Mandal wrote:

Castes . . . have kept Hindu society divided in a hierarchical order for centuries. This has resulted in a close linkage between the caste rankings of a person and his social and economic status. This manner of stratification of society gave the higher castes deep-rooted vested interests in the perpetuation of the system. (McDonald, 1991: 28)

The hard evidence for the case was strong. Of four classes of government jobs, only 5% of the Class I posts (the highest) were held by OBCs, despite the fact that they represented over half the national population. In fact, 90% of Class I posts were held by members of upper castes representing only 25% of the population. Even Dalits, who had had the benefit of compensatory discrimination, were still significantly underrepresented, with their reserved posts often going unfilled (Jaffrelot, 2003: 343).

In its conclusions, the Mandal report recommended that OBCs also receive compensatory discrimination and that 27% of government jobs and educational seats be set aside for them.

The possibility of further reservations, reducing the number of posts available for highly educated, but not necessarily wealthy, high caste young people, brought violent reaction. With BJP support, anti-reservation riots broke out among students in the western state of Gujarat in 1981 and 1985. In the latter event, the army had to be called out to control the violence (Kohli, 1992: 261). The government, then under Congress leadership, chose to delay discussion of the matter. But in 1990, the Janata Dal returned to power and simply announced the implementation of reservations for OBCs. The result was rioting that killed hundreds across the country and a rash of suicide protests. Upper caste students, "who had seen education and jobs as their way forward and now found a chasm appearing under their feet," doused

Table 8.1. Mandal Commission Report on Allocation of Central Government Jobs

	SCs and STs	OBCs	Forward Castes	Total
Percent of Population	22.5%	52.0%	25.5%	100% (683.3 million)*
Class I	5.7%	4.7%	89.6%	100% (174,026)
Class II	18.2%	10.6%	71.2%	100% (1,112,925)
Class III & IV	24.4%	19.0%	56.6%	100% (484,687)
All Classes	18.7%	12.6%	68.7%	100% (1,571,638)

Key: SC = Scheduled Castes, ST = Scheduled Tribes, OBC = Other Backward Castes
Sources: *As per 1981 census: Visaria & Visaria, 1998: 27
All other statistics: Omvedt, 1993: 55

themselves with flammable liquids, and lit themselves afire in public protest (Omvedt, 1993: 281). Over 150 people attempted suicide, and 63 succeeded (Jaffrelot, 2003: 347).

Front page photographs and cover story accounts of the student suicides fueled the flame that fed the Hindu nationalist furor. The Janata Dal government fell, due to the withdrawal of BJP support, and Congress returned for the time being. In 1992, the reservations were upheld in principle by the Supreme Court, but anti-reservation sentiment at the popular level continued to grow and to become more vocal. The battle over caste reservations was dividing the Hindu community. And, the BJP's challenge was to represent high caste interests, while at the same time present a united Hindu front. It did this through the use of carefully selected images and symbolic acts.

In 1990, at the height of the anti-reservation riots, the patriarchal guru of the BJP, L.K. Advani, decorated a Toyota to resemble a Hindu chariot, and with much media fanfare, engaged in a holy pilgrimage, or *rath yatra*, starting from Gujurat in the middle of the country, and heading to Ayodhya in the north. Advani traveled over 10,000 kilometers in a self-proclaimed identification with the god Ram. Saffron clad activists accompanied him, holding meetings and singing militant songs. Devotees traveled to meet him along the way, with men giving gifts of their own blood and women donating their *talis* (marriage necklaces) to the cause (Jaffrelot, 1996: 416ff). Fearful of the possibility of rioting, the government arrested Advani after a month of travel and before he had reached his destination.

The object of the *yatra* was a visit to a Muslim mosque by the name of Babri Masjid, the very mosque that Hindu nationalists were claiming to be on the site of Ram's birthplace. It had been built in the 16th century by the Emperor Babur, who purportedly had demolished a previously existing Hindu temple to do so. In 1853, Hindu nationalists had physically attacked the Babri Masjid to destroy it for Ram. In 1883, they had formally requested of the government, and had been denied, the right to build a temple on adjacent land. In 1949, they had broken into the mosque, placing within it an icon of Ram. And, in 1986, the VHP had targeted it for agitations, along with a list of other mosques that were said to be sitting on the sites of previous temples. So, Advani's choice of a destination for his *rath yatra* was well considered, as was the government's decision not to permit him to arrive.

In the 24 months following Advani's arrest (and release), *sevaks* organized across the country, consecrated bricks etched with the names of their places of origin, and traveled in holy pilgrimage to bring them to Ayodhya for the construction of the Ram temple. Then, on Dec. 6, 1992, they hoisted the saffron flag of Hinduism, stormed the mosque, and destroyed it in a few short hours. Idols and portraits of Ram were brought in, and a temporary temple was constructed on the site. For the most part, the police fled the scene. But those clashes with police that resulted in deaths of *sevaks* produced martyrs for the cause whose ashes were subsequently carried in procession throughout India (Brass, 1997: 27).

The BJP's official response to the destruction of the Babri Masjid was characteristically ambiguous. Utter Pradesh, the state in which Ayodhya is located, was BJP controlled, and had blocked federal interference in the event (Brass, 1996: 246). But, Advani, who was present at the destruction, seemed genuinely distressed by the outcome and resigned his government post to take responsibility for the violence (Jaffrelot, 1996: 456). Others in the party called the event a "miscalculation." Later, however, the party "abandoned its apologetic stance," and participated in Hindu victory processions that sparked riots in Bombay and elsewhere, including one in Karnataka that resulted in 73 deaths (Jaffrelot, 1996: 476, 463). In Utter Pradesh, the riots were so severe that the central government had to impose President's rule to maintain order.

The destruction of the mosque in Ayodhya has become a symbol of the new Hindu militancy and of pride in Hindu values. Of course, the intent was to unite Hindus by vilifying Muslims. But arguably, there was a message of social conservatism for the Hindu community as well. Omvedt (1995: viii) suggests that Dalits and women were warned in the event to remember their traditional roles:

> In destroying the Babri Masjid on December 6, 1992, the forces of *Hindutva* issued a declaration of caste war, not simply an assault against the Muslim community . . . This was a declaration of war against dalits, adivasis [tribals], women, the bahujan samaj [Shudra Party], the toiling and productive castes and classes who have always been held as inferior by *varnashrama dharma*. That

war has to be fought, at the level of culture and symbolism and not simply that of politics and economics; and not simply with the weapons of "secularism" but over every inch of the terrain of Indian history and identity that the Hindu-nationalists have staked a claim to.

At the Babri Masjid, the "angry Hindu" asserted himself, and declared himself unwilling to cooperate any further with the democratic and secular values of the current form of the nation state.

In 1996, the BJP won the general elections for central government for the first time. The party was so controversial, however, that it was unable to form a government for longer than 13 days. In 1998, it was elected again, but by a larger majority. This time, it successfully formed a government and remained in power for five years. As a socially conservative party of the upper castes in a nation with masses of lower caste people, the BJP's ability to hold on to power was surely due to its "silver tongued" prime minister, Atal Bihari Vajpayee (1926-) (Thakur and Sharma, 1999). Vajpayee had begun his career as a member of the RSS in the 1940s and was a close associate of Advani's. But he was educated, with an MA in political science, careful in his speech, and "a man of compromise" (Jaffrelot, 1996: 309). It was Vajpayee's image as a moderate that garnered enough legitimacy for the party to retain its position in government.

Still, Vajpayee did not fail to represent his party's interests during the five years of his prime ministership. On March 19th of 1998, he was sworn into office. On May 11th of the same year, he threatened Pakistan by announcing the successful conducting of an underground test of nuclear armaments. Four more tests followed, resulting in similar tests and threats by Pakistan, economic sanctions by the rest of the world, and a United Nations resolution against dangerous saber rattling. Then, with attention duly diverted outside the country, on July 7th, Vajpayee announced the retention of SC/T and OBC reservations in a bid to win over the lower castes to the Hindu fold (Thakur and Sharma, 1999: 131, 194). This time, there was little protest from the high caste constituency, and the BJP was able to consolidate power by representing itself as a party for all Hindus.

Given India's history of commitment to democracy and to socialism, the BJP's success has surprised most political analysts. Arguably, the party represents reactionary values in a modern context. Its constituency is largely urban, middle class, and upper caste. Yet it is not completely lacking in rural or lower caste support as well. Basu (1996: 59-60) suggests that the BJP's success is due to 1) its ability to moderate its political rhetoric when losing ground, and to strengthen it when gaining, and 2) its ability to present "contradictory images" to its diverse public:

The BJP must devise appropriate strategies for different arenas and constituencies. Conversely, people are likely to support the BJP for diverse reasons, which often have little to do with communal hostility. In New Delhi, for example, the middle classes may support the BJP because they favor a stronger, more authoritarian state with more ambitious foreign policy objectives, whereas slum dwellers may support the BJP because it promises to legalize their dwellings. (Basu, 1996: 59)

These are strategic reasons for its success. But, I would suggest, philosophical reasons exist as well. The BJP is offering Indians a distinct national identity, based on religious symbolism, values and practices, that provides a sense of security in the face of the onslaught of globalization (a phenomenon which I will explore in the next chapter). It is promising them safety at the price of freedom and love.

CULTURE WARS

In the past, the caste- and gender-based hierarchies of Hindu society have had the support of the state. Fukazawa reports that in pre-colonial Maharashtra "the caste system . . . was not a 'spontaneous' social order of the people but very much a state order of society, controlled and protected by the state" (cited in Chakravarti 2000: 13-14). The British East India Company did little to threaten this order. But as democracy evolved under the British Raj, and even more so as its full implications were beginning to be realized after independence, a disjuncture between political values and social ones emerged. Jaffrelot (2003: 3) suggests:

> The institutional mechanisms of the Republic of India are superimposed on a social system that is dominated by the hierarchical logic of castes, and therefore seems *a priori* largely incompatible with the individualist and egalitarian values of democracy. India, at least in its earlier incarnations, may therefore be an extreme case of political democracy without social democracy.

For fifty years, observers have thought that the dichotomy between public and private life so prevalent in the West would resolve the problem of caste and democracy in India (Singer, 1980). But, as the Hindu nationalists have realized (along with Muslim communities in other places), a secular democratic arena is not neutral as regards religion. Thus, the BJP defends the nation state as indigenous, but labels secularism and democracy as western (Basu, 1996: 60). Furthermore, what happens in the public arena has a way of eroding structures in the private arena. Traditionally oppressed groups, such as

women, untouchables, and the poor, who encounter new ideas in the public
square may no longer be willing to carry on as usual in the village or at home.
No doubt with this possibility in mind, Hindu nationalists are attempting to
reverse the direction of influence, that is, to bring private arena Hindu values
into the public arena to shore up the traditional order.

Hindu conservatives do have reason to fear. There has in fact been an ero-
sion of legitimacy for upper caste authority, undercutting both Brahminism
and patriarchy (Basu and Kohli, 1998: 2). And, the addition of reservations
for OBCs has made it clear that there are further losses yet to be endured by
the traditional elite. Basu (1998: 247) remarks:

> . . . lower castes have broadened the parameters of democracy by demanding
> greater rights and opportunities. The violence associated with caste conflict is
> usually instigated by the upper castes to prevent subordinate groups from ac-
> quiring greater power. . . . Where caste-based reforms would foster a more eq-
> uitable system, Hindu nationalism would do the opposite.

The expansion of democratic principles, rooted historically in Christian influence, has seriously endangered the legitimacy of the Hindu cosmic order.

Hindutva, then, is a "primordial" reaction (Geertz, 1973) to this threat. It
attempts to protect Hinduism by melding together race, language, culture, and
religion into a total defense. Such primordialism is often dangerously violent.
Geertz (1973: 261) writes:

> Economic or class or intellectual disaffection threatens revolution, but disaffec-
> tion based on race, language, or culture threatens partition, irredentism, or
> merger, a redrawing of the very limits of the state, a new definition of its do-
> main. Civil discontent finds its natural outlet in the seizing, legally or illegally,
> of the state apparatus. Primordial discontent strives more deeply and is satisfied
> less easily. If severe enough, it wants not just Sukarno's or Nehru's or Moulay
> Hasan's head, it wants Indonesia's or India's or Morocco's.

And, Webster (1992: 150) notes that "since Independence Dalits have experienced not the widespread caste Hindu 'change of heart' Gandhi had promised, but a growing 'backlash' against whatever modest gain Dalits have
made." Conservative Hindus are on the move.

The Dalit community has not failed entirely to respond. There have been a
number of forms of protest. One of these has been to follow Ambedkar's example of conducting high profile mass conversions out of Hinduism. In 1981,
1,000 members of an untouchable village in Tamil Nadu converted to Islam.
With wide media coverage, thousands more Dalits converted across the country, waiving their rights to compensatory discrimination as ex-untouchables.

Hindu nationalists reacted with a political campaign to introduce the "Freedom of Religion" bill, banning "forced" conversions and requiring government permits for the construction of any new religious buildings (Jaffrelot, 1996: 287). Not dissuaded, on November 4th of 2001, Dalits held an enormous rally in Delhi, where 50,000 people publicly converted to Buddhism. Their leader, Ram Raj, chairman of the All-India Confederation of Scheduled Castes and Scheduled Tribes Organizations, himself converted, and encouraged Dalits across the country to reject Hinduism in favor of the religion of their choice. The Christian community was present, with the leadership of the All India Christian Council on the platform, pledging support for Dalits regardless of religious affiliation.[9]

Another form of protest has been to engage in icon politics. While caste Hindus have been putting up posters and images of Ram (a mythical king reigning over a unified Hindu community), Dalits have been putting up photographs and statues of Ambedkar (an historical figure who uncovered the divisions in the Hindu community). In 1994, in the state of Uttar Pradesh alone, there were 60 incidents of violence, and 21 people killed, accompanying the installation of Ambedkar statues. In 1995, Mayawati, a female Dalit chief minister of Uttar Pradesh set up 15,000 Ambedkar statues across the state, and renamed Agra University as Ambedkar University. She also ran Dalit village development programs, gave grants to Dalit primary school children, and reserved 20% of police inspector's positions for Dalits. The reaction from the caste communities of the state was to swell the ranks of the BJP (Jaffrelot, 2004: 412ff). And, for their part, in February of 2003, while still in control of the central government, the BJP government unveiled a portrait of Savarkar to be hung in a hall of parliament along with Gandhi and Nehru. Opposition party members walked out on the unveiling.

Yet, perhaps a silent majority of ordinary Dalit communities are responding to the pressures of Hindu conservatism by adopting the middle caste strategy of sanskritisation. They are taking up the religious rites and social practices of the castes above them in order to prove their worth. The market women I interviewed are members of such communities. This is despite the fact that they live in a state that has been relatively progressive. Under colonialism, Karnataka's kings promoted reforms advantageous to women and to lower castes. Post-independence, the state had one of the country's first lower caste chief ministers, Devaraj Urs, who instituted land reform and reservation schemes for Dalits. Perhaps reforms such as these have functioned to release the pressure that might have been mounted against the high castes and men to make more radical changes in the social order. In any case, it would seem that market women are choosing the reform offered to them by social conservatives, rather than the revolution that would fully liberate them.

NOTES

1. Baird (2001: 152) states that the Hindu code bill was intended as a first step toward a uniform civil code (UCC) for all women, based on "reason, equality, modernity, and public opinion." Though he favored the construction of such a code, Nehru did not want to alienate the Muslim community too early in the process. Hence he supported a "Hindu" code, anticipating that Muslims would eventually be willing to adopt it (Lamb, 1967: 190).

2. Kohli's figures are based on government survey data on crime and on the work of Paul Brass (1997: 240), who defines them as "incidents of communal violence." See also Nayar (1975: 17).

3. Gandhi was assassinated by Nathuram Vinayak Godse, who was also associated with the Hindu Mahasabha. Savarkar was both friend and mentor to Godse, who, in fact, visited him on his way to Delhi to do the killing.

4. Ironically, the term Sindh was given to India by Alexander the Great to indicate the people beyond the river, i.e. the Indus River, to the east of Greece (Ludden, 1996: 7). Yet these foreign origins have not prevented Hindu nationalists from assuming the term and its derivatives to be both indigenous and divinely ordained.

5. *Swayamsevak* means religious devotion in the form of voluntary service to one's own people (*swayam* = "one's own," *sevak* = "service"). It contrasts sharply, then, with Jesus' injunction to love the other in the form of a stranger on the road (see chapter one).

6. Brass (1997: 27) notes, "This formidable movement [i.e. *Hindutva*] . . . propagates a different lesson from that taught by the greatest of all Indian mass mobilizers, Mahatma Gandhi. Instead of Swaraj defined as self-mastery, Hindu nationalists offer communal pride; instead of love for an alien oppressor who must nevertheless be fought, they offer hatred and pogroms against a weaker minority; instead of constructive work to improve the lives of the ordinary people of the country, they propose to create a great military industrial state and to build nuclear weapons to intimidate neighboring countries and gain the respect of foreign powers."

7. While many families, especially in villages, do not own television sets, it has been customary to set TVs up in central places and to invite everyone to watch on an occasion such as this one.

8. The emergence of the OBCs as a political bloc was the result of a general shift in the conception of caste. Sharma (1997: 133) remarks, "The discourse on caste has changed a great deal. Instead of talking about untouchability, pollution-purity and accessibility to educational and occupational opportunities, caste is being used as a resource for mobilization to reach all the possible corners of social life. Caste-based demands are being made as assertions of rights of the people." Mayer (2000: 62) agrees that, "The dominant morphology of caste is no longer primarily that of ranking, rather it is of separation; and the normative basis is less that of purity than it is of difference within which lies familial solidarity."

9. Van der Veer (2001: 22) comments: "It is remarkable to see that in both the American colony and the Indian colony it is the Christian dissenters who try to erect a 'wall of separation' between church and state . . . The effects in both cases . . . were

not that dissimilar in allowing an expansion of religious activity in civil society." And, Webster (1997: 67) suggests that despite caste divisions in the Church, "Christ is being presented and worshiped not merely as a source of heavenly escape from the dehumanizing consequences of the caste system, but also as the embodiment of the liberative power of God in the life of Dalit Christians and of the world in which they now live."

Chapter Nine

Entering the Global Market

Market women are untouchable, female, and poor. Having examined the origins of their untouchable and female statuses in chapters six and seven respectively, and having traced the history of the influence of Christianity in challenging the Hindu conceptions of these statuses in chapter eight, I now turn to the matter of their poverty.

Of course, market women are poor most immediately because they have been born into poor families. They have no inheritance, no education, and little or no help from husbands, who are generally underemployed. They have become petty commodity traders out of the dire necessity to feed themselves and their children. This pattern is typical of market women in other parts of the world as well, where "frequently women will enter the market as an extension of household tasks they perform as well as to make possible the economic survival of those households and, particularly to secure the survival of their children" (Seligmann, 2001: 3). Trading for the purpose of subsistence is socially acceptable for women even in cultures that restrict their movements outside the home. Trading as a profession, with intent to grow the business, is typically inappropriate female activity. Cross-culturally, "the economic fertility associated with capital accumulation is considered to be appropriate for men, not women, whose work should be primarily directed toward biological reproduction and economic reproduction of the household" (Seligman, 2001: 5). Since petty trading fits the latter bill, yielding too little gain to make capital accumulation possible, but enough to reproduce the household (Basu, 1992: 265), women are able to take it up to feed their families.[1]

Yet, it would seem that, once in the market, women should be able to grow their businesses into larger scale operations, further mitigating their poverty. This essentially never happens in India. In my own research, I initially attributed the failure of market women's businesses to grow to a "precapitalist mentality." Market women do not seem to have thought of reinvesting through capital accumulation, such as by purchasing carts or kiosks, or of expanding by hiring help. Their concerns reflect a mentality of maintenance. They only want to make enough money to feed and house their families and to pay back their loans. That accomplished, they hope to be able to spend more time at home. Most would consider their lives to have improved if they could but find enough family income to quit trading entirely.

Yet this maintenance mentality is not merely the product of precapitalist thinking. Central and west African market women develop trading networks and hierarchies that allow them to expand their businesses. Some become regional business "queens" (Clark, 2001; Horn, 1994). The difference is that while these societies also link women's extra-domestic economic activities to domestic needs, they do not on that account negatively evaluate women's active participation in public arenas. In India, a "good" woman is restricted to the domestic arena. Hence, work in the market is seen as a necessary evil, rather than an opportunity. When asked about it, market women express values that mirror the culture entirely; better women, including both those that are higher ranking and those that are wealthier, should not *need* to work outside the home at all.

In addition to cultural restrictions on women's activities, there are practical reasons why it is difficult to grow a petty commodity business to more profitable levels. One of these is the relative powerlessness of the seller as against his or her "backward linkages," i.e. moneylenders and suppliers. In a study of petty commodity traders of Calcutta, Dasgupta (1992) demonstrates that the scarcity of capital, together with the overabundance of sellers, makes it possible for middle traders to coerce the terms of financial agreements and to control supply. Sellers, if they wish to do business at all, cannot negotiate for better arrangements, and must yield inordinate proportions of the profits to their suppliers. Dasgupta (1992: 1451) comments:

> The urban economy through the *mahajan* [middle trader] is constantly working to reduce the share of surplus that goes to the petty trader. This control of the relationship extends through his control of the price and quantity the petty trader can sell. The petty trader's lack of control over his backward linkages and the market mechanism results from his lack of access to resources.

The lack of direct access to money and supplies subordinates the petty trader to middle traders.

Ironically, enduring higher levels of subordination can yield somewhat higher profits to the seller (Dasgupta, 1992: 1451). Agreements range from low levels of subordination to high as follows: producer sellers, strict cash transactions, selling on commission, and short term credit. The more subordinated the seller is, the more secure the source of money and goods, and the higher the profits will be. The more independent the seller is, the more she or he must operate on a small margin, sometimes even at a loss. So, attempts to detach from backward linkages in order to expand businesses are risky at best. Most female petty traders are dealing in produce with short credit arrangements. They are enduring relatively high levels of subordination, and sacrificing the possibility of expansion, in order to receive a slightly higher profit and some security. So, their maintenance mentality is pragmatic, in part.

POVERTY AND RECIPROCITY

Market women are engaged in work that yields only minimal returns for very intense labor. Without shops, stalls, or storage of any kind, they must be physically able to carry their entire stock. They purchase goods from supply sites, transport them to sitting spots, sell on small margins, try to absorb losses due to bad weather, spoiling produce, or cantankerous customers, and commit much of their meager gains to the repayment of their loans. That they can do this work and make a profit at all is due to the services that they provide, such as minor processing (shelling peas or weaving flower garlands), bulk breaking to very small amounts (a tomato at a time), providing a flexible product mix, transporting perishable products in the absence of refrigeration, and selling at convenient locations. That they do not make a higher profit than they do for these services is due, ultimately, to the large number of other impoverished sellers available to do the work.

Still, to an anthropologist it is not surprising that, even in circumstances of grinding poverty, market women emphasize not the fact that they are in competition with one another, but the fact that they need one another, as demonstrated through systems of generalized reciprocity. As I have described in chapters two and three, market women help one another to find loans, sponsor one another in highly prized sitting spots, and even conduct one another's businesses when needed. Furthermore, in the evenings they return to common neighborhoods where they give one another meals, share market information, and assist one another with childcare and domestic chores.

I asked market women to describe to me the nature of the connections between money, friends, and family. Essentially all agreed that relationships, whether friends or family, can be a good source of money in times of need, and that people with money should share with others. Far from separating financial from social obligations, market women *expect* that money and relationships will be, and should be, intertwined. Varunamma, who is sixty years old, expresses it this way:

> What we earn in life is only people. That is our property, money, and everything. If we have people, then we can easily get property. I believe more in people strength than in material wealth. People take care of us when we are in trouble. We need money, [but] money doesn't care about us . . . Relatives are themselves [a kind of] property.

Kalamma, who is well known in her community for sponsoring women poorer than herself, both inside and outside the market, explains the obligation to help:

> One should be kind to poor people and should not neglect them. One should develop friendships with them. One should invite them for lunch if they are hungry. One should treat them properly and see to their necessities. We have to keep them in our houses and treat them like family until they can stand on their own legs.

Varunamma agrees that "Poor people must help poor people. We can share lunch together. [That way,] both get help in times of emergency." Nagamma says that "friendship is the most important thing," and Laxmi, who is desperately poor herself, says that "People are most important. Property will not come to help you after death . . . Poor people need people. They need friendship. They need friends other than family members . . . Money is poison."

Yet, it is also true that the mixing of money and relationships is a constant source of small grievances, and some mild cynicism. Chennamma begins by affirming, "You can get friends if you have money. But we have no desire for money. We want people; we want friends," but later complains, "Everyone shows up when I have money. But I am penniless. So nobody cares." In part, the problem is that the high obligation to help can seriously deplete one's own resources. Mariamma says:

> We can get crowds of friends if we have money . . . [But then] we easily lose the money which we have earned. If we have a lot of friends, we are forced to give them money, and then we are in loss. So we don't want to have too many friends. [Still,] we help by giving meals and clothing to the poor and needy. The more we help others the more our children will be looked after by God.

Remembering that relationships can be in competition with one another, Javaramma comments that giving too much money to friends causes the family to suffer.

Yet, in a life filled with risk—of business losses or failure, of one's own or family members' ill health, of early deaths and incapacitation for work—such reciprocity is a long term investment in financial stability, despite its immediate inconvenience. All "gifts" given in times of plenty can be cashed in for returns in times of need. Reciprocity, both horizontal between friends and vertical between sellers and their patrons, creates a flexible network of supply of money, food, and clothing.

A good reputation is invaluable. In order to remain in the network, one must be *pramanika*, "authentic, credible, true, just . . . upright, honest" (Bucher, 1983: 340), a characteristic that is measured by the timely repayment of small loans, a willingness to lend stock, a reluctance to quarrel, and the avoidance of all stealing or lying. Good behavior is reinforced by the gossip chain and by direct confrontation. Granovetter (1985: 490) identifies the role of social embeddedness in economic behavior, making the point that trust is less the result of a generalized sense of morality or of coercive institutions than of the simple pressure to live up to obligations produced by face-to-face relationships:

> The embeddedness argument stresses . . . the role of concrete personal relations and structures (or "networks") of such relations in generating trust and discouraging malfeasance. The widespread preference for transacting with individuals of known reputation implies that few are actually content to rely on either generalized morality *or* institutional arrangements to guard against trouble . . . Better than the statement that someone is known to be reliable is information from a trusted informant that he has dealt with that individual and found him so. Even better is information from one's own past dealings with that person.[2]

So, a good reputation is a kind of savings, and reciprocal ties are a hedge against financial risk. Puttabasamma expresses it simply: "Money and friendship. A person needs both."

THE INDIAN ECONOMY

Understanding market women's poverty requires not only an analysis of their immediate economic circumstances, but an account of the history that has constructed those circumstances, and a description of the institutions that currently connect and subjugate them to global forces.

India is no newcomer to the global economy. David Washbrook (1990) has described the country's relationship to capitalism over the past four hundred years. Following Wallerstein's (1979) analysis of world systems into core, semiperipheral, and peripheral economies, Washbrook identifies India as initially having been a core country in the precolonial world system of the Indian Ocean. It had well developed merchant communities regulated by guilds, extensive banking systems, and high levels of capital investment producing luxury goods (p. 488). In fact, it was these very sorts of institutions that proved attractive to British mercantile capitalists, who saw in them the means to dominating the region.

> Scribal groups possessed literate cultures and advanced administrative and accountancy skills; military groups possessed longstanding martial traditions and paramilitary organizations; petite bourgeois trading and banking groups had business systems and networks of connections going back to the medieval period. It was precisely because the British did not have to invent, and therefore pay for, any of this that these intermediary agencies were so useful: the British harnessed their dynamic potential and rode them to a new world empire. (Washbrook, 1990: 490)

India, then, was incorporated into the emerging capitalist world system early precisely because of its full-fledged administrative, financial, and military institutions.

Furthermore, incorporation was not entirely without Indian cooperation. Through the entire first half of the colonial period, the Indian merchant community had much to gain from their associations with the East India Company. There were, of course, the gains to be made from trade itself. And, colonial structures benefited the middle classes. As the Company consolidated its power in the region, it progressively transported English law to India. In 1793, for instance, Lord Cornwallis introduced the concept of land as private property when he revamped the *zamindari* system of Bengal. Traditionally, *zamindars* had been tax collectors with the responsibility to keep law and order and the right to retain some of the revenue for themselves. They did not have rights to evict the cultivators or alienate their holdings. Taxes were negotiated after harvests, based on serfs' ability to pay, and remitted to the king who had made the appointment. Cornwallis mistook *zamindars* for landlords, and, in an attempt to introduce "better" administration, issued deeds to them and insisted that tax rates be contracted in advance. The net result was a transfer of power from serfs to local *zamindars,* who could now evict them, and from local *zamindars* to absentee *zamindars,* i.e. city bankers and moneylenders, when poor harvests made it impossible to pay taxes at the contracted rate (Wolpert, 2004: 197).[3] Structural changes such as these enhanced capital accumulation in the Indian merchant community as much as in the Company in the 17th and 18th centuries.

In the second half of the colonial period, however, British capital significantly replaced Indian capital, as the Raj instituted a policy of deindustrialization designed to reduce India to an agricultural state (Washbrook, 1990: 493). Government monopolies had already been declared on salt, pepper, saffron, cocaine and other profitable goods. Now, tea, indigo, coffee, and jute plantations were established, and taxation favoring English over Indian manufacturing, particularly textiles, was instituted. The wholesale dumping of cheaply produced goods on Indian markets set up the classic colonial exchange of raw materials for manufactured products, crippling Indian industry and establishing a net flow of wealth to England. By the twentieth century, "The desperate poverty and backwardness of peasant India were as much constituted by the forces of the international market economy as by anything else" (Washbrook, 1990: 480).

Still, Washbrook makes the point that India was never fully reduced to a mere supplier of raw materials and markets (p. 502). Such would have qualified it for peripheral status in the world system. Instead, India's role in providing institutions that mediated British political and economic hegemony elsewhere qualified it for semiperipheral status. Two of these institutions were Indian migrant labor, which was used to work mines and plantations all over the colonial world, and the Indian Army, which was used not only to police India, but to expand the Empire throughout the region. The Indian Army was:

> the army of British imperialism, formal and informal, which operated worldwide, opening up markets to the products of the industrial revolution, [and] subordinating labor forces to the domination of capital . . . The Indian army was the iron fist in the velvet glove of Victorian expansionism. (1990: 481)

For the British, India was as the right hand of the whole enterprise.

After World War I, England's exchange with India became increasingly less profitable. Indian nationalists, including Gandhi, had been deeply disappointed that their loyalty during the war had not been rewarded with more equitable treatment. Furthermore, the drain on India's economy was becoming increasingly evident. The nationalists intensified their demand for self-rule, spawning mass agitations and boycotts, and thereby increasing the cost of administering the country. At the same time, revenues began to decline. India was losing world market share due in part to the nervous withdrawal of British capital. The government began to "twist and turn," sometimes favoring economic alliances with India's merchant classes and sometimes favoring political alliances with the Brahmin literati, in an increasingly desperate attempt to administer the country without losing the economic benefits of colonial exchange:

> The colonial imperative dictated conservative policies aimed at preserving a stable 'tradition'; the capitalist imperative dictated commitment to a social transition which threatened to undermine both colonial authority and core economic

influence. The consequence was the progressive paralysis of both colonialism and capitalist development. (Washbrook, 1990: 500)

In the end, the British withdrew, unable to negotiate the contradiction that had emerged between developing the country and exploiting it.

With this history, then, it is not surprising that the early years of the democracy were characterized by socialist protectionism. The nationalists blamed the capitalist world system for India's poverty, and declared their intent to bring equity and development by means of central planning. This end was never pursued with the extreme means employed by the Soviet or Chinese governments. As a Fabian, Nehru was committed to democratic freedoms and a gradual evolution toward socialist ideals. He declared at the outset that India would have a mixed economy, giving full government control to just three industries (the railways, munitions, and atomic energy) (Lamb, 1967: 201), and permitting some integration with the world system (Omvedt, 1993: 28). Still, mindful of the heavy price India had paid for its participation in global capitalism, he pursued a protectionist policy of government regulation, high tariffs, and import substitution, in the main.

The elimination of poverty was Nehru's chief domestic concern. He chaired the five-year planning commissions himself, promoting economic growth, an equitable distribution of wealth, and the "values and attitudes of a free and egalitarian society" (Nanda, 1998: 209). The first plan (1951-1956) focused on land reform, abolishing the *zamindari* system, establishing land-holding ceilings, and setting up rural development programs. Much of this reform was derailed by local landed elite, party bosses in the Congress machine, who partitioned and transferred their lands on paper in order to keep them. As late as 1972, well after the Nehru era, 10% of rural households still held 55% of the land, while 50% of rural households held only 10% of the land (Nanda, 1998: 215). With approximately 80% of the population in agricultural villages, the failure to redistribute the land accounted for much of India's continuing problem with poverty after independence.

The second and third plans (1956-1961; 1961-1965) focused on both agricultural and industrial growth. These plans had real impact. Between 1951 and 1961, agricultural production rose 41%, industrial production rose 94%, and steel production more than doubled, making steel one of India's primary exports to the rest of Asia (Nanda, 1998: 209). Also, between 1950 and 1965, infrastructure was expanded, with electric generating capacity tripling, and the number of kilometers of paved and unpaved roads doubling (Lamb, 1967: 214-215). Domestic savings as a proportion of the GDP rose from 10% to 15% between 1955 and 1965, and life expectancy went up from 40 years to 50 years between 1951 and 1966 (Nanda, 1998: 209).

Socialist economic policy, then, was far from unsuccessful at producing growth. Yet, poverty was equally far from being eliminated. Nehru himself became severely disillusioned toward the end of his life as the socialist dream seemed to elude him. Some of the difficulty derived from the now familiar problems of a large state bureaucracy and government over-regulation; of government bureaucrats who were corrupt and inefficient; and of the poor quality of goods produced under a policy of import substitution. Some of the difficulty was due to the negative impact on the economy of rising taxes and foreign debt. And, some of the difficulty was in the failure to control population growth. Between 1951 and 1961, the population grew by twice what was anticipated (2.5% vs. 1.25%), absorbing many of the gains made from wealth production (Nanda, 1998: 209). In any case, at the time of Nehru's death in 1964, a full 40% of the population still lived below the poverty line (ibid, 212).[4]

Indira Gandhi's administration, perhaps, had more impact. Under her tenure, the Green Revolution (beginning in 1969) turned India from a food importer to a food exporter. Gandhi used the media during the Emergency (1975-1977) to campaign heavily for hard work as a kind of "worship," and to encourage capital investment. While she maintained the socialist rhetoric of her father, Gandhi's approach was entirely pragmatic. She allowed private enterprise to thrive, and, in 1981, she took the initial step toward economic liberalization by accepting a loan from the International Monetary Fund (IMF). Hers "was a uniquely Indian syncretism of socialism and capitalism, of state-supported free enterprise" (Wolpert, 2004: 403). Still, Gandhi retained high levels of protectionism, continued the five year plans, redoubled efforts to control population growth, and instituted a more successful program of land reform than her father's. The poverty rate, after having risen above 60% in the late 1960s, fell throughout the 1970s and 1980s to below 35% during her term of office (World Bank, 2000: 12).

Rajiv Gandhi overtly advocated liberalization in the late 1980s, contributing to the "prolonged, halting, but definite shift away from a state-directed economy" (Omvedt, 1993: 177). And, in June of 1991, the most significant liberalization took place when Manmohan Singh, a Harvard trained economist and committed free market advocate, then finance minister of Narasimha Rao (Congress Party), devalued the rupee, reversed import substitution, lowered trade barriers, and assisted the privatization of key industries. He also accepted the terms of a structural adjustment program as condition for another IMF loan. The most immediate effect was an increase in both the poverty rate and the absolute number of poor, as deregulated food prices and inflation jumped up (Dev & Ranade, 1999: 52). Over time, though, the poverty rate slowly declined to 29% in 2004.[5] Currently, the poverty rate is at its lowest since independence. But there are still nearly 300,000,000 people living on less than one US dollar per day, and a bottom 40% of the population that are spending 78% of their income on food alone (ibid: 54).

Looking back, the process of liberalization seems to have been almost completely independent of political platforms and rhetoric. When the BJP came to power, the party's nationalist saber rattling initially frightened the stock markets. Yet the BJP's primary constituency has always been middle-class and urban. Writing at the time of it's first (failed) election to central government in 1996, Patnaik and Chalam (1996: 273) said:

> The BJP solidly supports the present protagonists of liberalization—a package which includes 'free' foreign collaboration by the big business class as well as catering for the dreams of the upper middle class of acquiring consumer durables (now available in the market) freed from the strait-jacket of import-substitution.

So, liberalization continued unabated during the five years of the BJP's tenure in central government. In 2004, in a major election upset, Congress ousted the BJP from power, causing the stock markets to oscillate once again with fear that the old socialist party would reverse the trend. They need not have worried. The party president, Sonia Gandhi (wife of Rajiv), appointed to the prime ministership none other than Manmohan Singh, liberalization's chief architect. With Singh at the helm, India's full incorporation into the global capitalist world system now seems assured.

There is no doubt that liberalization has brought growth, consumer goods and an expanded middle class to India. The GDP, which hovered around 3.5% during the Nehru years, now regularly reaches 7% and higher. Purchase of consumer goods has expanded dramatically:

> Color televisions; computers; Bajaj scooters and Hondas and Lunas for the women of the family; refrigerators, pressure cookers and mixers to ease the work of the housewife; videos to film the weddings of the children; designer jeans and the new 'ethnic look' fashioned in expensive boutique versions of traditional bright peasant and nomad dresses; cities transformed by new hotels and expensive vegetarian restaurants and even fast-food places along with gaudy new temples, . . . and above all the Maruti car . . . now turned into the prize status symbol of the rising upper-middle class. (Omvedt, 1993: 187)

The middle class is estimated to be at 250 million people, nearly as large as the entire population of the United States (though only a quarter of India's population). And an estimated 61,000 Indians are now millionaires in US dollars (Sullivan, 2004: 16). Furthermore, the economic future looks "bright." India's middle class is educated and English-speaking, making it an attractive source of labor for the American service industry. Jobs from telemarketing to customer support to accounting can be outsourced via telephone and the internet. Already in 2004, India captured 66% of the world's offshore business outsourcing revenue (ibid).

Yet, the results of the most recent election have made it clear to politicians and policy makers alike that not all Indians feel they are benefiting from the inflow of wealth brought on by liberalization. Quoting statistics such as the ones above, the BJP ran on a platform of "India Shining." The slogan backfired, as millions of rural poor, who had yet to see any positive effects of India's integration into the global economy, turned out to vote against the incumbents, while urban middle class supporters stayed confidently at home. In 1997, Paul Brass wrote prophetically:

> The long-term political danger of a policy which caters increasingly to the urban consuming middle classes is that it may threaten the persistence of the parliamentary system itself in which the votes of the rural peasantry and the rural and urban poor continue to far outweigh those of the urban middle classes. It is necessary, therefore, to revise the traditional view of the urban middle classes as the main supporters of systems of political democracy. In developing countries, their expanding consumption demands can be met only by ignoring or repressing the needs of the majority. (p. 392)

It was this conflict of interests between the middle and lower classes that was most revealed in the ousting of the BJP in 2004. The poor still constitute a significant percentage of the electorate, and they do not intend to be forgotten in the middle class rush toward accumulation.[6]

CAPITALISM AND POVERTY

"Unfettered" capitalism has the following virtues: 1) an increasing degree of specialization producing growth in technology and therefore in the potential standard of living, 2) the freedom of contract-based economic relationships, breaking the sometimes oppressive bonds of the "moral" community, 3) a value on honesty that permits the pursuit of legitimate self-interest (for women as well as for men), 4) a tendency to encourage democracy (though not inevitably so),[7] and most clearly, 5) the ability to mass produce previously unimaginable types and amounts of material wealth. Its primary vices are two: 1) an accelerating problem with the distribution of the wealth it creates and 2) a focus on the material world, promoting values such as efficiency, utility, and consumption, that increasingly crowd out other values, such as family, community, or religious faith.[8]

Evaluating the impact of global capitalism on the poor in India purely according to material gains, it is true that even those at the bottom have benefited from scientific and technological advances. Small pox, for instance, a terrible thief of children, has been eradicated for rich and poor families alike. Diets have improved, with the poor consuming more refined cereals, eggs, and milk (Dev and Ranade, 1999: 54). A variety of manufactured products are available to even the poorest homes, such as the light, durable, plastic pots that have replaced the heavy, breakable pottery women used to carry on their heads to get water. And, of course, advances in infrastructure, such as utilities and transportation, have benefited everyone.

Yet, this does not mean that life at the bottom has necessarily become more viable. Despite the refinement of their diet, the proportion of the rural population that is malnourished has increased, rather than decreased, from 66% in 1983 to 70% in 1993 (Dev and Ranade, 1999: 55). The percentage of low birth weight babies, an indicator of mothers' malnutrition, has increased from 28% in 1990 to 34% in 2001. Infant mortality has fallen because of better access to medical services. But many families are yet unable to adequately nourish breastfeeding mothers.[9] And, child labor continues unabated, with an estimated 100 million working children between the ages of 5 and 14 (ibid, 65). The result is that even the most conservative voices are predicting that liberalization will produce "a greater divide between the poor and the rest, even as the new government struggles to reconcile election promises with economic realities" (Sullivan, 2004: 15).

Market women are a product of economic reform. Studies (Arora, 1999; Dewan, 1999; Seligman, 2001:5) show that emerging economies, particularly under the influence of structural adjustment programs, force women into the informal economy, either out of the household when men's employment fails, or out of the formal sector when women are "downsized" from industries that are becoming more "flexible" and competitive:

> Thinking in global terms, one could say that informal activities, especially women's marketing, are in many but not all cases, the result of the gradual outflanking of nation-bound capitalism. As global economic systems come to predominate, composed of large trading blocs, the informalization of the economy also increases. (Seligman, 2001: 20)

Liberalization produces two things: 1) an expanding middle class, and 2) a drop in income for the poor. The marketplace is a particularly welcoming arena for the latter because of its ability to "soak up" large numbers of uneducated and unskilled people, and to keep them minimally alive (Alexander and Alexander, 2001: 67).

This is not to say that petty trading is encouraged by the government, or that petty traders are valued by the higher classes that use their services. Seligmann (2001: 16) notes:

> The presence of these unruly traders selling on sidewalks and in storefronts, without paying licenses and taxes, evokes images of disorder, of development gone awry, and of market failure. The sprawling urban barrios and sidewalks congested with women hawking wares, their children sitting beside them, bespeak the failure of development and government control.

As a result, market women are not treated well. They are chased off by police for sitting in unauthorized spots, verbally abused by ruffians, and generally stigmatized with very low rank. The marketplace welcomes them at one level and abuses them at another.

Furthermore, as liberalization proceeds, market women's economic circumstances are likely to become more difficult. First, increasing numbers of poor are entering the marketplace, making gains from trade harder and harder to come by. Then, refrigerated supermarkets and shopping malls are being built that will eventually reduce the number of available customers. And finally, the government is likely to try harder to control the informal economy by formalizing purchasing and credit arrangements, regulating the use of space, and, of course, imposing taxes. Over the long term, the marketplace as an economic arena will shrink in size, providing less and less of a refuge for people in need of an income.

Clearly then, the role that government plays, or fails to play, in the process of global integration will be critical to the future of the poor in India. The value of socialism was in its overtly stated goals: to protect the national economy from rapacious forces in the global market, and to protect and promote the poor in class-based competition within the country. Its means of achieving the former goal was economic protectionism. Its means of achieving the latter goal was to regulate the economy with labor laws and price controls, and to provide essential services such as infrastructure, agricultural development, primary and secondary education, basic healthcare, and social security. The architects of structural adjustment programs have frowned heavily on such policies for inhibiting growth. But, it is possible that four decades of socialist policy have actually played a crucial role in *preparing* India to enter the global economy now. The "four tigers" of Asia (Hong Kong, Singapore, South Korea, and Taiwan), whose high growth rates were initially attributed to the advantages of free market enterprise, have been shown to have benefited from periods of significant government involvement. That involvement has included not only the provision of services, such as gender inclusive primary education and preventative healthcare, but also direct intervention in the economy, such as effective land reform and the selection and promotion of export industries (Dreze and Sen, 1995: 37-42). While these governments have encouraged foreign investment, they have heavily restricted capital flight, and have promoted both import substitution and state owned enterprises (Jomo, 2003: 5). If India has had lower growth rates than the "Tigers" to date, it may be because it has had less (or less effective), rather than more, government intervention.

In any case, as is well known, the primary difficulty with using growth rates as a measure of national wellbeing is that they say nothing at all of the internal distribution of the wealth. Sen (1999: 47) notes that while China, Sri Lanka, and Kerala have lower gross national products than South Africa, Gabon, Namibia, and Brazil, they have much higher life expectancy rates, due to the provision of government sponsored healthcare and education. In fact, globally, when one accounts for public spending on health, the positive correlation between GNP and life expectancy "entirely vanishes" (Dreze and Sen, 1995: 44). Truly *national* wellbeing depends upon a good distribution of the wealth, and a good distribution of the wealth requires good government.

Dreze and Sen (1995: 51ff) have compared two states in India to make this latter point: Kerala and Uttar Pradesh (U. P.). Kerala, as we have already seen, has a good distribution of wealth and gender equity due to decades of democratically supported Marxist government programs. U. P. has an exceedingly poor distribution of wealth and almost no gender equity due to its feudal structure of powerful landlords (ex-*zamindars*) who resist change. Kerala has a poverty rate of only 8%, while U. P. has a poverty rate of 46%, and Kerala has an adult female literacy rate of 86%, while U.P.'s rate is just 25%. Given the international correlation between rising standards of living and falling birthrates, it is not surprising, then, that in Kerala the fertility rate has dropped to 1.8% without coercive measures, while in U.P. it is a stunning 5.1%, the very highest rate in the country (p. 47). So, Dreze and Sen conclude, economic development requires good government in at least the following three arenas: 1) the provision of "well-functioning public services," such as schooling, healthcare, social security, and relief, 2) the promotion of true democracy through the creation of a safe space for "the political organization of deprived sections of the society" (p. 54), and 3) a willingness to engage in effective wealth redistribution, because "in many circumstances, distributional concerns are *congruent* with other social objectives, including economic efficiency" (p. 96) [emphasis in the original].

At the national level, such government policies can be instituted, protecting the poor and marginalized from both internal and external exploitation. But, these days, national governments are very much at the mercy of global forces. And, at the global level, institutions of legal oversight that might sponsor social services and education, promote full political participation, or provide mechanisms of redistribution, are badly lacking. Townsend and Gordon (2002: xiv) remind us that, despite a half century of World Bank and IMF efforts to eradicate poverty using free market principles:

> There is no evidence of marked change in the huge extent of poverty in the world. In some regions—especially Sub-Saharan Africa and the transitional economies of Eastern Europe and the republics of the former Soviet Union—it has increased noticeably.

The world's wealth is exceedingly poorly distributed. According to the United Nations Development Programme, in 1999, the richest 200 people in the world (.00000003% of the population) had assets in excess of the poorest 41% of the population. In fact, the richest *three* people in the world had more wealth than the combined GNP of the 43 least developed countries (Townsend and Gordon, 2002: 9). In terms of income, the richest 10% controlled 50% of the world's supply, while the poorest 50% controlled only 10% of that supply (p. 386). Furthermore, there is evidence that global wealth may be "trickling up" (p. 6). Between 1988 and 1993, the top quartile of the world's population *increased* its income share by almost 15%, while the bottom quartile *lost* more than 12% (p. 387), this in only five years![10] It would seem that, far from eliminating poverty, the current world capitalist system, like the previous colonial one, is badly exacerbating it.

Statistics such as these raise the question of whether global capitalism is sustainable for the long run. Without redistributive mechanisms, wealth has become increasingly unequally distributed, resulting not only in the tremendous suffering of those at the bottom, and not only in the commercialization of those at the middle and the top, but in the general instability of the system as a whole. For a time, development economists attempted to make the argument that inequality was a temporary, but necessary, phase in the rise of a fully capitalist economy. Simon Kuznets championed this view, citing a correlation he had found between inequality and high growth rates in "emerging" economies. Various civic and political leaders then used Kuznets' argument to justify their own countries' income and wealth disparities with "trickle down" theory, suggesting that the poor will benefit in due time if market forces are allowed to operate without government interference.

By now, however, the evidence is presenting a different picture. In a review of empirical studies of economic development, Aghion et. al. (1999) have demonstrated an association, not between inequality and growth, but between inequality and *volatility* in the growth rate (due to decreasing returns to small numbers of wealthy investors). Tadaro (2000: 179) finds that, far from "trickling down," wealth further concentrates internally as national economies are incorporated into the global one. He cites a study of 43 developing countries:

> It was found that the primary impact of economic development on income distribution has generally been to decrease both the absolute and the relative incomes of the poor. There was no evidence of any automatic trickle-down of the benefits of economic growth to the very poor. On the contrary, the growth process experienced by these 43 LDCs ["less developed countries"] has typically led to a "trickle-up" in favor of the small middle class and especially the very rich.

Tadaro suggests that wealth disparities eventually inhibit growth rates for the following reasons: 1) poverty reduces the economic productivity of those at the bottom, 2) lacking social security, the poor have larger numbers of children to care for them in old age and cannot afford to educate them, 3) the rich spend their money on conspicuous consumption, rather than on investment, and send their savings abroad, 4) wealth in the hands of the rich is spent on foreign goods, while in the hands of the poor it is spent on local goods, thereby encouraging the national economy, and 5) failing to incorporate the masses into "public participation in the development process" can bring about a political rejection of the project as a whole (p. 182). Reducing inequality through redistribution, on the other hand, can have a positive effect on growth rates for these same reasons. Both Tadaro and Aghion et. al. conclude that there is "an important efficiency role for *sustained* redistribution" [emphasis in the original] (Aghion, 1999: 1656). Without government sponsored redistributive mechanisms, high growth rates produce inequality, which then hinders further growth.

In fact, a variety of theorists since Marx have suggested that there may be even deeper reasons to suspect capitalism's sustainability. Writing in the early 20th century, Joseph Schumpeter (2003), who believed that the capitalist order was economically viable for the long run,[11] nonetheless predicted a political withdrawal into socialism due to the cycle of destruction inherent in capitalist progress (p. 375). In 1942, he wrote:

> Capitalism, then, is by nature a form or method of economic change and not only never is but never can be stationary . . . The fundamental impulse that sets and keeps the capitalist engine in motion comes from the new consumers' goods, the new methods of production or transportation, the new markets, the new forms of industrial organization that capitalist enterprise creates. . . . *This process of Creative Destruction is the essential fact about capitalism.* It is what capitalism consists in and what every capitalist concern has got to live in. (1975: 82-3) [emphasis added]

Contemporary Marxists, such as David Harvey, have picked up the term 'creative destruction,' and identified its coercive aspects (Harvey, 1992: 105). Competition fuels expansion that results in overproduction and inevitably diminishing returns on investments. Companies losing revenues must innovate; those that do so successfully destroy older technologies and modes of production in partially unpredictable ways:

> The struggle to maintain profitability sends capitalists racing off to explore all kinds of other possibilities. New product lines are opened up, and that means the creation of new wants and needs. Capitalists are forced to redouble their efforts to create new needs in others, thus emphasizing the cultivation of imaginary appetites and the role of fantasy, caprice and whim. The result is to exacerbate insecurity and instability, as masses of capital and workers shift from one line of production to another, leaving whole sectors devastated, while the perpetual flux in consumer wants, tastes, and needs becomes a permanent locus of uncertainty and struggle. (Harvey, 1992: 106)

There are two results of building a system upon creative destruction: 1) an entire industry (marketing) whose business it is to fuel consumerism,[12] and 2) the continual reappearance of sweatshops and other types of oppression, as companies struggle to stay afloat by reducing labor costs. Workers are divided into two groups: those who are suitably employed (at least for the moment) and are targeted for consumption, and those who are under- or unemployed and must struggle simply to survive in a world filled with consumer goods just out of their reach.

The working poor do consume, and not just of necessities. Osella and Osella (1999: 1018) point out that conspicuous consumption "may be even more important for those at the peripheries of capitalism and modernity than for those at the centre." The struggle for social position can rival the struggle for economic survival. Furthermore, much is promised to people at the periphery. Media from billboards to television depict the status symbols and comforts of middle class life that are said to be now available to everyone. As any anthropologist will recognize, "tastes" are highly constructed by the culture. And in "cultures of poverty" consumption of symbols of prestige (expensive tennis shoes in the United States, or wrist-watches in the two-thirds world) is at its most devastating.

The focus on consumption in the middle and upper classes may not be economically devastating, but it is surely morally degenerative. It causes them to forget their neighbor. United Nations general secretary Kofi Anan's "amazing facts" include that Americans spend $17 billion per year on pet food, $4 billion more than needed to provide for basic health and nutrition for everyone in the world; Europeans spend $11 billion per year on ice cream, $2 billion more than needed to provide clean water and safe sewers for everyone in the world; and Americans spend $8 billion per year on cosmetics, $2 billion more than needed to provide basic education to everyone in the world. Statistics such as these lead Townsend & Gordon (2002: 73) to conclude that "Ending poverty is largely a matter of lack of political will. It is not a problem of lack of money or scientific knowledge on how to eradicate poverty." People simply do not want to share.[13]

Meanwhile, the appearance of sweatshop conditions in the two-thirds world, more than rivaling the oppressive conditions of 19th century Europe, is the signal that the world system is gearing up to produce yet more goods for wealthy consumers. Even in developed countries, real minimum wages have fallen, and labor unions have been weakened, due to the impact of global competition.

> Telephone operators working for AT&T are expected to deal with one call every 28 seconds as a condition of contract, lorry drivers push themselves to extremes of endurance and court death by taking pills to keep awake, air traffic controllers suffer extremes of stress, assembly-line workers take to drugs and alcohol, all part and parcel of a daily work rhythm fixed by profit-making rather than by the construction of humane work schedules. (Harvey, 1992: 231)

Free trade zones limit labor regulation in the interest of providing impoverished countries with jobs, and national identity becomes a marketable characteristic of products, "Made in Indonesia." In fact, nationalism itself can be a means of capturing working class loyalties for capitalist interests (Harvey, 1992: 236). Certainly, in India, the conservative trading classes, through the *Hindutva* movement, are attempting to buy out lower class political resistance. Consumption requires production, and capitalist production requires a class "which possesses nothing but its capacity to labour" (Marx, 1972b: 178).

Two-third's world nations are experiencing a highly coerced entrance into the global economy. On the one hand, there is a celebration of the local and of cultural difference, due in part to its marketability, while on the other, there is a "straightjacket" for economic performance that reduces the state to a mere lackey of international business concerns. Nowhere is this more clear than in the financial markets. McMichael writes:

> The loss of currency control by governments threatens nations' economic and political sovereignty. Speculation destabilizes currency values, compromising planning. In 1992, the former chairman of Citicorp described the currency traders . . . as conducting "a kind of global plebiscite on the monetary and fiscal policies of governments issuing currency." He found this system to be "far more draconian than any previous arrangement, such as the gold standard or the

Bretton Woods system, because *there is no way for a nation to opt out.*" (2004: 125) [emphasis added][14]

Without global political institutions to protect the interests of two-thirds world and laboring people, the culture of consumption, driving modes of production, is exacerbating the concentration of wealth that so threatens the system as a whole.

THE KINGDOM OF CAPITALISM[15]

Notable in this process is the remarkably *religious* tone used in the defense of the capitalist world system. It is "as if a miracle were expected,"[16] "a recipe for how modernization will universally yield rationality, punctuality, democracy, the free market, and a higher gross national product" (Appadurai 1997: 9). Friedland and Robertson (1990: 4) suggest that neoliberal doctrine regarding the market has become "a modern secular religion." Korten (1995: 69) calls it "a fundamentalist religious faith . . . to question its doctrine has become virtual heresy."[17]

The basic tenets of the religion include existential beliefs in radical individualism, instrumental rationality, and progress, that produce normative beliefs in efficiency, competition, private property, and growth. Such values encourage policies of deregulation, trickle down, and reduced government. When these policies produce economic decline, as they did around the world in the 1980s, or in post-Soviet Russia in the 1990s, the dismal effects are excused as a) the results of earlier policies, or b) a failure to implement the model more severely (Carrier, 1997: 8). Counter-evidence has little impact on religiously held views. Furthermore, as with any religion:

> One of the reasons the model has the force and appeal that it does is that it roots the Market in what is construed as fundamental human nature. The Market is presented as embodying essential humanity and the ethics that spring from it. It is, in effect, what people would do spontaneously among themselves if left alone, if their propensity to truck, barter and exchange were not constrained. (Carrier, 1997: 19)

Capitalism, as a religion, claims merely to be reflecting human nature the way that it "really is." And human nature is characterized as being rooted in only one experience: the eternal gap between what we have and what we want.

Yet, as Marshall Sahlins (1972: 1) reminds us, "wants may be 'easily satisfied' either by producing much or desiring little."[18] The older virtue of reigning in our appetites through self-discipline is missing from the current form of the capitalist religion, as is the concern for others that would temper the pursuit of our own interests. Most disturbingly, for a Christian, the illusion of self-sufficiency that this competing religion offers to the relatively wealthy, loosens their dependence upon God Himself, causing them to break both of the commandments of Jesus, "Love God and love your neighbor." So, at the same time that market women are being encouraged to pursue prestige through sanskritisation, they are also being encouraged, even coerced, to rely upon the free market to save them from poverty. No doubt, this is a form of liberation from traditionalism. But it is not the whole liberation of the person and of the community that Jesus himself would have intended for them.

NOTES

1. The restriction on women's business activities explains the dichotomy between sex and business size described in chapter two (see Table 2.2).

2. Granovetter goes on to say, "This is better information for four reasons: (1) it is cheap; (2) one trusts one's own information best – it is richer, more detailed, and known to be accurate; (3) individuals with whom one has a continuing relation have an economic motivation to be trustworthy, so as not to discourage future transactions; and (4) departing from pure economic motives, continuing economic relations often become overlaid with social content that carries strong expectations of trust and abstention from opportunism."

3. Wolpert (2004: 196) says that, "Private ownership of land in traditional Indian society was virtually unknown. Between the raja or *padishah* [king], who ruled over and 'protected' all his domain, and the vast 'herd' (*ri'yat*) of peasant tillers of the soil, there were, naturally, various intermediaries, endowed with a variety of landed interests." But none of these had full property rights.

4. I am aware of the difficulties in calculating a poverty rate. For a survey of the subject, see Todaro (2000: chapter 5). Despite these difficulties, the identification of a "poverty line" is useful in giving a general estimate of the proportion of the population suffering from significant want.

5. All 2004 statistics are from "India at a Glance," produced by the World Bank at www.worldbank.org.

6. Sheth (2002: 216) makes the point that the strength of Congress' appeal has always been in its ability to avoid dichotomizing the electorate by either caste or class. "Its politics was largely addressed to link vertically middle-class rule to lower caste support. And the ideology used for legitimation of this vertical social linkage in politics was neither class ideology nor caste ideology; it was the ideology of 'nation-building.'"

7. Hirschman (2003) surveys the literature on the relationship between "progress" in the political and economic spheres. The modern histories of developing countries demonstrate "linkages" between the two spheres, rather than autonomy, but an uneven evolution toward democracy and prosperity, with sometimes one and sometimes the other taking the lead.

8. Hirschman (1982) contests this idea with a fascinating journey through the history of economic thought, suggesting that market interactions can construct, as well as destruct, social ties. I do not find the argument convincing, however, because there is a reversal of order of priority in market based as against reciprocal (social) relationships. In reciprocal ties, the exchange of goods is subordinated to the promotion of the relationship. In market ties, the relationship is subordinated to the utility of the exchange. In the latter, then, relationships are easily engaged or severed, and are manipulated for ulterior purpose because they are not ends in themselves. To the degree that more diffuse and general loyalties occur in market ties, these are in spite of, not due to, market forces.

9. World Bank data available at http://devdata.worldbank.org.

10. These statistics are from a World Bank study done in 2000 and reported by B. Milanovic ("True World Income Distribution, 1988 and 1993: First Calculation Based on Household Surveys Alone." *World Bank, Development Research Group,* Washington, DC: World Bank). The upper and lower middle quartiles fell too, by 10% and 5% respectively.

11. In this, he distinguished between the capitalist "order" (fundamental institutions) and the capitalist "system" (business cycle). The latter might endure periodic crises, he said, without necessary detrimental effects to the former (2003: 352).

12. Harvey (1992: 352) quotes Alan Sugar, chairman of the Amstrad Corporation: "If there was a market in mass-produced portable nuclear weapons then we'd market them too."

13. Mother Teresa.

14. Lewellen (2002: 16) notes that no small bit of violence has accompanied the expansion of free market capitalism: "While a few Third World countries, notably Chile and Brazil, embraced neoliberalism with apparent enthusiasm, most were pulled into the fold almost literally kicking and screaming; structural-adjustment riots, strikes, and even revolutions became common . . . without the oil shocks, the resultant debt crisis, and the collapse of Soviet communism, Third World countries would not have been forced into the neoliberal system."

15. David Maybury-Lewis has coined this phrase in his Millennium film series on "tribal wisdom for the modern world." The phrase is in the episode entitled, "A Poor Man Shames Us All."

16. Also a phrase by Maybury-Lewis in the same film.

17. The two most penetrating critiques of this religion, in my estimation, are by Bailey (2003), an anthropologist, and Blaug (1992), an economist.

18. See also Sen's (1977) excellent article on commitment in economic choice making.

Chapter Ten

Love God—Heart, Soul, and Mind:
Summary and Conclusions

One of the reasons why it is difficult to perceive radical changes . . . is that the actors themselves are often unwilling to face the fact of change. Men whom historians can later see to have been reformers and innovators are written off as deviants and trouble makers. Gandhi appeared in this light to many British administrators, as no doubt did Jesus Christ to most of the Jews and Romans. To have admitted that such men might be the heralds of a new social or political or religious structure is also to allow that there is something amiss with the existing social structure. (Bailey, 2001a: 203)

There is indeed "something amiss" with the existing structure of the social world. On that account, in this work, I have rejected the stance of the morally neutral scientist. I believe that such a stance is neither possible nor valuable. Michael Polanyi, in his critique of scientific objectivity, suggests that scientists claiming moral neutrality end up interjecting the morality of their choice into their work, and into culture, by sleight of hand:

Men may go on talking the language of positivism, pragmatism, and naturalism for many years, yet continue to respect the principles of truth and morality which their vocabulary anxiously ignores . . . A utilitarian interpretation of morality accuses all moral sentiments of hypocrisy, while the moral indignation which the writer thus expresses is safely disguised as a scientific statement. And on other occasions, these concealed moral passions reassert themselves, affirming ethical ideals either backhandedly as a tight-lipped praise of social dissenters, or else disguised in utilitarian terms . . . The public, taught by the sociologist to distrust its traditional morality, is grateful to receive it back from him in a scientifically branded wrapping. Indeed, a writer who has proved his hard-headed perspicacity by denying the existence of morality will always be listened to with especial respect when he does moralize in spite of this. Thus

the scientific disguise of our moral aspirations may not only protect their sub-
stance against destruction by nihilism, but even allow them to operate effectively by stealth. (1974: 233-4).

Rather than denying our involvement in morality and culture, I believe that
we scientists should declare our positions clearly and simply, and indicate
their origins. I am a Christian. So, my own morality, and the one I advocate
in the public arena, is determined by the words of Jesus: "You shall love the
Lord your God with all your heart, and with all your soul, and with all your
mind . . . [and] You shall love your neighbor as yourself."

The fact that I am a Christian is especially relevant because I am an anthropologist. Anthropology's subject is people. And people cannot be understood
apart from certain basic assumptions about the nature of the human condition.
It is no accident that the term "anthropology" was originally a theological one.
Basic assumptions about the human condition derive from basic assumptions
about God and all of life. So, to be clear, my assumptions as a Christian include the following: 1) that God exists and has created humanity, 2) that God
is loving in such a way as to be angry with evil for its abuse of his creation,
while yet patient with its removal, 3) that humanity commits evil due to its enslavement to sin and to selfishness, 4) that Jesus, as the Son of God, came to
liberate humanity from this enslavement and to inaugurate a new Kingdom, 5)
that an inner transformation of the heart is needed to free the individual, 6) that
a break with biological family and with the conservative values of social structure is needed to fully enter the Kingdom, and 7) that the work of the Kingdom of God is to produce revolutions in the kingdoms of this world through
the impact of the Church on society, revolutions of both love and justice.

If these assumptions are correct, then humanity is to be viewed compas-
sionately for its suffering, but also critically for its failure to receive the hope
offered by God in Christ and to make the changes that that hope inspires. Oppression, the human failure most directly addressed in this volume, is a sin of
two parties. The oppressors are obviously and primarily culpable for their evil
actions towards those over whom they have power. But the oppressed are also
to blame for instances in which they may cooperate in the matter. A reluctance
to lose social benefits, along with an (understandable) fear of the consequences of resistance, may cause them to passively perpetuate systems of injustice. It is this type of compromise with injustice that I see in the phenomenon of sanskritising Dalits. In the case of caste, neither oppressor nor
oppressed is willing to admit that "there is something amiss with the existing
social structure."

Anthropology's typical approach to morality (despite its neutral dis-
claimer) has been to vilify western peoples and institutions, because they

have had power, and to romanticize nonwestern peoples and institutions, because they have lacked it. Such simple moralizing produces ambivalence over indigenous structures of power, such as caste and gender, in which traditional forms of oppression occur. I certainly do not dispute the critique of colonialism, nor of contemporary capitalist imperialism. But neither do I presume the subjects of my study to be merely ignorant victims of their circumstances, that is, to lack moral responsibility. The limitations on their lives are real and evident. Market women cannot easily get the money and influence they need to make significant changes. And even their minor attempts to challenge the system produce quick and effective, often violent, reactions. Yet, when given real opportunity, market women seem inclined to a social conservatism that secures their own continuing oppression. They are not willing to take the risks that would be associated with a real revolution in their circumstances. The Christian theology of enslavement to sin and self makes sense of this reaction, and suggests that religious liberation, or an internal conversion, is what is needed first, if change in external circumstances is to occur and to produce real justice.

SUMMARY

To review, market women are oppressed by economic, gender, and caste-based structures. First, they are in the market selling because they have to be. Their children and other family members depend on them for an income. And the market is a sponge, soaking up the remnants of unskilled labor cast off by the modernizing economy. Because India as a whole is a poor country, that remnant is large. So market women must enter into business, competing with one another for sitting spaces, for loans, and for customers. Despite the competition, market women cooperate with one another by creating networks of reciprocity to support them through crises and to stabilize the foreseeable future. But daily they struggle to survive financially, with little margin for error. Produce is perishable, and prices fluctuate significantly. Loans are necessary to provide capital and must be repaid regardless of business profits or losses. And, despite exceedingly long hours at work, market women only minimally make enough money to provide for themselves and their families. They are poor.

These circumstances reflect a situation of economic oppression. Born into poverty, market women simply do not have the power, education, or skills to significantly improve their lot. Their industry and remarkable optimism are their primary assets, and these virtues are largely responsible for the fact that they are minimally successful. Yet, market women do not speculate about growing their businesses or in any way transcending their place in the market channel. Their efforts are focused almost entirely on the constant attempts to find new loans. They live with a day to day mentality and are generally reluctant to think of the future, hoping merely to "die with no loans." This is no uniquely Indian form of fatalism. It is the fatalism that tempts anyone in difficult and seemingly insurmountable circumstances, and that is too readily accepted in the face of the consequences of challenge.

Because market women are poor, they have grown up uneducated, married early, and begun work early as well. Because they are women, they have had to endure the neglect and abuses of men, both husbands and sons, who themselves cannot find adequate place in society. Market women are frequently beaten and betrayed by their husbands. They have to plead and cajole to get any financial support. Their sons, who are supposed to take care of them in old age, often do not. So market women end up supporting the men in their families themselves, if only to gain protection from other men. Others in their immediate networks do little to confront this situation, and women themselves accept their treatment at the hands of men as a matter of good or bad luck. These circumstances reflect a situation of gender oppression. In their relations with men, market women have responsibility without power. And men enjoy power, especially in the home, without being held adequately responsible.

Because they are Dalits, market women have had to bear the full weight of the caste system's stigmatization. Caste oppression is experienced in the rough tones, sharp words, and other remnants of untouchability that women endure daily from suppliers and customers. An untouchable woman is at the bottom of the heap. And the constant reminders of this fact in social discourse are even now very evident to any outsider. Market women generally receive these insults, both overt and covert, without much protest, lest they disturb the sources of their sustenance. But in conversation amongst themselves, and in their diligent, energetic attempts to save money for a better life for their daughters, one can see a glimmer of resistance. They are supporting their communitys' efforts to move up.

Urban Dalits are moving up both by taking advantage of the economic opportunities offered by the government and by adopting the middle-caste strategy of sanskritisation. Sanskritisation involves emulating higher caste ritual practices. For women, these include the female rites of passage, the restrictions on women's remarriage, and the giving of dowry. Though they received bridewealth themselves, market women are saving dowries for their daughters. The acceptance of bridewealth has always signified the social degradation of communities that permit women to work outside the home. The giving of dowry has signified the prestige of communities that restrict women to the domestic arena. Hence the shift from bridewealth to dowry marks a rejection of low rank. Market women are hoping to marry their daughters into more prestigious, but also more restricted, circumstances. Hence, to the degree that they do have hope for the future and a willingness to resist, market women are investing in a change that affirms and supports the basis for traditional forms of caste and gender oppression.

It is Hinduism that has defined traditional caste and gender values in India. Metaphysical notions of purity and pollution arrange castes into a hierarchy that equates rank with moral worth. Dalits are placed at the bottom of the scale as "untouchables." The hierarchy is legitimized by the twin concepts of *dharma*, the doing of the duty of one's station as the highest moral good, and *karma*, the promise that duty will be rewarded or punished in the next life. Untouchable rank is justified as the result of bad behavior in previous lives, and at the same time mitigated with promises of rebirth to better circumstances. A similar argument is made for women. Even poverty is explained in like manner. Hence, a passive conformity, despite suffering, is expected in this life. Justice is to be had in the next.

Market women are aware of the contemporary political value on equality, and they take advantage, when they can, of the government efforts to improve the circumstances of women, Dalits, and other marginalized groups. They are skeptical of the doctrine of *karma* which has been used to legitimize their low rank. Furthermore, they insist that they share a common humanity, and therefore a common moral worth, with the higher castes. "We are people too." Yet, they affirm all of the basic tenets of Hinduism, worship Hindu gods, and make every effort to emulate high caste Hindu practices. Some women are more conservative in this matter, and some are more liberal. But, on the whole, market women are adopting the values and ritual practices of Hinduism, the religion that constructed their situation in the first place.

It is here that market women's agency, and therefore their responsibility, can most clearly be seen. There can be no doubt that external structures of economy, gender, and caste place women in their current circumstances, limit their opportunities, and punish them for nonconformity. The culpability for failure to love others as neighbors rests with those who institute and maintain these oppressive structures. Yet, market women themselves choose socially conservative paths toward improving their lot. They make every effort to present themselves as good members of their families and communities, and as good Hindus. To the best of their abilities, they follow the prescriptions they are given for morality, and thereby contribute to their own oppression. They are perhaps excessively "good" women.

This compromise with evil is to be expected of any of us who have not yet received the power that comes from a transformation of the heart, and who live solely in the kingdoms of this world. Human kingdoms are built, not upon the benign social contract, but upon the fear of neighbors. Mired as we human beings all are in slavery to selfish desire, fears of ill intent in others, and of the anarchy that might result should that intent be realized in action, cause people everywhere to construct systems, from family to state, that ensure their own security at the price of others' freedom. Even those who least benefit from such orders may choose to limit their own freedom for the minimal security they can attain through the system. On the whole, they prefer an oppressive system to no system at all. The solution is not, of course, no system. Rather, it is, said Jesus, to join another Kingdom, and thereby to make a break with the biologically-based, socially conservative orders of this world. It must be said that even many Christians have failed to understand Jesus' teachings on this point.

Hinduism, together with the caste structure that it creates, is unapologetically a socially conservative order. That is, it promises security at the expense of freedom. Furthermore, it sacrifices some peoples' freedom in the interest of others. And, it provides religious sanction to this injustice by denying the realities of time and change, and by rejecting the validity of human passions in favor of the pure action that is duty to the system itself. I am not suggesting that there is no value in Hinduism or caste. Together, these institutions have established a viable life for Indians over three millennia. But, I am suggesting that the Hindu caste system is oppressive. It is order at the expense of people.

In contrast to the social conservatism produced by fear of others that is found in all human institutions, Christianity commends a superhuman love that is generous with others because it rests in the security of God's sovereignty. The Christian ethic of love is based on an affirmation of human passion and a consequent involvement in, rather than detachment from, one another's lives. It produces institutions that promote human freedom – not the pseudo-freedom of uninhibited selfishness, but the true freedom of self-expression and service that arises out of deliverance from slavery to sin and self. And, it refuses to permit any to be sacrificed in the interests of others in the construction of an overall order.

Christian influence on Hindu India, and on the caste system in particular, is as old as Christianity itself. The Syrian churches of Kerala date back to the first century. But, syncretism with the existent social order can significantly hinder the full revolution that Christianity might bring to oppressed peoples. Untouchables in Kerala, as elsewhere, were bound by intertwined institutions of symbolic stigmatization, social exclusion, religious restriction and degraded economic status and tasks. And, by the 16th century, the Syrian Christians were fully accommodated to caste, not only in society but in the church as well. They offered no challenge to the treatment of untouchables in Hindu society.

Even in the 18th and 19th centuries, it was only after the attempts to understand and accommodate caste had failed to produce true churches, that Christian missionaries began to resist the system. Increasingly, they determined that caste, which demands segregation due to differences in essential worth, was fundamentally incompatible with the Church, which demands fellowship arising out of a common redemption. Missionaries not only accepted untouchables into full church membership, they also insisted that high caste converts sit together with low to accept the Eucharist, a symbol of humility and equality. As a result, some high caste converts were lost, but many low caste and untouchable converts were gained through the mass movements of the late 19th and early 20th centuries.

The response of the Hindu community to the Christian critique of caste was divided. Some, particularly educated, Hindus worked together with Christians to advocate for the reform of Hindu society. Others formed reactionary associations that became the precursors to the modern Hindu fundamentalist movement. Since most nationalist leaders were reform minded Hindus, at Independence a constitution was established that outlawed caste and protected ex-untouchables with mandated compensatory discrimination. Dalits received a quota of 15% reserved seats in education and government. But, in a move to protect Hinduism, Christian converts were declared no longer disadvantaged and therefore ineligible for benefits. The result was the end of the mass movements. Yet today, despite the loss of benefits, most Christian converts of Dalit background are better off than their Hindu counterparts, both socially and economically, due in part to the assistance provided them by the Church and in part to the enhanced self-respect they claim from the process of conversion.

Nineteenth century missionaries also critiqued the treatment of women. Practices such as female infanticide, child marriage, the stigmatization of widows, and *sati*, together with beliefs in inherent pollution and periodic untouchability, had combined to subjugate women to husbands and to caste. Early missionaries such as William Carey, working together with Hindu reformers such as Ram Mohan Roy, lobbied the colonial government in favor of legislation to protect women and to provide them with benefits such as labor regulation, education, and inheritance. Eventually, an indigenous women's movement formed that supported nationalists in the campaign for independence, and at the same time promoted full citizenship for women in the new democracy.

After independence, however, tensions between religious communities and their "rights" to restrict women caused the government to back off from further reforms. The result was a dramatic decline in women's political participation, and a drop in the female to male ratio of the population, as patriarchy reasserted itself. Recent efforts by the central government to encourage full participation in the democracy have put women into local government in huge numbers. But the socially conservative mood of the country conditions many women to support traditional values in an effort to assist their castes in the process of sanskritisation. And sanskritisation, as we have already seen, entails the disempowerment of women.

In part, the failure to protect women is a result of the naïve belief that the public arena of a modern nation state can, or should, be kept free of religious influence. In the West, a highly artificial split between public and private arenas is advocated. The public arena is state controlled, and its purpose is to protect civil rights and to promote participation in the political process. Religion is relegated to the private arena, where an ethic of 'tolerance' is to provide the picket fences that will prevent conflict between neighbors in a plural environment. Van der Veer challenges this conception, as do I: public orders are based on fundamental values that emerge from religions. Furthermore, any serious adherent of a religion knows that faithfulness requires all of life, including those parts deemed "public," to be influenced by religious beliefs. It is therefore simply not possible to construct a public arena that is truly neutral on the matter of religion. To the degree that Westerners have thought it was, it is because they have *presumed* that Christian values would underlie that arena: values such as love, justice, freedom, equality, and human dignity.

Hindu fundamentalists have recognized the contradiction. The provision of human rights to all people in Hindu society would significantly undercut the very foundations of the order. Untouchables provide ritual and farm labor. Women provide domestic and child-care work. To offer outside avenues of service and expression to these oppressed groups is to alter traditional society at the deepest level. It simply will not work to be secular on the job or in the marketplace, and Hindu at home.

It is the daily experience of this contradiction between public and private arenas that has fueled the flame of the *Hindutva* movement, which, I would suggest, is really a grassroots backlash against the influence of Christian values. The BJP, when it took the central government in 1998, immediately attempted to alter the constitution to make India a Hindu nation. They failed at this due to the fact that there are yet many Indians, in government and elsewhere, who do not agree with their vision. But, even now, *Hindutva's* influence on ordinary, middle-class Hindus is very strong, both inside and outside of the country. And even many women and Dalits are buying into the notion that pride in their identity as Indians necessitates a return to the Hindu cosmology and order.

While it is true that Christian influence has threatened the Hindu order, it is not true that Christianity is a threat to Indian identity. That threat comes from another corner. Nation states all over the world are under siege due to the impact of globalization. Globalization is the latest form of expansion of the world capitalist system, which emerged in the 16th century with the establishment of colonial forms of exploitation. India had been deeply involved from the beginning as the "right hand" of the British Empire. So, when independence came, its nationalist leaders were careful to set up a protected economy and to address questions of poverty and marginalization. Much was accomplished during the period of socialism, but poverty was not eliminated. And now, after a half century of withdrawal, India is reentering the capitalist world order through economic liberalization.

The most immediate effect of liberalization is to divide the lower class into two: those who rise to become an expanding middle class, and those who drop off into abject poverty. The latter group end up in the informal economy, as agricultural labor is released from villages due to new farming technologies, and domestic, construction, and other kinds of unskilled labor is released in cities due to new urban technologies. Many of these "released" people end up in petty trading because it is low skilled work and has easy entrance.

But, petty traders are all the more subject to the forces of the global economy. They are controlled most immediately by their "backward linkages," that is, their money and goods suppliers. And their livelihoods are contingent upon market processes well beyond their sphere of influence. In fact, in the future, the open-air marketplace itself may shrink to become the cultural relic it is in the West, as refrigeration and transportation make supermarkets both possible and accessible. Hence, market women, as products of globalization, are occupying a temporary space, one that provides for them only minimally in the present, and may not provide for them at all in the future.

Capitalism produces tremendous amounts of wealth. But it distributes that wealth poorly, and it promotes an ethic of hedonism. Its false notion of freedom as individual license erodes responsibility to community and results in an increasing divide between rich and poor, both nationally and internationally. As the poor get poorer, and face the difficult issues that market women face such as how to feed their children and themselves, the rich get richer and face equally difficult but unrecognized issues such as where to find true significance in a shifting kaleidoscope of competitive consumption. If the poor need the rich for their sustenance, the rich surely need the poor for their own moral regeneration.

Capitalism, said Weber, is a product of Protestantism. Hard work and frugality are the Protestant virtues that fuel reinvestment and capital growth. Yet Weber himself recognized that capitalism has rejected its moral roots in Christianity. True freedom, which is from selfishness, has become the pseudo-freedom to pursue individual tastes without conscience. Hard work, intended to glorify God, has become slavery to success. The Christian injunctions to rest on the Sabbath and care for creation have become moral license to pursue the most superficial pleasures at exorbitant ecological costs. And, for those who hold religiously to neoliberal doctrines, even the most moderate forms of government regulation, constraints that might check the worst effects of the pursuit of selfishness, have become anathema.

How can this have happened? In chapter one, I suggested that Marx's defense of the second commandment of Jesus, to love one's neighbor as one's self, has resulted paradoxically in abuses of the state that derive from the rejection of the living God and the consequent apotheosis of humanity. Here, I suggest that capitalism's purported defense of freedom has resulted in economic abuses that derive, actually, from the same mistake—the rejection of the living God. Schumpeter (1975: 127) predicted this:

> The capitalist process rationalizes behavior and ideas and by so doing chases from our minds, along with metaphysical belief, mystic and romantic ideas of all sorts. Thus it reshapes not only our methods of attaining our ends but also these ultimate ends themselves.

Capitalism rejects religion as an ultimate end, and by shifting our attention to our own interests, makes us the gods of our own lives.

CONCLUSIONS

Jesus' two commandments contain a priority: love God, *and then* love others as yourself. Since the Enlightenment, western humanists have projected a utopian future in which humanity will solve its own problems without the help of God. A casual glance at the record will surely indicate that this experiment has failed, and failed badly. By some estimates, the 20th century has been the bloodiest century in human history. There have been two world wars, countless civil wars, and endemic problems with unrest. Perhaps it is possible to blame religion for some of these conflicts. But the vast majority have been disputes between ethnic groups, usually of the same religion, over control of the state. And the state has been fought over because it is the last remaining source of protection from the coercive powers of the global economy. It would seem that we are in the grip of fear of the greatest human project to date, the Tower of Babel as it were. Humanity is not doing very well without God.

We need the true God to teach us to love. Without Him, we are only capable of loving ourselves and our own people. We need to learn to love others. The apostle John reminds us that "we love because He first loved us" (I John

4:19). It is God Himself who provides for us *both* freedom and security. With our own needs fulfilled, we are empowered to take the risks and make the sacrifices needed to provide for others. And with our own future secured, we are able to use power differently. Jesus instructed his disciples:

> You know that the rulers of the Gentiles lord it over them, and their great ones are tyrants over them. It will not be so among you; but whoever wishes to be great among you must be your servant, and whoever wishes to be first among you must be your slave; just as the Son of Man came not to be served but to serve, and to give his life a ransom for many. (Matt. 20: 25-28)

Such an ethic is not generally attractive to people in positions of worldly power. Commonly, they dismiss it by declaring it an impractical ideal. But to those in circumstances of powerlessness, it can be very appealing indeed. Webster (1992:182) quotes the 19th century missionary, J.F. Burditt:

> From the outset the Gospel appears to find its prime objective point, its magnetic pole, among the poor, the lowly, the oppressed, and the outcaste. And if again this earth were trod by the blessed feet of the Son of God, can we doubt that far beyond the confines of the rich, respectable, self-satisfied upper classes, he would press with yearning compassion, and His voice of infinite tenderness would be heard again crying to the most sinful, and wretched and lost, "Come unto Me all ye that labour and are heavy-laden and I will give you rest."

It is those whom life has already humbled, who most readily understand their need for a Savior. Those who have "everything" are blinded by the illusion of self-sufficiency to their need for Him.

Yet, Jesus promised that all who look for God will find him (Matt. 7:7). The discovery of God, transforming the hearts and minds of the converted, will produce the freedom and justice that we all long for in society.

On one occasion, Jesus compared the Kingdom of God to a mustard tree. A mustard tree begins as a small seed. But it grows to be a mighty tree, and "the birds of the air make nests in its branches." It was in terms of this parable that I first understood the full circumstances of the market women of India. Market women are Hindus. But, because of Christian influence, so far, they have been able to make their nests in the branches of a tree that promotes justice, the justice that emerges out of the love of God and the love of neighbors as oneself.

References

Abbott, Dina
   1999   "Paying the Price of Femininity: Women and the New Hinduism" in *Culture and Global Change.* Edited by Tracey Skelton and Tim Allen. New York: Routledge.

Aghion, Philippe, Eve Caroli, and Cecilia Garzia-Penalosa
   1999   "Inequality and Economic Growth: the Perspective of the New Growth Theories." *Journal of Economic Literature* XXXVII: 1615-1660.

Agnes, Flavia
   1995   "Redefining the Agenda of the Women's Movement within a Secular Framework" in *Women and the Hindu Right.* Edited by Tanika Sarkar and Urvashi Butalia. New Delhi: Kali for Women, 136-157.

Alexander, Jennifer
   1987   *Trade, Traders and Trading in Rural Java.* New York: Oxford University Press.

Alexander, Jennifer and Paul Alexander
   2001   "Markets as Gendered Domains: the Javanese Pasar." in *Women Traders in Cross-Cultural Perspective: Mediating Identities and Marketing Wares.* Edited by Linda Seligmann. Stanford, CA: Stanford University Press, 47-69.

Allen, Michael and S.N. Mukherjee, eds.
   1990   *Women in India and Nepal.* Asian Studies Association of Australia. Bangalore: Sterling Publishing Ltd.

Anderson, Benedict
   1991   *Imagined Communities: Reflections on the Origin and Spread of Nationalism.* New York: Verso.

Antony, M.J.
   1989   *Women's Rights: What Every Woman Should Know about her Rights and the Law.* Delhi: Hind Pocket Books.

Appadurai, Arjun
   1997 *Modernity at Large: Cultural Dimensions of Globalization.* Minneapolis, MN: University of Minnesota Press.

Arora, Dooly
   1999 "Structural Adjustment Program and Gender Concerns in India." *Journal of Contemporary Asia* 29 (3): 328-361.

Bailey, F.G.
   2003 *The Saving Lie: Truth and Method in the Social Sciences.* Philadelphia, PA: University of Pennsylvania Press.
   2001a *Stratagems and Spoils: A Social Anthropology of Politics.* Boulder, CO: Westview Press.
   2001b *Treasons, Stratagems, and Spoils: How Leaders Make Practical Use of Beliefs and Values.* Boulder, CO: Westview Press.
   1971 *Tribe, Caste and Nation.* Manchester: Manchester University Press.
   1967 *Caste and the Economic Frontier.* Manchester: Manchester University Press.

Baird, Robert D.
   2001 "Gender Implications for a Uniform Civil Code" in *Religion and Personal Law in Secular India: a Call to Judgment.* Edited by Gerald James Larson. Bloomington, IL: Indiana University Press.

Basham A.L.
   1959 *The Wonder that was India.* New York: Grove Press.

Basu, Amrita
   1998 "Conclusion" in *Community Conflicts and the State in India.* Edited by Amrita Basu and Atul Kohli. Delhi: Oxford University Press.
   1996 "Mass Movement or Elite Conspiracy? The Puzzle of Hindu Nationalism" in *Contesting the Nation: Religion, Community, and the Politics of Democracy in India.* Edited by David Ludden. Philadelphia: University of Pennsylvania Press.
   1995 "Feminism Inverted: the Gendered Imagery and Real Women of Hindu Nationalism" in *Women and the Hindu Right.* Edited by Tanika Sarkar and Urvashi Butalia. New Delhi: Kali for Women, 158-180.
   1993 "Feminism Inverted: the Real Woman and Gendered Imagery of Hindu Nationalism" in *Bulletin of Concerned Asian Scholars* 25 (4): 29.

Basu, Amrita and Atul Kohli
   1998 "Introduction" in *Community Conflicts and the State in India.* Edited by Amrita Basu and Atul Kohli. Delhi: Oxford University Press.

Basu, Alaka Malwade
   1992 "The Status of Women and the Quality of Life Among the Poor." *Cambridge Journal of Economics* 16: 249-267.

Bayly, Susan
   1999 *Caste, Society and Politics in India from the Eighteenth Century to the Modern Age.* The New Cambridge History of India, Vol. 4, No. 3. Cambridge: Cambridge University Press.

Beck, Brenda E. F.
   1970 "The Right-Left Division of South Indian Society." *The Journal of Asian Studies* XXIX: 779-798.

Becker, Gary S.
   1998   *Accounting for Tastes*. Cambridge, MA: Harvard University Press.
Bellah, Robert, et. al.
   1985   *Habits of the Heart: Individualism and Commitment in American Life.* New York: Harper and Row.
Bennett, Lynn
   1983   *Dangerous Wives and Sacred Sisters*. New York: Columbia University Press.
Beteille, Andre
   2000   "Caste in Contemporary India" in *Caste Today*. Edited by C.J. Fuller. New York: Oxford University Press. 150-179.
   1996   "Varna and Jati." *Sociological Bulletin* 45 (1): 15-27.
Bible, The
   1989   New Revised Standard Version. Grand Rapids, MI: Zondervan Publishing House.
   1985   New King James Version. Chicago: Moody Press.
Blaug, Mark
   1992   *The Methodology of Economics: Or How Economists Explain.* Cambridge: Cambridge University Press.
Borthwick, Meredith
   1990   "The Bhadramahila and Changing Conjugal Relations in Bengal," in *Women in India and Nepal.* Edited by Michael Allen and S.N. Mukherjee. Bangalore: Sterling Publishing Ltd., 105-135.
Brass, Paul R.
   1997   *The Politics of India Since Independence,* 2nd edition. New York: Cambridge University Press.
Briggs, Jean L.
   1981   *Never in Anger: Portrait of an Eskimo Family*. Cambridge, MA: Harvard University Press.
Bucher, Rev. J.
   1983   Kannada-English, and English-Kannada Dictionary, Chiefly Based on the Labours of Dr. F. Kittel. New Delhi: Asian Educational Services.
Caldwell, John C.
   1982   *Theory of Fertility Decline*. New York: Academic Press.
Carrier, James G.
   1997   *Meanings of the Market: the Free Market in Western Culture.* New York: Berg.
Carstairs, G. Morris
   1975   *The Twice-Born: A Study of a Community of High-Caste Hindus*. Bloomington, IN: Indiana University Press.
Cassady, Ralph Jr.
   1974   "Exchange by Private Treaty." *Studies in Marketing*, No. 19. Austin, TX: Bureau of Business Research, University of Texas at Austin.
Chakravarti, Uma
   2000   *Rewriting History: the Life and Times of Pandita Ramabai.* New Delhi: Kali for Women.

Chowdhry, Prem
   1997 "Customs in a Peasant Economy: Women in Colonial Haryana" in *Recasting Women: Essays in Indian Colonial History.* Edited by Kumkum Sangari and Sudesh Vaid. New Brunswick, NJ: Rutgers University Press, 302-336.
Clark, Gracia
   2001 "'Nursing Mother Work' in Ghana: Power and Frustration in Akan Market Women's Lives" in *Women Traders in Cross-Cultural Perspective: Mediating Identities and Marketing Wares.* Edited by Linda Seligmann. Stanford, CA: Stanford University Press, 103-126.
Colson, Elizabeth
   1974 *Tradition and Contract: The Problem of Order.* Chicago: Aldine Publishing Co.
Dasgupta, Nandini
   1992 "Linkage, Heterogeneity and Income Determinants in Petty Trading: the Case of Calcutta." *World Development* 20 (10): 1443-1461.
Deliege, Robert
   1999 *The Untouchables of India.* New York: Berg.
   1993 "The Myths of Origin of the Untouchables." *Man* 28: 533-549.
Derrida, Jacques
   1995 *The Gift of Death.* Chicago: Chicago University Press.
Devadas, Rajammal P., G. Ramathilagam, and K. Arulselvam
   1990 "Equality of Women through Education and Employment and Challenges to Social Justice" in *Women in India: Equality, Social Justice and Development.* Edited by Leelamma Devasia and V.V. Devasia. New Delhi: Indian Social Institute, 10-20.
Dev, S. Mahendra and Ajit Ranade
   1999 "Persisting Poverty and Social Insecurity: A Selective Assessment" in *India Development Report: 1999-2000.* Edited by Kirit S. Parikh. Indira Gandhi Institute of Development Research. New Delhi: Oxford University Press, 49-67.
Dewan, Ritu
   1999 "Gender Implications of the 'New' Economic Policy: a Conceptual Overview." *Women's Studies International Forum* 22 (4): 425-429.
Dhruvarajan, Vanaja
   1990 "Religious Ideology, Hindu Women, and Development in India." *Journal of Social Issues* 46 (3): 57-69.
Dirks, Nicholas B.
   2001 *Castes of Mind: Colonialism and the Making of Modern India.* Princeton: Princeton University Press.
Dreze, Jean and Amartya Sen
   1995 *India: Economic Development and Social Opportunity.* New Delhi: Oxford University Press.
Dubois, Abbe J.A.
   1999 *Hindu Manners, Customs and Ceremonies.* Delhi: Book Faith India.

Dumont, Louis

1970 *Homo Hierarchicus*. Chicago: University of Chicago Press.

Eliade, Mircea

1991 *The Myth of the Eternal Return; or, Cosmos and History*. Princeton, NJ: Princeton University Press.

Elliot, Elizabeth

1987 *A Chance to Die*. Grand Rapids, MI: Baker Book House.

Embree, Ainslie T., editor

1988 *Sources of Indian Tradition, Vol. 1*. New York: Columbia University Press.

Forrester, Duncan B.

1980 *Caste and Christianity: Attitudes and Policies on Caste of Anglo-Saxon Protestant Missions in India*. London: Curzon Press.

Friedland, Roger and A. F. Robertson, editors

1990 *Beyond the Marketplace*. New York: Aldine de Gruyter.

Friedman, Thomas L.

1999 *The Lexus and the Olive Tree*. New York: Farrar Straus Giroux.

Fuller, C. J.

2000 *Caste Today*. New York: Oxford University Press.

1992 *The Camphor Flame: Popular Hinduism and Society in India*. New York: Penguin Books.

Fulton, Robert Brank

1960 *Original Marxism Estranged Offspring*. Boston: The Christopher Publishing House.

Galenter, Marc

1970 "Changing Legal Conceptions of Caste," in *Structure and Change in Indian Society*. Edited by M. Singer and B.S. Cohn. Chicago: University of Chicago Press.

Geertz, Clifford

1973 *The Interpretation of Cultures*. New York: Basic Books.

Ghurye, G. S.

1993 *Caste and Race in India*. Bombay: Popular Prakashan.

Gough, Kathleen

1973 "Harijans in Thanjavur," in *Imperialism and Revolution in South Asia*. Edited by Kathleen Gough and H. Sharma. New York: Monthly Review Press, 222-245.

Granovetter, Mark

1985 "Economic Action and Social Structure: the Problem of Embeddedness." *American Journal of Sociology* 91:481-510.

Gupta, Charu

2002 *Sexuality, Obscenity, Community: Women, Muslims, and the Hindu Public in Colonial India*. New York: Palgrave.

Hardgrave, Robert Jr.

1969 *The Nadars of Tamilnadu: The Political Culture of a Community of Change*. Berkeley: University of California Press.

194 References

Harper, Susan
2000 *In the Shadow of the Mahatma: Bishop V.S. Azariah and the Travails of Christianity in British India.* Grand Rapids, MI: Eerdmans.
Harvey, David
1992 *The Condition of Postmodernity.* Cambridge, MA: Blackwell.
Hay, Stephen, ed.
1988 *Sources of Indian Tradition*, Vol. II., 2nd edition. New York: Columbia University Press.
Hirschman, Albert O.
2003 "The On-and-Off Connection Between Political and Economic Progress" in *The Economics of Structural Change, Vol. 1*. Edited by Harald Hagemann, Michael Landesmann, and Roberto Scazzieri. Northampton, MA: Elgar, 343-348.
1982 "Rival Interpretations of Market Society: Civilizing, Destructive, or Feeble?" *Journal of Economic Literature* XX (Dec.): 1463-1484.
Hopkins, Edward W., ed.
1995 *The Ordinances of Manu.* Translated by Arthur Coke Burnell. New Delhi: Munshiram Manoharlal Publishing.
Horn, Nancy
1994 *Cultivating Customers: Market Women in Harare, Zimbabwe.* Boulder, CO: Lynne Rienner Publishers.
Hudson, D. Dennis
2000 *Protestant Origins in India: Tamil Evangelical Christians, 1706-1835.* Grand Rapids, MI: Eerdmans Publishing Co.
Irschick, Eugene
1969 *Politics and Social Conflict in South India.* Berkeley: University of California Press.
Jaffrelot, Christophe
2003 *India's Silent Revolution: the Rise of the Lower Castes in North India.* New York: Columbia University Press.
1996 *The Hindu Nationalist Movement in India.* New York: Columbia University Press.
Jayakumar, Samuel
1999 *Dalit Consciousness and Christian Conversion: Historical Resources for a Contemporary Debate.* Oxford: Regnum International.
Jeffrey, Robin
1992 *Politics, Women and Well-Being: How Kerala Became 'a Model.'* London: MacMillan Press.
John of the Cross, St.
1958 *Ascent of Mount Carmel.* Garden City, NY: Doubleday and Co.
Jomo K. S.
2003 *Southeast Asian Paper Tigers?: from Miracle to Debacle and Beyond.* New York: RoutledgeCurzon.
Karlekar, Malavika
1982 *Poverty and Women's Work: a Study of Sweeper Women of Delhi.* New Delhi: Vikas Publishing House.

King, Martin Luther, Jr.

    2001a "Where do we go from here?" in *A Call to Conscience: The Landmark Speeches of Dr. Martin Luther King, Jr.* New York: Time Warner Audiobooks.

    2001b "I've Been to the Mountaintop" in *A Call to Conscience: The Landmark Speeches of Dr. Martin Luther King, Jr.* New York: Time Warner Audiobooks.

Kohli, Atul

    1992 *Democracy and Discontent: India's Growing Crisis of Governability.* New York: Cambridge University Press.

    1989 *The State and Poverty in India.* New York: Cambridge University Press.

Kolenda, Pauline

    1985 *Caste in Contemporary India: Beyond Organic Solidarity.* Prospect Heights. IL: Waveland Press.

    1964 "Religious Anxiety and Hindu Fate," in *Religion in South Asia.* Edited by E. B. Harper. Berkeley: University of California Press, 71-81.

Korten, David C.

    1995 *When Corporations Rule the World.* West Hartford, Conn: Kumarian Press.

Krygier, Jocelyn

    1990 "Caste and Female Pollution," in *Women in India and Nepal.* Edited by Michael Allen and S.N. Mukherjee. Bangalore: Sterling Publishing Ltd., 76-104.

Kuber, W. N.

    1991 *Ambedkar: A Critical Study.* New Delhi: People's Publishing House.

Lamb, Beatrice Pitney

    1967 *The Nehrus of India: Three Generations of Leadership.* New York: The Macmillan Company.

Leach, Edmund R.

    1961 "Two Essays Concerning the Symbolic Representation of Time," in *Rethinking Anthropology.* London: The Athlone Press, 124-136.

Lee, Richard Borshay

    1969 "A Naturalist at Large: Eating Christmas in the Kalahari." *Natural History,* December.

Levy, Robert I.

    1973 *Tahitians: Mind and Experience in the Society Islands.* Chicago: University of Chicago Press.

Lewellen, Ted C.

    2002 *The Anthropology of Globalization: Cultural Anthropology Enters the 21st Century.* Westport, CN: Bergin and Garvey.

Lieten, G.K.

    1996 "Hindu Communalism: Between Caste and Class." *Journal of Contemporary Asia* 26 (2): 236-252.

Ludden, David

    1996 *Contesting the Nation: Religion, Community, and the Politics of Democracy in India.* Philadelphia: University of Pennsylvania.

MacIntyre, Alasdair

    1984 *Marxism and Christianity.* Notre Dame: University of Notre Dame Press.

Mandelbaum, David G.

1972 *Society in India*, Vol. I and II. Berkeley: University of California Press.
Mani, Lata

1997 "Contentious Traditions: the Debate on *Sati* in Colonial India." in *Recasting Women: Essays in Indian Colonial History.* Edited by Kumkum Sangari and Sudesh Vaid. New Brunswick, NJ: Rutgers University Press, 88-126.
Manshardt, Clifford, ed.

1949 *The Mahatma and the Missionary: Selected Writings of Mohandas K. Gandhi.* Chicago, IL: Henry Regnery Co.
Marx, Karl

2000 *Karl Marx: Selected Writings.* Edited by David McLellan. Oxford: Oxford University Press.

1988 *The Communist Manifesto*. New York: W. W. Norton.

1972a "Critique of Hegel's Philosophy of Right" in *The Marx-Engels Reader.* Edited by Robert C. Tucker. New York: W. W. Norton, 11-23.

1972b "Wage, Labour and Capital" in *The Marx-Engels Reader.* Edited by Robert C. Tucker. New York: W. W. Norton, 167-190.
Mauss, Marcel

1990 *The Gift: the Form and Reason for Exchange in Archaic Societies*. New York: W.W. Norton.
Mayer, Adrian

2000 "Caste in an Indian Village: Change and Continuity 1954-1992" in *Caste Today.* Edited by C. J. Fuller. New York: Oxford University Press. 32-64.
McDonald, Hamish

1991 "Class Interests Erode Caste Designations, Ancient and Modern" in *Far Eastern Economic Review,* May 2.
McMichael, Philip

2004 *Development and Social Change: a Global Perspective.* Thousand Oaks, CA: Pine Forge Press.
Mencher, Joan P.

1974 The Caste System Upside Down, or the Not-So-Mysterious East. *Current Anthropology* 15 (4): 469-478.
Mendelsohn, Oliver and Marika Vicziany

2000 *The Untouchables: Subordination, Poverty and the State in Modern India.* Cambridge, UK: Cambridge University Press.
Meneses, Eloise Hiebert

2000 "No Other Foundation: Establishing a Christian Anthropology." *Christian Scholar's Review* XXIX(3): 531-549.

1987 "Traders and Marginality in a Complex Social System." *Ethnology* XXVI(4): 231- 244.

1986 "Aspects of Cheating in a South Indian Market." Unpublished Manuscript. University of California, San Diego.
Midha, Seema

1990 "Women, Law and Social Justice" in *Women in India: Equality, Social Justice and Development.* Edited by Leelamma Devasia and V.V. Devasia. New Delhi: Indian Social Institute, 69-78.

Moffatt, Michael
  1979 *An Untouchable Community in South India: Structure and Consensus.* Princeton: Princeton University Press.
Mukherjee, S.N.
  1990 "Raja Rammohun Roy and the Status of Women in Bengal in the Nineteenth Century" in *Women in India and Nepal.* Edited by Michael Allen and S.N. Mukherjee. Bangalore: Sterling Publishing Ltd., 155-178.
Murray, Sandra
  1984 "All in the Family: a Study of Family Life in a Jat-Sikh Village." Unpublished manuscript. University of California, San Diego.
Murthy, U. R. Anantha
  1978 *Samskara: A Rite for a Dead Man.* New York: Oxford University Press.
Nabar, Vrinda and Shanta Tumkur
  1997 *The Bhagavadgita.* Hertfordshire, England: Wordsworth Classics.
Nair, Janaki
  2000 *Women and Colonial History: A Social History.* Bangalore: National Law School of India University.
Nanda, B. R.
  1998 *Jawaharlal Nehru: Rebel and Statesman.* Delhi: Oxford University Press.
Neill, Stephen
  1971 *A History of Christian Missions.* Baltimore, MD: Pelican Books.
Newbigin, Lesslie
  1996 *Truth and Authority in Modernity.* Valley Forge, PA: Trinity Press International.
  1991 *Truth to Tell: the Gospel as Public Truth.* Grand Rapids, MI: Eerdmans Publishing Co.
  1989 *The Gospel in a Pluralist Society.* Grand Rapids, MI: Eerdmans Publishing Co.
Nussbaum, Martha C.
  2000 *Women and Human Development: The Capabilities Approach.* Cambridge, MA: Cambridge University Press.
O'Connor, Daniel
  2001 "United Society for the Propagation of the Gospel, 1701-2000: Chronicling Three Centuries of Mission." *International Bulletin of Missionary Research* 25 (2): 75-79.
O'Flaherty, Doniger
  1981 *The Rig Veda: An Anthology.* New York: Penguin Books.
Omvedt, Gail
  1995 *Dalit visions.* New Delhi: Orient Longman.
  1993 *Reinventing Revolution: New Social Movements and the Socialist Tradition in India.* New York: M. E. Sharpe.
Osella, Filippo and Caroline Osella
  1999 "From Transience to Immanence: Consumption, Life-Cycle and Social Mobility in Kerala, South India." *Modern Asian Studies* 33 (4): 989-1020.

Palriwala, Rajni and Indu Agnihotri

    1996   "Tradition, the Family, and the State: Politics of the Contemporary Women' Movement" in *Region, Religion, Caste, Gender and Culture in Contemporary India.* Edited by T. V. Satyamurthy. Madras: Oxford University Press, 503-521.

Parvathamma, C.

    1971   *Politics and Religion.* New Delhi: Sterling Publishing

Patnaik, Arun and K.S.R.V.S. Chalam

    1996   "The Ideology and Politics of Hindutva" in *Region, Religion, Caste, Gender and Culture in Contemporary India.* Edited by T. V. Satyamurthy. Madras: Oxford University Press, 252-280.

Pearson, Gail

    1990   "The Female Intelligentsia in Segregated Society – Bombay, a Case Study" in *Women in India and Nepal.* Edited by Michael Allen and S.N. Mukherjee. Bangalore: Sterling Publishing Ltd., 136-154.

Polanyi, Michael

    1974   *Personal Knowledge: Toward a Post-Critical Philosophy.* Chicago: Chicago University Press.

Prashad, Vijay

    2000   *Untouchable Freedom: a Social History of the Dalit Community.* New York: Oxford University Press.

Raheja, Gloria Goodwin

    1999   "The Illusion of Consent; Language, Caste, and Colonial Rule in India" in *Colonial Subjects: Essays on the Practical History of Anthropology.* Edited by Peter Pels and Oxcar Salemink. Ann Arbor: University of Michigan Press.

Robbins, Richard H.

    1999   *Global Problems and the Culture of Capitalism.* Boston, MA: Allyn and Bacon.

Sahlins, Marshall

    1972   *Stone Age Economics.* New York: Aldine de Gruyter.

Sanneh, Lamin

    1993   *Encountering the West: Christianity and the Global Cultural Process: The African Dimension.* New York: Orbis Books.

Sarkar, Tanika and Urvashi Butalia, eds.

    1995   *Women and the Hindu Right.* New Delhi: Kali for Women.

Sastri, Nilakanta

    1994   *A History of South India.* Madras: Oxford University Press.

Satyamurthy, T. V., ed,

    1996   *Region, Religion, Caste, Gender and Culture in Contemporary India.* Social Change and Political Discourse in India, Vol. 3. Madras: Oxford University Press.

Savarkar, V.D.

    1999   *Hindutva: Who is a Hindu?* Mumbai: Swatantryaveer Savarkar Rashtriya Smarak, Pandit Bakhle.

Schumpeter, Joseph A.
  2003 "The Instability of Capitalism" in *The Economics of Structural Change, Vol. 1: Economic Structure and Change: Concepts and Theories*. Edited by Harald Hagemann, Michael Landesmann, and Roberto Scazzieri. International Library of Critical Writings in Economics Series. Edited by Mark Blaug. Northampton, MA: An Elgar Reference Collection.
  1975 *Capitalism, Socialism and Democracy*. NY: HarperPerennial.

Seligmann, Linda
  2001 "Introduction: Mediating Identities and Marketing Wares" in *Women Traders in Cross-Cultural Perspective: Mediating Identities and Marketing Wares*. Edited by Linda Seligmann. Stanford: Stanford University Press, 1-24.

Sen, Amartya
  1999 *Freedom as Development*. New York: Anchor Books, Random House.
  1977 "Rational Fools: a Critique of the Behavioral Foundations of Economic Theory." *Philosophy and Public Affairs* 6 (4): 317-344.

Sen, Ilina
  1996 "Women's Politics in India" in *Region, Religion, Caste, Gender and Culture in Contemporary India*. Edited by T. V. Satyamurthy. Madras: Oxford University Press, 444-462.

Shah, Ghanshyam, ed.
  2002 *Caste and Democratic Politics in India*. Delhi: Permanent Black.

Sheth, D. L.
  2002 "Caste and Class: Social Reality and Political Representation" in *Caste and Democratic Politics in India*. Edited by Ghanshyam Shah. Delhi: Permanent Black, 209-233.

Shivakumar, Chitra
  1982 *Education, Social Inequality, and Social Change in Karnataka*. Delhi: Hindustan Publishing Corporation.

Singer, Milton
  1980 *When a Great Tradition Modernizes: an Anthropological Approach to Indian Civilization*. Chicago: University of Chicago Press.

Smith, Adam
  1937 *The Wealth of Nations*. New York: Random House.

Srinivas, M. N.
  1966 *Social Change in Modern India*. Los Angeles: University of California Press.

Stokes, Eric
  1963 *The English Utilitarians and India*. Oxford: Clarendon Press.

Sullivan, Aline
  2004 "Politics Obscure a Robust Economy." *International Herald Tribune*. June 26-27.

Suresh, V.
  1996 "The Dalit Movement in India" in *Region, Religion, Caste, Gender and Culture in Contemporary India*. Edited by T. V. Satyamurthy. Madras: Oxford University Press, 355-387.

Thakur, C.P. and Devendra P. Sharma
  1999 *India under Atal Behari Vajpayee: the BJP Era.* New Delhi: USB Pub-
         lishers.
Todaro, Michael P.
  2000 *Economic Development.* 7th edition. New York: Addison Wesley Longman.
Townsend, Peter and David Gordon, eds.
  2002 *World Poverty: New Policies to Defeat an Old Enemy.* Bristol, UK: Policy
         Press.
Troeltsch, Ernst
  1992 *The Social Teachings of the Christian Churches.* Louisville, KY: Westmin-
         ster / John Knox Press.
Tucker, Robert C.
  1972 *The Marx-Engels Reader.* New York: W.W. Norton & Co.
  1964 *Philosophy and Myth in Karl Marx.* New York: Cambridge University Press.
van der Veer, Peter
  2001 *Imperial Encounters: Religion and Modernity in India and Britain.* Prince-
         ton: Princeton University Press.
  1994 "Syncretism, Multiculturalism and the Discourse of Tolerance" in *Syn-
         cretism / Anti-syncretism: the Politics of Religious Synthesis.* Edited by
         Charles Stewart and Rosalind Shaw. New York: Routledge, 196-211.
Van Leeuwen, Arendt
  1964 *Christianity in World History: The Meeting of the Faiths of East and West.*
         New York: Charles Scribner's Sons.
Visaria, Leela and Pravin Visaria
  1998 *Reproductive Health in Policy and Practice: India.* Washington DC: Popu-
         lation Reference Bureau.
Vlassoff, Carol
  1994 "From Rags to Riches: The Impact of Rural Development on Women's Sta-
         tus in an Indian Village." *World Development* 22 (5): 707-719.
Vyasulu, Poornima and Vinod
  1999 "Women in Panchayati Raj: Grassroots Democracy in India, Experience
         from Malgudi." Meeting on Women and Political Participation: 21st Cen-
         tury Challenges, March 24-26, 1999, New Delhi. Management Develop-
         ment and Governance Division, United Nations Development Programme
         and the United Nations Office of Project Services.
Walker, F. Deaville
  1960 *William Carey: Missionary Pioneer and Statesman.* Chicago: Moody Press.
Wallerstein, Immanuel
  1979 *The Capitalist World-Economy.* Cambridge: Cambridge University Press.
Washbrook, David
  1990 "South Asia, the World System, and World Capitalism." *The Journal of
         Asian Studies* 49 (3): 479-508.
Weber, Max
  1976 *The Protestant Ethic and the Spirit of Capitalism.* New York: Charles Scrib-
         ner's Sons.

Webster, John C. B.
  1997 *From Role to Identity: Dalit Christian Women in Transition.* I.S.P.C.K.
         Delhi: Cambridge Press.
  1992 *A History of the Dalit Christians in India.* San Francisco: Mellen Research
         University Press.
White, Sarah C.
  1992 *Arguing with the Crocodile: Gender and Class in Bangladesh.* New Jersey:
         Zed Books.
Wolpert, Stanley
  2004 *A New History of India.* 7th edition. New York: Oxford University Press.
World Bank
  2000 *India: Reducing Poverty, Accelerating Development.* New Delhi: Oxford
         University Press.
Yoder, John Howard
  1994 *The Politics of Jesus.* Grand Rapids, MI: William B. Eerdman's Publishing
         Co.
Yunus, Muhammad
  2001 "The Grameen Bank" in *Global Studies: India and South Asia.* Edited by
         James H. K. Norton. Guilford, CT: McGraw-Hill / Dushkin Co., 186-189.

Index